THE BOOK
OF JUBILEES

Translated by
R. H. CHARLES

Canon of Westminster; Fellow of Merton College;
Fellow of the British Academy

With an Introduction by
G. H. BOX

Lecturer in Rabbinical Hebrew, King's College,
London; Hon. Canon of St. Albans

DOVER PUBLICATIONS
Garden City, New York

Bibliographical Note

The Book of Jubilees, first published by Dover Publications in 2010, is an unabridged republication of the work originally published by the Society for Promoting Christian Knowledge by The Macmillan Company, London and New York, in 1917.

Library of Congress Cataloging-in-Publication Data

Book of Jubilees. English.
    The Book of Jubilees / Anonymous ; translated by R.H. Charles ; with an introduction by G.H. Box.
      p. cm.
    Originally published: London : Society for Promoting Christian Knowledge ; New York : Macmillan Co., 1917.
    ISBN-13: 978-0-486-47659-9
    ISBN-10: 0-486-47659-6
     1. Charles, R. H. (Robert Henry), 1855–1931. 2. Title.

BS1830.J7A3 2010
229'.911—dc22

2009047765

Manufactured in the United States of America
47659610   2021
www.doverpublications.com

THE BOOK
OF JUBILEES

INTRODUCTION

SHORT ACCOUNT OF THE BOOK

THE Book of Jubilees, or, as it is sometimes called, " the little Genesis," purports to be a revelation given by God to Moses through the medium of an angel (" the Angel of the Presence," i. 27), and containing a history, divided up into jubilee-periods of forty-nine years, from the creation to the coming of Moses. Though the actual narrative of events is only carried down to the birth and early career of Moses, its author envisages the events of a later time, and in particular certain events of special interest at the time when he wrote, which was probably in the latter years of the second century B.C., perhaps in the reign of the Maccabean prince John Hyrcanus. Though distinguished from the Pentateuch proper (" the first Law," vi. 22), it presupposes and supplements the latter. The actual narrative embraces material contained in the whole of Genesis and part of Exodus. But the legal regulations given presuppose other parts of the Pentateuch, especially the so-called " Priest's Code " (P), and certain details in the narrative are probably intended to apply to events that occurred in the author's own time (the latter years of the second century B.C.). The author himself seems to have contemplated the speedy inauguration of the Messianic Age, and in this respect his point of view is similar to that of the Apocalyptic writers. But his work, though it contains one or two passages of an apocalyptic character, is quite unlike the typical apocalypses. It is largely narrative based upon the historical narratives in Genesis and

Exodus, interspersed with legends, and emphasizing certain legal practices (such as the strict observance of the Sabbath, circumcision, etc.), and laying much stress upon their eternal obligation. But his main object was to inculcate a reform in the regulation of the calendar and festivals, in place of the intercalated lunar calendar, which he condemns in the strongest language. He proposes to substitute for this a solar calendar consisting of 12 months and containing 364 days. The result of such a system is to make all festivals, except the Day of Atonement, fall on a Sunday; the author also fixes the date of the Feast of Weeks (Pentecost) on Sivan 15th (in place of the traditional Sivan 6th). He obviously believes that the prevailing system has produced grave consequences in religious practice. The proper observance of the feasts, which had been prescribed by divine authority, is, according to his view, rendered impossible so long as the right principles for regulating the calendar are ignored. These principles are justified from the written Law, and are represented as having been ordained in heaven. To what party or tendency in Judaism did the author belong? Various answers have been given to this question, which will be fully discussed below. It is very difficult to believe, as Dr. Charles contends, that the author was a Pharisee, for the positions he advocates are in many respects fundamentally opposed to later Pharisaic practice. In particular, how can any member of the Pharisaic party, which from its beginning championed popular religious custom, have advocated a solar calendar? More can be said for the view that the author was a member of the Hasidim or " pious " (who must not be confounded with the Pharisees), while in a recent important discussion Leszynsky has made out a strong, if not quite convincing, case for Sadducean authorship. The Book has sometimes been styled a Midrash, but such a descriptive term needs some qualification. It claims to be a revelation, and not a mere exposition of Genesis and

Exodus. At the same time, there is a certain Midrashic tendency observable in the way the author rewrites the older narratives, which reminds one of the work of the Chronicler as compared with the earlier canonical books which he remodelled. But *Jubilees* is not at all like the typical Midrash of the later Rabbinical period; it is more independent, and resembles rather such works as the " Chronicles of Jerahmeel," or the earlier (narrative) part of the " Apocalypse of Abraham."

The Book, which was probably composed in Hebrew, is divided into fifty chapters, and appears to be complete.

TITLES

The Book was known under various titles, most of them in Greek as referred to in later Greek writers. The most important are " Jubilees " (= τὰ Ἰωβηλαῖα or οἱ Ἰωβηλαῖοι) and " the little Genesis " (= ἡ λεπτὴ Γένεσις and variants). Both of these seem to go back to Hebrew originals, and there would thus appear to have been two authoritative Hebrew titles of the original Hebrew work, viz. *ha-yôbĕlîm* (or *sēfer hā-yôbĕlôth*), and *Berēshîth zûtā*. In the latter the epithet " little " [1] refers not to the extent of the work, but to its relatively inferior position as compared with the canonical Genesis. It is also noteworthy that a clear reference to our Book is made in the recently recovered fragments of a " Zadokite Work." [2] The passage runs as follows (xx. 1) :

And as for the exact statement of their periods to put Israel in remembrance in regard to all these, behold it is treated accurately in the Book of the Divisions of the Seasons according to their Jubilees and their Weeks.

This is remarkably like the opening words of the Prologue of our Book : *This is the history of the division*

---

[1] Applied also to certain minor midrashîm ("midrash zûtā," etc.).

[2] First published by Schechter in 1910 (Cambridge Press).

of the days . . . of the events of the years according to their (year-) weeks, according to their jubilees. . . .
Cf. also the colophon at the end of the Book :
    Herewith is completed the account of the division of the days.

Other titles of our Book are : *The Apocalypse of Moses* (Syncellus) ; *The Testament of Moses* (the Catena of Nicephorus) ; *The Book of Adam's Daughters* (perhaps applied only to a portion of *Jubilees*) ; *The Life of Adam* (perhaps an amplified excerpt of our Book).

Versions and Original Language

The complete text of the Book is extant in an Ethiopic Version, which is also the most accurate that has survived. Four MSS. of it are known, and are preserved in European Libraries, the two most important in the National Library in Paris and in the British Museum respectively. A critical edition of the text, based on all the known MSS., has been published by Dr. Charles (Oxford, 1895), which was preceded by an important one by Dillmann (published 1859). Fragments of a Greek, Latin and (possibly) a Syriac version are also extant. The fragments of the Greek version are contained in numerous citations in Justin Martyr, Origen, Diodorus of Antioch, Isidore of Alexandria, Epiphanius, Syncellus and other writers. The Latin version, of which about one-fourth has been preserved, is very valuable for the criticism of the text. The fragments that have survived were first published by Ceriani (in his *Monumenta Sacra et Profana*, 1861), and have been edited by Rönsch (1874), and more recently by Charles (in his edition of the Ethiopic text referred to above). What may possibly be a fragment of a Syriac Version of our Book is contained in a British Museum MS. (Add. 12154, fol. 180) entitled " Names of the Wives of the Patriarchs according to the Hebrew Book called Jubilees." But whether this is really part of a complete version is very doubtful (see Charles, *op. cit.*, Appendix iii.).

It is generally agreed that both the Ethiopic and Latin versions were translated from the Greek which, it may be inferred from the large number of quotations scattered about in different writers over a wide period, must have been widely diffused. The fact that a Greek text underlies these versions is clear from such phenomena as the presence, in the Ethiopic, of transliterations of Greek words (*e. g.* ἡλίου, "of the sun," in xxxiv. 11); proper names are transliterated as they appear in Greek, not in Hebrew; and certain textual corruptions can only be explained by reference to an underlying Greek text. Similar phenomena characterize the Latin version. Thus in xxxviii. 12, "timoris" = δειλίας, which is corrupt for δουλείας; and sometimes the Greek has been misunderstood, as *e. g.* in xxxviii. 13, "honorem" = τιμήν, which should have been rendered by "tributum."

It is more difficult to determine whether a Semitic original underlies the Greek, and, if that be the case, whether the original Semitic text was Hebrew or Aramaic. It must be admitted that in a number of passages where the text of the canonical Genesis is cited the Ethiopic agrees with the LXX against all other authorities (see Charles' *Jubilees*, p. xxxiv). But these cases are not, on the whole, either numerous or important.[1] On the other hand, the Ethiopic often agrees with the LXX, supported by other authorities (especially the Samaritan text and version) against the Masoretic Hebrew text, and there are other variations in the textual phenomena. From a survey of these phenomena Charles deduces the conclusion, no doubt rightly, that " our book attests an independent form of the Hebrew text of the Pentateuch. . . . Our book represents *some form of the Hebrew text of the Pentateuch midway between the forms presupposed by the LXX and the Syriac.*"[2]

[1] They *may* be due to assimilation in the Greek Version with the LXX.   [2] *Jubilees*, p. xxxviii.

It agrees with the LXX, or with combinations into which the LXX enters, more often than with any other authority or group of authorities. On the other hand, it is often independent of the LXX, and in a considerable number of cases attests readings, with the support of MT and Sam., against the LXX, and manifestly superior to the latter. It is noteworthy that it never agrees with M against all the other authorities. These phenomena suggest that the composition of *Jubilees* is to be assigned to " some period between 250 B.C. (LXX version of the Pentateuch) and A.D. 100 [when M was finally fixed], and at a time nearer the earlier date than the latter." [1]

A number of considerations may be adduced which suggest that the original language of *Jubilees* was Hebrew. Thus mistranslations of Hebrew words occur, *e. g.* in xliii. 11, the word rendered (as corrected) " I pray thee," is, in the Ethiopic, " in me "— a confusion of the Hebrew *bî* = δέομαι (Gen. xliv. 18) with the Hebrew word (spelt in exactly the same way) which = " in me ; " there are also numerous Hebraisms surviving in the Ethiopic and Latin versions,[2] as well as paronomasiae based upon Hebrew words.[3] It is noteworthy, also, that the author lays special stress upon the sacred character of Hebrew, which was originally the language of creation (cf. xii. 25–26; xliii. 15). Moreover, he represents his work as having emanated from Moses, and a genuinely Mosaic work would naturally be written in Hebrew. Finally, certain parts of *Jubilees*, or of something remarkably like *Jubilees*, have survived in Hebrew form in certain Hebrew books, especially the *Chronicles of Jerahmeel*, and the Midrash Tadshe. It is not improbable, also, that a Hebrew form of *Jubilees* was known to the compiler of the *Pirke de R. Eliezer* (see Friedlander's Introduction to the latter book, p. xxii). The only ground for suggesting that the Semitic

[1] *Op. cit.*, p. xxxix.
[2] Cf. *e. g.* xxii. 10, " eligere in te " = Heb. *bāḥar bĕ.*
[3] See Charles, *op. cit.*, p. xxxiii for details.

original may have been Aramaic rather than Hebrew is the presence of certain Aramaizing forms of proper names (e. g. *Filistin*, with the termination *n* instead of *m*) in the Latin version. But in all these cases the Ethiopic transliteration has *m* (not *n*), and it seems probable that the Aramaizing forms in these cases are due to the Latin translator, who there is other ground for supposing was a Palestinian Jew. We may, therefore, safely conclude that the original language of our Book was Hebrew.

Affinities with other Literature

Though there is no reason to doubt the essential unity of our Book (that is to say, that it was composed and written in its present form by one author), it is equally clear that this writer incorporated earlier traditions and legends into his work. Thus he refers explicitly to Noachic writings (xxi. 10; cf. x. 13), and has apparently incorporated two considerable sections of a " Book of Noah " in vii. 20–39 and x. 1–15. It is well-known that this Noachic Book was also one of the sources of the Book of Enoch, 1 Enoch, vi.–xi., lx., lxv.–lxix. 25, and cvi.–cvii. being probably derived from it. There is reason, also, to believe that the author of *Jubilees* was acquainted with some form of the Book of Enoch (1 Enoch). According to Charles the parts of 1 Enoch with which our author was acquainted are 1 Enoch vi.–xvi., xxiii.–xxxvi. and lxxii.–xc. He seems clearly to refer to the last section in iv. 17 :

And he [Enoch] was the first among men that are born on earth who learnt writing and knowledge and wisdom and who wrote down the signs of heaven according to the order of their months in a book, that men might know the seasons of the years according to the order of their separate months.

Here the Enoch-book referred to forms a description of 1 Enoch lxxii.–lxxxii. (" the Book of the courses of the Heavenly Luminaries "), while iv. 19 (*And*

*what was and what will be he saw in a vision of his
sleep, as it will happen to the children of men throughout
their generations until the day of judgement; he saw
and understood everything, and wrote his testimony,
and placed the testimony on earth for all the children
of men and for their generations*) forms an exact description of the " Dream-Visions " in 1 Enoch lxxxiii.–xc.[1]
There are also a number of parallels with the *Testaments of the XII Patriarchs*, but these are not sufficient
to show dependence on either side; the phenomena
rather suggest that both writers are using common
sources: cf. xxviii. 9; xxx. 2–6, 18, 25; xxxi. 3–4,
13, 15, 16; xxxii. 1, 8; xxxiii. 1, 2, 4; xxxiv. 1–9;
xxxvii.–xxxviii.; xli. 8–14, 24–25; xlvi. 6–9.

It has already been mentioned that a knowledge of
our Book seems to be presupposed in some of the
later Jewish literature. Thus the *Chronicles of
Jerahmeel*, a late compilation written in Hebrew,
contains much material common to *Jubilees;* at
times it reproduces the actual words of the text of
the latter. Another late Jewish work, the Midrash
Tadshe, contains passages which are largely identical
with portions of the text of our Book. This Midrash
was compiled in its present form by Moses ha-
Darshan in the eleventh century A.D., but is based
upon a much earlier work by R. Pinchas b. Jair
(end of second century, A.D.), who utilized materials
from our Book. Besides the above, our Book appears
to have been known to the compiler of the Samaritan
Chronicle (twelfth century, A.D.), and also to the
compiler of the *Pirke de R. Eliezer* (finally redacted
in the ninth century A.D.). In fact, in both cases
there is implicit a certain amount of polemic (especially in calendar-matters) against the positions
advocated in *Jubilees*. But besides this, there is a
remarkable parallelism in subject-matter between
our Book and the *Pirke de R. Eliezer*, to which
Friedlander calls attention. He points out that
both " are alike in being practically Midrashic para-

[1] For further parallels see Charles, *Jubilees*, pp. lxviii ff.

phrases and expansions of the narratives contained in the Book of Genesis and part of the Book of Exodus. . . . Both books deal with the Calendar . . . and in this respect they recall the Books of Enoch." Both " have chapters setting forth the story of the Creation (*Ma'aseh Bereshith*). . . . The past is recalled and the future revealed. The nature of God, angels and man is unfolded. We read of sin and grace, repentance and atonement, good and evil, life and death, Paradise and Gehenna, Satan and Messiah." [1]

Numerous references to *Jubilees* occur in Christian literature (patristic period and later), where long extracts from the Book are often cited, and by name. These have been collected by Charles (*op. cit.*, pp. lxxvii ff.), who also cites a number of parallels between our Book and the New Testament. But these are somewhat vague, and are hardly sufficient to establish any real or direct connexion.

The Special Aims and General Character of the Book

It is obvious that *Jubilees* is dominated by certain interests and antipathies. It is to a large extent polemical in character, and its author desires at once to protest against certain tendencies which, in his view, threaten true religion, and to inculcate certain reforms. Incidentally it commends certain religious practices, and endeavours to invest them with enhanced sanctions. In the forefront, as its name (" the Book of Jubilees ") suggests,[2] stands the question of the Calendar. It is all important in the author's view that the divinely ordained principle according to which history is divided up by year-weeks (*i. e.* periods of 7 years) and Jubilees (*i. e.* periods of 7×7 years) is recognized (cf. i. 26 f.). Accordingly, he gives a history from Creation to Moses, in which the sequence of events is recorded and dated exactly

[1] *Op. cit.*, p. xxii.
[2] This is obscured by such titles as " the little Genesis," " the Apocalypse of Moses," etc.

by jubilee-periods, or portions of such. This leads up to a final section in which the law respecting jubilees and sabbatical years is solemnly enjoined. The writer's aim seems to have been nothing less than a reformation of the Jewish Calendar. The prevailing system has led to the nation " forgetting " new moons, festivals, and sabbaths (and (?) jubilees);[1] in other words, it has produced grave irregularities in the observance of matters which were of divine obligation.

A cardinal feature of the writer's system is the jubilee-period, which consists of 7×7 (i. e. 49) years. Here we are confronted with a difficulty. The passage in Lev. (xxv. 8–14) which ordains the observance of the jubilee-year expressly identifies this, in the present form of the text, with the fiftieth year (Lev. xxv. 10 and 11). But it is incredible that the author of our Book would deliberately have violated the express injunctions of the Pentateuch on such a matter, and we are driven to conclude that he had a text before him in which the word " fiftieth " was absent.[2] The wording of verses 8 and 9 is ambiguous, and allows of the explanation that the jubilee-year was the forty-ninth and not the fiftieth. It is quite possible that in verses 10 and 11 " fiftieth " has been added to the text, in the interests of the rival explanation that ultimately prevailed, for, as has been pointed out already, our Book presupposes a text of the Pentateuch that is independent of and earlier than M.T. This explanation suffers from the difficulty that the LXX and other ancient versions (including the Samaritan text) support the currently received reading. But it is not improbable that on such a matter the influence of orthodox views may have operated to bring their text of the verses into harmony with the currently accepted theory.[3]

---

[1] vi. 34; cf. i. 10.
[2] So Leszynsky, *Die Sadduzäer*, pp. 156 ff.
[3] It should be noted that the Talmud (T.B., *Ned.*, 61a) refers to the view (held by R. Jehuda) that the jubilee-period was forty-nine years.

But more revolutionary is the writer's advocacy of a solar calendar. In ii. 9 he says, " God appointed the sun to be a great sign upon the earth for days and for sabbaths, and for feasts and for years and for jubilees and for all seasons of the years." In Gen. i. 14 this function is assigned to the sun *and the moon ;* but in our Book the moon is deliberately excluded. The writer objected fiercely to the traditional calendar which was based upon the changes of the moon, and was adjusted to the solar year by means of inter-calation. How can his apparent violation of the express wording of Scripture be explained? His answer would probably have been that the solar year of 364 days (cf. vi. 32) was actually the system implied in the Pentateuch. It has been pointed out by Bacon [1] that in the P sections of the Flood-narrative in Genesis a year of 364 days is pre-supposed. It is said that the Flood began on the 17th day of the second month, and ended on the 27th day of the second month the following year, *i. e.* reckoning by the ordinary lunar months, 12 months ($= 12 \times 29\frac{1}{2}$ days) or 354 days + 10 days (to make up the solar year), or 364 days in all, this completing the one whole year which, according to the Babylonian source, was the length of the Flood's duration. Thus the author of *Jubilees* had a dogmatic basis within the text of the Pentateuch itself for his view that the true year was a solar one of 364 days. He may very well have believed that whatever may be the exact significance of Gen. i. 14, it could not override this fact. It is interesting to notice that this tradition of a solar year of 364 days should be implicit in the P sections of Genesis. There are strong reasons for believing that the author of *Jubilees* was a priest, and, as such, may have been acquainted in some special way with this priestly tradition. There are, however, difficulties in connexion with the reckoning of such a solar year. It is obvious that a year of 12 months, each

[1] In *Hebraica,* vol. viii. (1891–2), cited by Charles on vi. 32.

of which contains 30 days, will only yield a total of 360 days. It has been supposed that our author overcame this difficulty by inserting one intercalary day at the beginning of each quarter. Thus each three months would contain 31 + 30 + 30 (= 91) days. But this solution will not harmonize with the date assigned by our author to the Feast of Weeks, which is the " middle " of the third month (xvi. 13). Scholars are agreed that the 15th of Sivan is meant. Now the Feast of Weeks was to be celebrated on the fiftieth day, counting from the " morrow " after the Sabbath of Passover (Lev. xxiii. 15 f.). The Pharisees, as is well known, interpreted " Sabbath " here to be the first day of the Feast (Nisan 15th), whatever the day of the week on which it fell, and reckoned from Nisan 16th, which would bring the Feast of Weeks to Sivan 6th. Another view, with which our Book agrees, interpreted " sabbath " as = " week " (as in fact it has this meaning throughout the rest of the verse). Then render : *And ye shall count unto you from the morrow after the (festival) week, from the day that ye bring the wave-sheaf, seven complete weeks shall there be, until the morrow after the seventh week ye shall number fifty days* : the festival-week would be Nisan 15–21, and its " morrow " Nisan 22 ; reckoning 28 days to the month, this would leave 6 days in Nisan + 28 days in Iyar + 15 in Sivan = 49 + Nisan 22 = 50 days. This seems to have been the reckoning of our author. Moreover, since the year he advocates contains 364 days, the festivals would always fall upon the same day of the week, and as Nisan 1st the first day of Creation fell, according to his scheme, on the first day of the week, *i. e.* Sunday, it must always fall on that day ; thus Nisan 14th and 21st would always fall on a Sabbath, while Nisan 22nd and Sivan 15th would always fall on a Sunday. To make the Feast of Weeks fall on the 1st day of the week was a Sadducean practice, and one that it is inconceivable that any Pharisee can ever have sanctioned or tolerated. It will be noticed, however, that the view of our author, according to which the Feast of Weeks falls on Sivan 15th, implies a reckoning of 28 days to the months Nisan and Iyar. How is this to be reconciled with a solar year of 12 months? Eppstein supposes that our author used two reckonings, one for the civil year of 12 months, 8 of 30, and 4 of 31 days, and an ecclesiastical year of 13 months each containing 28 days. But it is difficult to believe that the writer used two systems side by side. A better solution would be that he added a week to every third month, which would make each 3 months consist of 28 + 28 + 35 days (total 91 days), or 4 + 4 + 5 weeks. It is evident that his calendar-system is based upon the number 7; thus each month consists of 4 × 7 (or 5 × 7) days, while the year consists of 52 × 7 days, the year-week of 7 years, and the jubilee of 7 × 7 years. On this reckoning the Feast of Weeks would still fall on the 15th of Sivan, but the 15th would not strictly be the "middle" of that month, which, *ex hypothesi*, consisted of 35 days. It might, however, be used loosely for such a date. Perhaps, too, the author desired to avoid specifying more particularly this date, because current Sadducean practice (based upon a different length of days assigned to the months) would not quite harmonize with it.[1] With regard to the Passover, it is noticeable that our author interprets the phrase "between the two evenings" (at which time the Passover lamb was to be slain, cf. Exod. xii. 6; Lev. xxiii. 5) to mean the third part of the day (xlix. 10); *i. e.* assuming the day to contain 12 hours, we may fix the third part as from 2 to 6 p.m. This, again, contradicts Pharisaic practice. Notable, too, is the mention of wine in connexion with the Passover: *All Israel* [*i. e.* in Egypt] *was eating the flesh*

---

[1] Thus the Abyssinian Jews (Falashas), maintaining old practice, reckon the 50 days from Nisan 22, as our author does, but fix Sivan 12 as the date for the Feast of Weeks, as they use alternate months of 30 and 29 days. It should be noted that the author of 1 Enoch lxxii.–lxxxii. also advocates a year of 364 days.

of the paschal lamb and drinking the wine (xlix. 6).
Now this was a Pharisaic custom in later times, and
has no basis, apparently, in the canonical account in
Exodus. In view, however, of the fact that our
author usually follows the prescriptions of Scripture
with scrupulous care, the question arises whether he
did not, in fact, derive this from the Pentateuch.
Leszynsky suggests [1] that the word rendered " bitter
herbs " in Exod. xii. 8 (" with bitter herbs shall
they eat it ") was interpreted by our author to mean
" wine "—the word simply means " bitter," or " what
is poisonous," and a cognate form is used in connexion
with wine in Deut. xxxii. 32. It is certainly curious
that our author makes no mention of " bitter herbs "
in connexion with the Egyptian Passover.

The Feast of Tabernacles, too, as described in our
Book (xvi. 10–31), has certain peculiar features.
In particular, the specifically Pharisaic custom of
pouring water on the altar [2] at the Feast is not mentioned or recognized. Now as early as the time of
Alexander Jannæus (102–76 B.C.) the Pharisees
tried to enforce the adoption of this custom upon the
Sadducean priest-king, who, to show his contempt,
allowed the water, which should have been poured
solemnly on the altar, to run over his feet. The
protest that ensued was followed later by a massacre
of Pharisees. It is difficult to believe that our author,
a few years earlier, if he was himself a Pharisee, could
have been ignorant of this custom, which was based
upon old popular tradition. His silence concerning
it is much more probably deliberate. The custom
was objectionable, from the Sadducean standpoint,
because it had no basis in the written Law. The
custom of wearing wreaths upon the head which is
here prescribed (xvi. 30) is also unknown to tradition ;
nor has it, apparently, any Scriptural basis, unless it
was inferred as an act of rejoicing, from the words
" and ye shall rejoice before the Lord your God seven
days " (Lev. xxiii. 40), taken in conjunction with the

[1] *Op. cit.*, pp. 207 ff.   [2] Cf. *R.W.S.*[2], p. 401 f.

command (in the preceding clause) to take " branches of palm trees, and boughs of thick trees, and willows of the brook." Wearing a wreath of palm-leaves may have been regarded as one of the ways in which this command was to be fulfilled.

Even more striking are the sections which give directions about the observance of the Sabbath (l. 1–13 ; cf. ii. 29–30). These directions are very severe. The following actions are prohibited on the Sabbath under penalty of death : travelling by land or sea, buying or selling, drawing water, carrying burdens out of the house, killing or striking, snaring beasts, birds or fish, fasting or making war, marital intercourse. The last prescription is in direct opposition to Pharisaic practice, as is also the severe penalty imposed for non-observance of the various prescriptions. It is interesting to notice that these agree with the practice still maintained by the Falashas, Samaritans, and Ḳaraite Jews. Probably this rigid view of sabbath-observance was cherished in specially pious priestly circles at the time when our author wrote. In this connexion it may be noted that our Book, in its interpretation of the law about the fruit of newly-planted trees given in Lev. xix. 23–24, agrees with the view of the Samaritans and Ḳaraite Jews in directing that the first fruits of the fruit of the fourth year should be offered on the altar, and what remained given to the priests. According to Pharisaic practice what remained was to be eaten by the owners within the walls of Jerusalem.

Another point in which *Jubilees* upholds a view which is certainly not Pharisaic is on the question of the law of retribution, the so-called *lex talionis*. It is well known that while the Sadducees insisted on the strict letter of the Law, " an eye for an eye, and a tooth for a tooth," the Pharisees strove to mitigate its harshness by the substitution (except in the case of murder) of compensating money - payments. Moreover, the Mishna directs that where the death-penalty is inflicted it is to be carried out by the sword (cf. *Sanhedrin* ix. 1 : " These are to be be-headed "). Our Book, however, seems to wage a polemic against such views in no uncertain language :

Take no gifts for the blood of man,[1] *lest it be shed with impunity, without judgement ; for it is the blood that is shed that causes the earth to sin, and the earth cannot be cleansed from the blood of man save by the blood of him who shed it. And take no present or gift for the blood of man ; blood for blood* (xxi. 19 f.).

In iv. 31 f. the circumstances of Cain's death are described : *his house fell upon him and he died in the midst of his house ; for with a stone he had killed Abel, and by a stone was he killed in righteous judgement. For this reason it was ordained on the heavenly tables : " With the instrument with which a man kills his neighbour, with the same shall he be killed ; after the manner that he wounded him, in like manner shall they deal with him."*

It is true that a school of Pharisees (the School of Shammai) still, to some extent, upheld, in theory at any rate, the severer and older view. But this does not alter the fact that it was a distinctive tenet of the Sadducees; and it is difficult to believe that any Pharisee can, at any time, have used such unqualified language as that employed in the extracts given above.[2]

At this point we may well ask what was the author's attitude towards the belief in a future life? At the time when he wrote the doctrine of the resurrection of the body had become well established in certain Jewish circles. In the Book of Daniel it had received classical expression. It was a cherished belief of the Pharisaic party. Now our Book does not in any way accept such a belief. The one passage in which the language employed might, at first sight, suggest a hint of such a belief is a sentence describing the happiness of the righteous in the age of felicity which is to dawn :

[1] This would be allowed in certain cases of homicide (not deliberate murder) by the Rabbinical Law.

[2] Cf., however, xlviii, 14 note.

And at that time the Lord will heal His servants,
And they will rise up and see great peace,
And drive out their adversaries (xxiii. 30).

But here there is probably no reference to the idea of a resurrection. As Charles points out, the words " shall rise up " have here " apparently no reference to the resurrection, and mean merely that when God heals His servants (cf. Rev. xxii. 2) they become strong." The clause in the preceding verse, *all their days will be days of bl. ssing and healing* (cf. also i. 29) renders " this view the most probable." On the other hand, the opening words of xxiii. 31 :

And their bones will rest in the earth,
And their spirits will have much joy,

though they are susceptible of another interpretation, may point to a belief that the righteous dead are destined to enjoy a blessed immortality. But it is to be noticed that no emphasis is laid on the idea ; and in any case no countenance is given to the doctrine of resurrection. This attitude accords with the Sadducean position. What the Sadducees maintained was that the resurrection doctrine could not be proved from the Pentateuch. They did not assert that the personality was annihilated at death, or deny the doctrine of immortality—indeed, it is by no means impossible that some sections of the Sadducean party accepted this doctrine ; but in general their position towards this question—apart from that of the bodily resurrection—was cautious and reserved. And this certainly seems to be the attitude of our author. It should be noted that Sheol is represented—somewhat vaguely and in poetical passages—as a place of punishment for the wicked (vii. 29; xxii. 22; xxiv. 31). This looks like the converse of the idea that the righteous dead are destined to enjoy a blessed immortality. In this connexion a word may be said about the angelology and demonology of our Book. These are in a fairly advanced stage, and imply much the same development as is to be seen in 1 Enoch and the *Testaments of the XII Patriarchs*. There are three classes of angels, two of a superior order, the angels of the presence, and the angels of sanctification (cf. ii. 2, 18), and, besides these, a numerous inferior order who presided over natural phenomena (ii. 2). It is noteworthy that the two superior orders are represented as observing the Sabbath, and as fulfilling the prescriptions of the Law regarding circumcision, etc.; they even observe in heaven the great festivals, such as the Feast of Weeks (vi. 18).[1] Various activities are assigned to the angels in connexion with mankind throughout our Book.[2]

Over against the angelic orders there stands a well-organized demonic kingdom, presided over by "the prince of the Mastêmâ" (cf. xvii. 16; xlviii. 2; xviii. 9, 12, etc.).[3] Among the Satanic beings that appear in our Book is Beliar (i. 20).

What is the attitude of our author towards the Messianic Hope? The hope for the coming of the Messianic King who should spring from the old Royal House of David was always cherished among the masses of the people, and in times of unusual stress was apt to flame up in vivid expression. The Pharisees, who themselves sprang from the ranks of the people, were naturally influenced by this tradition, and gave literary expression to it in the *Psalms of Solomon* (70–40 B.C. ?). But at the time when our author wrote the desire for a Messianic King of the House of David was probably only latent. A period of national prosperity came in during the reign of John Hyrcanus, and the people generally were well content. It is not to be supposed, however, that the popular hope had completely died away. It was merely quiescent. On the other hand,

---

[1] Besides the above there were the seventy angelic patrons of the nations (xv. 31 and note) and the guardian angels of individuals (xxxv. 17).

[2] For details see Charles, *op. cit.*, p. lvii f.

[3] This is the right form of the expression (not "prince Mastêmâ"): "Mastêmâ" in derivation and meaning = "Satan" (cf. x. 8 note).

there was a party, which no doubt had its seat in the priesthood, and may represent the old Saducean party, that claimed for the priesthood not only sacerdotal but also ruling functions: Levi's descendants are not only to be priests, but also the civil rulers of the nation, and this view receives expression in our Book (cf. xxxi. 15). Now it is well known that the Pharisees objected to the double office being exercised by one person, and when Alexander Jannæus assumed the title of " king " this feeling broke out into open hostility. At a somewhat later time a Pharisaic author in the *Psalms of Solomon*, looking back upon the terrible events that followed the break-up of the Hasmonean dynasty, evidently regards the bloody chastisement which the Jews had to endure at that time from the hands of the Romans as the punishment inflicted on the people for having acquiesced in the usurpation by the Hasmoneans of the royal dignity which had been reserved for the Messianic prince of the House of David. Especially significant in this connexion is the promise recounted in our Book of Levi (xxxii. 1) : *And he abode that night at Bethel, and Levi dreamed that they had ordained and made him the Priest of the Most High God, him and his sons for ever.* This, originally the title of the priest-king Melchizedek (Gen. xiv. 18), was revived by the Maccabean princely High Priests, and there is some evidence that in certain (? Saducean) quarters it was expected that the Messiah would spring from the tribe of Levi, and even from the priestly ruling Maccabean house.[1] The one possible reference to the hope of a Messiah from Judah in our Book occurs in the blessing of Judah, xxxi. 18 :

> *A prince shalt thou be, thou and one of thy sons over the sons of Jacob ;*

Here Judah is addressed, and is singled out for special honour by the side of Levi. This was only

---

[1] Cf. *Test. Levi*, xviii. ; Reuben, vi. ; Ps. cx. 4 (? addressed to Simon Maccabæus). The Pharisees objected to the use of this title.

natural, as the Jews derived their name from the tribe of Judah, who may be regarded as a sort of symbol of the nation generally. But who is meant by " one of thy sons "? Some would see in this a reference to the expected Messiah, but if this be so it is very vague. It is much more likely that the historic David is meant. The priestly author is significantly silent about a Davidic Messiah. Any Messiah he may have hoped for would, according to his view, spring from the tribe of Levi. He does not accept the view that the Davidic dynasty is of eternal duration, even ideally. May he not, too, have been thinking, in the address to Judah, of Judas Maccabæus? [1] Judas by his warlike exploits had shed a new glory on the name " Judah." But Judas himself belonged to the priestly family of the Hasmoneans, and it would be easy for our author to see in him the embodiment of the glories of the tribe of Judah, without diminishing the claims of the priestly tribe to civil as well as sacerdotal primacy.

In the same context (xxxi. 20) two lines occur in the address to Judah which run as follows :

And when thou sittest on the throne of the honour of thy righteousness,

There will be great peace for all the seed of the sons of the beloved.

The exact meaning of these words is not clear. They can hardly refer to the expected Messiah from David's House, because in that case the context would demand the use of the third person, whereas the second person is employed and Judah is being addressed. Leszynsky suggests that here in the Hebrew original there may be an allusion to the Sadducees, suggested by a word-play in the Hebrew word for " righteousness " (*sedek*). But even so the sentence is not clear. Is our author still thinking of Judas Maccabæus? If so, he may mean " and when thou (Judas), in the person of thy High-Priestly successors, sittest as Priest-king on thy Sadducean

[1] So Leszynsky.

throne of honour." It must be admitted that this is not very convincing, and the sentence remains obscure and uncertain in meaning. But of the high position assigned by our author to the tribe of Levi there can be no doubt. The lofty position of High-Priest and civil ruler is assigned to Levi as a reward for the destruction of Shechem (cf. xxx. 17–23; xxxii. 1–3). As Kohler says: " The Levites are represented as the keepers of the sacred books and of the secret lore entrusted to them by the saints from of yore (xlv. 16; cf. x. 14). This indicates that the priests and Levites still included among themselves, as in the days of the author of the Book of Chronicles, the men of learning, the masters of the schools, and that these positions were not filled by men from among the people, as was the case in the time of Shammai and Hillel." Other features of our Book entirely accord with this. For instance, the glorification of the Patriarchs in which our author loves to indulge is the development of a tendency already marked in the Priestly Sections of the Hexateuch.[1] In *Jubilees* they become saints of the Law. Incidents which might reflect discredit upon them (such as that described in Gen. xii. 11–13) are omitted. Abram is represented as having known the true God from his youth (xi. 16–17; xii. 1 ff.). Jacob is " a model of filial affection and obedience." A noticeable feature is also the insistence upon the unique position of Israel among the nations, and its rigid separation from the latter. Circumcision is a sign of Israel's elect position (xv. 26) and a privilege which they enjoy in common with the two chief orders of angels (xv. 27). This is also true of the Sabbath, which the same angelic orders observe with Israel. It is needless to add that our author glorifies the Law, which is of heavenly origin and everlasting validity. This is his estimate of the Law in its narrow sense, *i. e.* the Pentateuch. It is by this criterion that he measures everything. It is true that *Jubilees*

---

[1] See Carpenter, *Hexateuch*, i. 123 (cited by Charles).

contains incidents and amplifications which are not
to be found in the written Torah. But the author
is careful to base everything that is of legal obligation upon the letter of the Law itself. Anything
that he allows himself to introduce by way of amplification or addition serves merely to enhance the
obligation of the written precept.

Finally, his eschatology is essentially that of one
who is primarily interested in the Law. In xxiii.
12–31, he introduces an apocalyptic passage which
gives a history of the Maccabean times from the
persecution of Antiochus Epiphanes to the Messianic
Kingdom, the advent of which is just at hand. A
dark picture is drawn of the inroads of Hellenism,
and of its disintegrating effects upon the observance
of the Law and the covenant (xxiii. 16–20); the
warlike efforts of the Maccabees to reclaim the
Hellenizers to Judaism are then described (xxiii.
20–22), and the cry of the nation for deliverance
from its calamities (xxiii. 23–25). Then follows a
passage (xxiii. 26–32) in which, as a consequence of
Israel's renewed study of the Law, a happier period
follows. The Messianic Kingdom is to be " brought
about gradually by the progressive spiritual development of man and a corresponding transformation
of nature." Its members are " to attain to the full
limit of 1000 years in happiness and peace." Prof.
Charles [1] adds : " The writer of *Jubilees*, we can
hardly doubt, thought that the era of the Messianic
Kingdom had already set in."

The important point to notice about this picture is
that the dawn of the happier Age is brought about
by renewed study and observance of the Law :

> *And in those days the children will begin to study
>   the laws,*
>
> *And to seek the commandments,*
>
> *And to return to the path of righteousness* (xxiii. 26).

The result is a gradual transformation of men and
their environment. There is no catastrophe. It is

[1] *Op. cit.*, p. lxxxvii.

doubtful whether the author clearly envisages a final judgement, though there may be an allusion to such, in rather vague language, in xxiii. 30 f. The tone throughout is priestly, and it can hardly be doubted that the author was a priest.

AUTHORSHIP AND DATE

According to Charles, the author was not only a priest but a Pharisee " of the straitest sect." We have already seen that many of the positions advocated in the Book are essentially un-Pharisaic in character. Such a fundamentally Pharisaic doctrine as the resurrection of the body is not accepted, and it is more than doubtful whether the author looked for the advent of a Davidic Messiah. Moreover, it is difficult to conceive any Pharisee at any time advocating the adoption of a solar calendar. Then, again, though there were, of course, Pharisaic priests in later times, when the influence of Pharisaism had become all-powerful, it would certainly be remarkable to find in the second century B.C. so priestly a writer as our author a member of the Pharisaic party. For that party arose from the ranks of the people. It was essentially a lay movement, and it championed popular religious, as opposed to priestly, tradition. All this has been instinctively felt by the Jewish scholars [1] who have discussed the problems connected with the authorship and general character of our Book. By these scholars our Book has been variously ascribed to Essene (Jellinek, 1855), Samaritan (Beer, 1856–7), Hellenist (Frankel, 1856), and Jewish-Christian (Singer, 1898) authorship. None of these views is entirely satisfactory. More can be said for the view that the author belonged to the party—if party it can be called—of the Hasidim (" Assideans " or " Hasideans ") who are referred to in 1 Maccabees.[2]

[1] With the distinguished exception of Dr. K. Kohler (in *JE*, s.v. *Jubilees*), who accepts Charles's view, though he suggests that the book may reflect early Hasidæan practice.

[2] Cf. 1 Macc. vii

These " pious " members of the Jewish community were devoted adherents of the Law, and banded themselves together to resist the Hellenizers even unto death. They must not be confounded with the Pharisees, who may, however, have been influenced by them. There is nothing to show that the earlier Hasidim accepted popular religious tradition which had no basis in the written Law. Indeed, the reverse is probable. We know that, in spite of their anti-Hellenism, they scrupled to oppose the legitimate High Priest, even when he was on the Greek side. On the other hand, it is doubtful whether they would have countenanced the claim that the priests should exercise civil rule, while, as we have seen, the author of *Jubilees* distinctly takes up this position, and appears to have been an admirer of the Maccabean Priest-Princes—at any rate, of John Hyrcanus [1] and Simon Maccabæus. Still there is a certain affinity between our author and the Hasidim, and if he was not actually a " Hasid," he may very well have been in sympathy with members of that party in fundamental religious positions. Recently Leszynsky,[2] has maintained the thesis that *Jubilees* was written by a Sadducean author, and, it must be admitted, makes out a strong case. Unfortunately, scholars are not yet agreed as to the real character and position of the Sadducean party, but of recent years there has been a growing consensus of opinion that the party had a real religious basis. It was not, as it is sometimes represented to have been, a mere political party of worldly opportunists who used religious questions as a stick to beat the Pharisees, who represented true religion, while the real interests

---

[1] It is true that John Hyrcanus favoured the Pharisees, according to Josephus (*Ant.*, xiii. 10, 5), who even speaks of him as their " disciple." But this probably means no more than that he adopted a conciliatory attitude towards them. He also had intimate friends among the Sadducees (Josephus, *Ant.*, xiii. 10, 6).

[2] *Die Sadduzäer* (1912), pp. 179–236.

of their opponents were to safeguard their privileged position and wealth. If such books as Sirach are really, in any sense, Sadducean, and if we weigh the evidence of Josephus impartially, we may conclude that the real Sadducees represented the conservative tradition of the old scribal schools which grew up under priestly influence. The Sadducees stood for the written Law of Moses against the oral tradition, derived from popular religious elements, represented by the Pharisees. What could not be proved from the Law they refused to accept. Their essential objection to the new doctrine of the resurrection of the body was that it could not be proved from the Law. They stood for priestly privilege against the democratic tendencies of the Pharisees, who wished to bring in the laity as much as possible. It was natural that this party should be strong among the priests, and especially among families connected with the High Priesthood. The best members of it were, no doubt, pious devotees of the Law. This is not to say that worldly-minded members of the party did not exist. No doubt there were such, and some such men may have found it convenient to attach themselves to the Sadducean party. There were also worldly and hypocritical adherents in the ranks of the Pharisees. But in neither case is it just to estimate the essential character of the party from such elements. The persistence of the Sadducean party for so long a time within Judaism suggests that it possessed elements of real vitality and vigour. No doubt, also, it was divided into sections—one such is known to us as the sect of the Bœthusians. In view of its long continuance as an active party, and its significance in the history of Judaism, it must have stood for something more than mere negations. While it rejected the resurrection doctrine, the hope of a Davidic Messiah, and the Pharisaic oral tradition, it upheld the sole binding force of the written Torah, and emphasized priestly privilege.

Judged by these criteria, our author may well have

been a pious Sadducean priest. It is not necessary, of course, to suppose that all the positions upheld in our Book were commonly accepted by the Sadducean party. Our author had views of his own, particularly regarding the calendar—which at the time when he wrote seems to have been a burning subject of debate —which would not necessarily have commended themselves to the party generally. It is to be noted that the positions he upholds on other matters often agree with those of the Samaritans and Falashas and Ķaraite Jews, who are well-known to represent old Sadducean views on various points.

On one point of detail the Ethiopic text of our Book does uphold a specifically Pharisaic view. In xvi. 18, Israel is spoken of as destined to become *a kingdom and priests and a holy nation*. This is an echo of Exod. xix. 6, but there the Hebrew text has *a kingdom of priests* (" And ye shall be unto me a kingdom of priests and an holy nation "). Now the alteration yielded by the text of our Book here reflects the Pharisaic exegesis of this passage; the same altera-tion appears also in Rev. v. 10 (cf. i. 6). The Pharisees were anxious to separate the kingdom from the priesthood, and expounded Exod. xix. 6 in this way, as the Jewish Targums attest. But the original text of our Book can hardly have been under any such influence. Such an exegesis would contradict the express claims made for the priesthood elsewhere in the Book. The Latin version, which has " a kingdom of priests " (as in the original Hebrew text in Exod. xix. 6), is no doubt right. Probably the Ethiopic scribe was influenced by the form of the text in Rev. v. 10, and introduced it here.

We may sum up by saying that the author was undoubtedly a pious priest, a devoted adherent of the Law, and an upholder of priestly tradition; he was certainly not a Pharisee, but has affinities with the Hasidim or " pious " of early Maccabean times; not improbably he was a Sadducean priest. The exact date of the composition of *Jubilees* cannot be

fixed with absolute certainty, but no doubt, as
Charles has argued, it falls some time within the reigns
of Simon Maccabæus or John Hyrcanus, the flourish-
ing period of the Hasmonean rule. This, at any rate,
may be inferred from the historical sketch embodied
in the apocalyptic passage, xxiii. 12–31, and is rein-
forced by a number of other considerations. The
date to which the various phenomena point is some
time in the last half of the second century B.C.

BIBLIOGRAPHY

The important edition of the Ethiopic text by
Charles has already been referred to, as well as his
English translation of the Book with Introduction
and Notes (1902). This translation has also been
reprinted (with an Introduction and Notes) in the
Oxford *Corpus* (vol. ii. Pseudepigrapha, 1913) and
is reproduced in the pages that follow.

The most recent, and in many respects the most
important, discussion of *Jubilees* is contained in
Leszynsky's *Die Sadduzäer* (Berlin, 1912), pp. 179–
236. Leszynsky's arguments have been referred to
fully above. Kohler's article in *JE*, vol. vii.
(" Jubilees Book of ") is interesting and useful.
Of earlier works the following are important :

Jellinek, *Ueber das Buch der Jubiläen* (1855) ;
Beer, *Das Buch der Jubiläen und sein Verhältniss zu
den Midraschim* (Leipzig, 1856) ; also *Noch ein
Wort über das Buch der Jubiläen* (1857) ;
Frankel in *Monatsschrift* (1856) ;
Singer, *Das Buch der Jubiläen oder die Leptogenesis*
(Stuhlweissenburg, 1898).

There is a good discussion in Schürer *GJV.*, iii.
371–384, with full Bibliography.

SHORT TITLES, ABBREVIATIONS AND BRACKETS
USED IN THIS EDITION

1 Enoch = The Ethiopic Book of Enoch.

2 Enoch = The Slavonic Book of Enoch.

Ap. Bar. = The Syriac Apocalypse of Baruch.

Pirke de R. Eliezer is cited according to the edition (English translation with notes by W. O. E. Oesterley, D.D., and G. H. Box, M.A.) of G. Friedlander (London, 1916).

MT = Masoretic text.

Sam. = Samaritan version, and Hebrew text in Samaritan characters when both agree.

Syr. = the Syriac version of the Old Testament.

Vulg. = Vulgate.

( ) Words or letters so enclosed are supplied by the editor from some other source.

[ ] Words so enclosed are interpolated.

† † Words so enclosed are corrupt.

Charles's *Jubilees = The Book of Jubilees translated from the Ethiopic Text*, by R. H. Charles, D.D. (London, 1902).

JE = Jewish Encyclopædia.

RWS[2] = *Religion and Worship of the Synagogue* (1911).

THE BOOK OF JUBILEES

Prologue

THIS is the history of the division of the days [1] of
the law and of the testimony, of the events of the
years, of [2] their (year) weeks, of their jubilees throughout all the years of the world,[3] as the Lord spake to
Moses on Mount Sinai when he went up to receive the
tables of the law and of the commandment, according
to the voice of God as He said unto him, " Go up to
the top of the Mount." [4]

God's Revelation to Moses on Mount Sinai
(i. 1–26 : cf. Ex. xxiv. 15–18).

I. And it came to pass in the first year of the 2450 A.M.
exodus of the children of Israel out of Egypt, in the (A.M. =
third month,[5] on the sixteenth day of the month, Anno
that God spake to Moses, saying : " Come up to Me Mundi)
on the Mount, and I will give thee two tables of stone
of the law and of the commandment, which I have
written, that thou mayst teach them." [6] 2. And
Moses went up into the mount of God, and the glory
of the Lord abode on Mount Sinai, and a cloud over-
shadowed it six days. 3. And He called to Moses on

[1] The Prologue sums up the contents of the Book as at
once a *history* and a *chronological system based upon the
number seven*.

[2] *i. e.* according to (their year-weeks) : a year-week = seven
years (cf. Lev. xxv. 8 f.).

[3] The writer apparently intended to write a history from
Creation to the establishment of the Messianic Kingdom.

[4] Cf. Exod. xxiv. 12.   [5] Cf. Exod. xix. 1.

[6] Cf. Exod. xxiv. 12.

35

the seventh day out of the midst of the cloud, and the appearance of the glory of the Lord was like a flaming fire on the top of the Mount. 4. And Moses was on the Mount forty days and forty nights, and God taught him the earlier and the later history [1] of the division of all the days of the law and of the testimony. 5. And He said : " Incline thine heart to every word which I shall speak to thee on this Mount, and write them [2] in a book in order that their generations may see how I have not forsaken them for all the evil which they have wrought in transgressing the covenant which I establish between Me and thee for their generations this day on Mount Sinai. 6. And thus it will come to pass when all these things come upon them,[3] that they will recognize that I am more righteous than they in all their judgments and in all their actions, and they will recognize that I have been truly with them. 7. And do thou write for thyself [4] all these words which I declare unto thee this day, for I know their rebellion and their stiff neck,[5] before I bring them into the land of which I sware to their fathers, to Abraham and to Isaac and to Jacob, saying : " Unto your seed will I give a land flowing with milk and honey. 8. And they will eat and be satisfied, and they will turn to strange gods, to (gods) which cannot deliver them from aught of their tribulation : " and this witness shall be heard for a witness against them.[6] 9. For they will forget all My commandments, (even) all that I command them, and they will walk after the Gentiles, and after their uncleanness, and after their shame, and will serve their gods, and these will prove unto them an offence and a tribulation and an affliction and a snare.[7] 10. And

---

[1] Cf. i. 26. According to the Jewish Midrash, also, God showed Moses "all the generations that should arise," as well as "all the minutiæ of the Law " (*Shemoth rabb.* xl.; *Megilla* 19*b*).

[2] Cf. Exod. xxxiv. 27. [3] Cf. Deut. xxx. 1.
[4] Cf. i. 27. [5] Cf. Deut. xxxi. 27.
[6] Cf. Deut. xxxi. 20. [7] Cf. Exod. xxiii. 33.

many will perish and they will be taken captive,[1] and will fall into the hands of the enemy, because they have forsaken My ordinances and My commandments, and the festivals of My covenant, and My sabbaths, and My holy place [2] which I have hallowed for Myself in their midst, and My tabernacle,[3] and My sanctuary, which I have hallowed for Myself in the midst of the land, that I should set My name upon it, and that it should dwell (there).   11. And they [4] will make to themselves high places and groves and graven images,[5] and they will worship, each his own (graven image), so as to go astray, and they will sacrifice their children to demons,[6] and to all the works of the error of their hearts.   12. And I will send witnesses unto them, that I may witness against them, but they will not hear,[7] and will slay [8] the witnesses also, and they will persecute those who seek the law, and they will abrogate and change everything so as to work evil before My eyes.   13. And I shall hide My face from them, and I shall deliver them into the hand of the Gentiles for captivity, and for a prey, and for devouring,[9] and I shall remove them from the midst of the land, and I shall scatter [10] them amongst the Gentiles.   14. And they will forget all My law and all My commandments and all My judgments, and will go astray as to new moons, and sabbaths, and festivals, and jubilees, and ordinances.   15. And after this they will turn to Me [11] from amongst the Gentiles with all their heart and with all their soul and with all their strength, and I shall gather them from amongst all the Gentiles,[12] and they will seek Me, so that I shall be found of them, when they seek Me

---

[1] N. Israel is referred to.

[2] *i. e.* the Temple in Jerusalem.

[3] The Tabernacle is apparently thought of as still in existence (in Jerusalem) during the time of the monarchy.

[4] *i. e.* Judah.   [5] Cf. 2 Chron. xxxiii. 3 ff.

[6] Cf. 2 Chron. xxviii. 3, xxxiii. 6.   [7] Cf. 2 Chron. xxiv. 19.

[8] Cf. Matt. xxiii. 34.   [9] Cf. 2 Kings xxi. 14.

[10] Cf. Deut. iv. 27, xxviii. 64.

[11] Cf. Deut. iv. 30.   [12] Cf. Jer. xxix. 14.

with all their heart and with all their soul.   16. And
I shall disclose to them abounding peace with righteousness, and I shall †remove them the plant of
uprightness†,[1] with all My heart and with all My
soul,[2] and they will be for a blessing and not for a
curse,[3] and they will be the head and not the tail.[4]
17. And I shall build My sanctuary [5] in their midst,
and I shall dwell with them, and I shall be their God
and they will be My people [6] in truth and righteousness.   18. And I shall not forsake them nor fail
them; [7] for I am the Lord their God."   19. And
Moses fell on his face and prayed and said, " O Lord
my God, do not forsake Thy people and Thy inheritance,[8] so that they should wander in the error of
their hearts, and do not deliver them into the hands
of their enemies, the Gentiles, lest they should rule
over them and cause them to sin against Thee.   20.
Let Thy mercy, O Lord, be lifted up upon Thy people,
and create in them an upright spirit,[9] and let not the
spirit of Beliar [10] rule over them to accuse them before
Thee, and to ensnare them from all the paths of
righteousness, so that they may perish from before
Thy face.   21. But they are Thy people and Thy
inheritance, which Thou hast delivered with Thy
great power [11] from the hands of the Egyptians :
create in them a clean heart and a holy spirit,[12] and
let them not be ensnared in their sins from henceforth
until eternity."   22. And the Lord said unto Moses :
" I know their contrariness and their thoughts and
their stiffneckedness,[13] and they will not be obedient
till they confess their own sin and the sin of their

---

[1] The obelized words are corrupt. Charles suggests
reading " And I will plant them the plant of uprightness in
the land."

[2] Cf. Jer. xxxii. 41.   [3] Cf. Zech. viii. 13.
[4] Cf. Deut. xxviii. 13.   [5] i. e. the second Temple.
[6] Cf. Lev. xxvi. 12 and often.   [7] Cf. Deut. xxxi. 6.
[8] Cf. Deut. ix. 26.   [9] Cf. Ps. li. 10.

[10] Beliar (Belial) is here, as in the *Ascension of Isaiah* (see
Introduction to that work), a Satanic being, apparently " the
prince of the devils."   [11] Cf. Deut. ix. 29.

[12] Cf. Ps. li. 10 (and ver. 20 above).   [13] Cf. Deut. xxxi. 27.

fathers.[1] 23. And after this they will turn to Me in
all uprightness and with all (their) heart and with all
(their) soul, and I shall circumcise the foreskin of
their heart [2] and the foreskin of the heart of their
seed, and I shall create in them a holy spirit, and I shall
cleanse them so that they shall not turn away from
Me from that day unto eternity. 24. And their souls
will cleave to Me and to all My commandments, and
they will fulfil My commandments, and I shall be
their Father and they will be My children. 25. And
they will all be called children of the living God,[3] and
every angel and every spirit will know, yea, they will
know that these are My children, and that I am their
Father in uprightness and righteousness, and that I
love them. 26. And do thou write down for thyself
all these words [4] which I declare unto thee on this
mountain, the first and the last, which shall come to
pass in all the divisions of the days in the law and
in the testimony and in the weeks and the jubilees
unto eternity, until I descend and dwell with them [5]
throughout eternity."

God commands the Angel to write (i. 27–29).

27. And He said to the angel of the presence : [6]
"Write[7] for Moses from the beginning of creation
till My sanctuary has been built among them for all
eternity. 28.[8] And the Lord will appear to the eyes

[1] Cf. Lev. xxvi. 40. [2] Cf. Deut. x. 16, xxx. 6.

[3] Cf. Hos. i. 10.

[4] viz. those contained in our Book (the *Book of Jubilees*)
as distinguished from the *Book of the First Law* (vi. 22 = the
Pentateuch), which was written by the angel himself.

[5] viz. in the perfect theocracy inaugurated by the Messianic
Kingdom.

[6] Cf. Isa. lxiii. 9; *Test. XII. Patr.*, Judah 25 : probably
Michael is meant. Note that the medium of communication
is an angel, and cf. Gal. iii. 19 (" The Law . . . ordained
through angels "). Later Judaism rejected this idea.

[7] *i. e.* not the Pentateuch, " but a history up to the Messianic
Kingdom " (Charles, in Oxford *Corpus*).

[8] Read this ver. after ver. 25.

of all,[1] and all will know that I am the God of Israel and the Father of all the children of Jacob,[2] and King on Mount Zion [3] for all eternity. And Zion and Jerusalem will be holy." 29. And the angel of the presence who went before the camp of Israel [4] took the tables of the divisions of the years [5]—from the time of the creation—of the law and of the testimony of the weeks, of the jubilees, according to the individual years, according to all the number of the jubilees [according to the individual years], from the day of the [new] creation †when† the heavens [6] and the earth shall be renewed and all their creation according to the powers of the heaven, and according to all the creation of the earth, until the sanctuary of the Lord shall be made in Jerusalem [7] on Mount Zion, and all the luminaries be renewed for healing [8] and for peace and for blessing for all the elect of Israel, and that thus it may be from that day and unto all the days of the earth.

The Angel dictates to Moses the Primæval History : the Creation of the World and Institution of the Sabbath (ii. 1–33 ; cf. Gen. i–ii. 3).

II. And the angel of the presence spake to Moses according to the word of the Lord, saying : Write the complete history of the creation, how in six days the Lord God finished all His works and all that He created, and kept Sabbath on the seventh day and hallowed it for all ages, and appointed it as a sign

---

[1] Cf. Rev. i. 7 (in the final theophany).

[2] Cf. i. 24 ; Jer. xxxi. 1.

[3] Cf. Isa. xxiv. 23.

[4] Cf. Exod. xiv. 19.

[5] From these the angel dictates to Moses (who writes) the Book of Jubilees.

[6] Text corrupt. Read " from the day of creation, till the heavens."

[7] *i. e.* in the Messianic Kingdom.

[8] Cf. Rev. xxii. 2.

for all His works. 2.[1] For on the first day He created the heavens which are above and the earth and the waters and all the spirits which serve before Him— the angels [2] of the presence, and the angels of sanctification,[3] and the angels [of the spirit of fire and the angels] of the spirit of the winds,[4] and the angels of the spirit of the clouds, and of darkness, and of snow and of hail and of hoar frost,[5] and the angels of the voices [6] and of the thunder and of the lightning,[7] and the angels of the spirits of cold and of heat, and of winter and of spring and of autumn and of summer,[8] and of all the spirits of His creatures which are in the heavens and on the earth, (He created) the abysses and the darkness, eventide (and night), and the light, dawn and day, which He hath prepared in the knowledge of His heart. 3. And thereupon we saw His works, and praised Him, and lauded before Him on account of all His works; for seven great works did He create on the first day. 4. And on the second

[1] 2–3 record the creations of the first day, seven in number, viz. heaven, earth, the waters, spirits, the abysses, darkness, light. According to *Pirḳe de R. Eliezer* iii., " eight things were created on the first day: namely, heaven, earth, the light, darkness, Tohu (chaos), Bohu (void), wind (or spirit), water." Perhaps *Tohu* and *Bohu* here = *abysses*.

[2] According to our Book the angels were created on the first day, and this probably represents the view of earlier Judaism. This was opposed by later Judaism, which objected to the idea that angels assisted in the work of creation on the days following the first. *Pirḳe de R. Eliezer* placed the creation of angels in the *second* day; some Rabbis on the *fifth* (cf. *Gen. rabb.* i. 5).

[3] Cf. ii. 18, xv. 27, xxxi. 14. These are the two chief orders of angels. The " angels of sanctification " sing praises to God.

[4] The various classes of angels that follow constitute the third or lowest order. They preside over the elements and natural phenomena; cf. 1 Enoch lx. 12–21, lxxv., lxxx.; 2 Enoch xix. 1–4. For the " angels of the winds," cf. Rev. vii. 1 f.; 1 Enoch xviii. 1–5, xxxiv.–xxxvi., lxxvi.

[5] Cf. 1 Enoch lx. 17–18.

[6] Cf. Rev. iv. 5, xi. 19, xvi. 18.

[7] Cf. 1 Enoch lx. 13–15.

[8] Cf. 1 Enoch lxxxii. 13–20.

day[1] He created the firmament in the midst of the waters, and the waters were divided on that day— half of them went up above and half of them went down below the firmament (that was) in the midst over the face of the whole earth. And this was the only work (God) created on the second day. 5. And on the third day[2] He commanded the waters to pass from off the face of the whole earth into one place, and the dry land to appear. 6. And the waters did so as He commanded them, and they retired from off the face of the earth into one place outside of this firmament, and the dry land appeared. 7. And on that day He created for them all the seas according to their separate gathering-places, and all the rivers, and the gatherings of the waters in the mountains and on all the earth, and all the lakes, and all the dew of the earth, and the seed which is sown, and all sprouting things, and fruit-bearing trees, and trees of the wood, and the garden of Eden, in Eden, and all (plants after their kind). These four great works God created on the third day. 8. And on the fourth day[3] He created the sun and the moon and the stars, and set them in the firmament of the heaven, to give light upon all the earth, and to rule over the day and the night, and divide the light from the darkness. 9. And God appointed the sun[4] to be a great sign on the earth for days and for sabbaths and for months and for feasts and for years and for sabbaths of years and for jubilees and for all seasons of the years. 10. And it divideth the light from the darkness [and] for

---

[1] Cf. Gen. i. 6–7; 2 Enoch xxvi.–xxvii. According to *Pirḳe de R. Eliezer* iv. the following were created on the second day : the firmament, angels, fire for flesh and blood, and the fire of Gehinnom.

[2] Cf. Gen. i. 9–13 (dry land, seas, herbage, fruit trees = 3 works). Our Book adds a fourth, the Garden of Eden (so also the Midrash *Bereshith rabb.* xv.; 2 Enoch xxx. 1). Another view was that Paradise (? the Heavenly Paradise) was created before the world; cf. 4 Ezra iii. 6 (note).

[3] Cf. Gen. i. 14–19; 2 Enoch xxx. 2–6.

[4] Note the intentional omission of the moon. The writer objected to a calendar based upon the changes of the moon.

prosperity, that all things may prosper which shoot and grow on the earth. These three kinds He made on the fourth day. 11. And on the fifth day [1] He created great sea monsters in the depths of the waters, for these were the first things of flesh that were created by His hands, the fish and everything that moves in the waters, and everything that flies, the birds and all their kind. 12. And the sun rose above them to prosper (them), and above everything that was on the earth, everything that shoots out of the earth, and all fruit-bearing trees, and all flesh. These three kinds He created on the fifth day. 13. And on the sixth day [2] He created all the animals of the earth, and all cattle, and everything that moves on the earth. 14. And after all this He created man, a man and a woman created He them, and gave him dominion over all that is upon the earth, and in the seas, and over everything that flies, and over beasts and over cattle, and over everything that moves on the earth, and over the whole earth, and over all this He gave him dominion. And these four kinds He created on the sixth day. 15. And there were altogether two and twenty kinds.[3] 16. And He finished all His work on the sixth [4] day—all that is in the heavens and on the earth, and in the seas and in the abysses, and in the light and in the darkness, and in everything. 17. And He gave us a great sign, the Sabbath day,[5] that we should work six days, but keep Sabbath on the seventh day from all work. 18. And all the angels of the presence, and all the angels of sanctification, these two great classes—He hath bidden us

[1] Cf. Gen. i. 20–23; 2 Enoch xxx. 7; 4 Ezra vi. 47 ff. According to our Book the three works of the fifth day were the great sea-monsters, fish and birds; according to *Pirḳe de R. Eliezer* ix. birds, fish and locusts.

[2] Cf. Gen. i. 24–28; 2 Enoch xxx. 8 f.

[3] Cf. ii. 23 (below).

[4] This is possibly the right reading of Gen. ii. 2a (so Sam. text, LXX, Syr.). It implies a severer view of Sabbath observance. The Masoretic text has " seventh."

[5] Cf. Exod. xxxi. 13.

to keep the Sabbath with Him [1] in heaven and on earth.   19. And He said unto us : " Behold, I will separate unto Myself [2] a people from among all the peoples, and these will keep the Sabbath day, and I will sanctify them unto Myself as My people, and will bless them ; as I have sanctified the Sabbath day and do sanctify (it) unto Myself, even so shall I bless them, and they will be My people and I shall be their God. 20. And I have chosen the seed of Jacob [3] from amongst all that I have seen, and have written him down as My firstborn son,[4] and have sanctified him unto Myself for ever and ever ; and I will teach them the Sabbath day, that they may keep Sabbath thereon from all work."   21. And thus He created therein a sign [5] in accordance with which they should keep Sabbath with us [6] on the seventh day, to eat and to drink, and to bless Him [7] who hath created all things as He hath blessed and sanctified unto Himself a peculiar people [8] above all peoples, and that they should keep Sabbath together with us.   22. And He caused His commands to ascend as a sweet savour [9] acceptable before Him all the days. . . . 23. There (were) two and twenty heads of mankind from Adam to Jacob, and two and twenty kinds of work were made [10] until

[1] The two chief orders of angels observe the Sabbath with God (and Israel).   The third order and the Gentiles are denied this privilege.
[2] Cf. 1 Kings viii. 53.
[3] Cf. Isa. xli. 8 (" Jacob whom I have chosen "), xliv. 1, 2.
[4] Cf. Exod. iv. 22 ; Ps. lxxxix. 27.
[5] For the Sabbath day as a sign between God and Israel, cf. Exod. xxxi. 13, 17 ; Ezek. xx. 12.
[6] i. e. with God and the superior angels.
[7] The Sabbath is to be a delight.
[8] Cf. Deut. vii. 6.   [9] Cf. 2 Cor. ii. 15 ; Eph. v. 2.
[10] It is probable that at end of 22 above there is a lacuna in the text (indicated by the dotted line).   Charles restores the missing words as follows : *As there were two and twenty letters, and two and twenty (sacred) books* [viz. in the Old Testament], *and two and twenty heads of mankind from Adam to Jacob, so there were made two and twenty kinds of work*, etc.

the seventh day; this [1] is blessed and holy; and the former [2] also is blessed and holy; and this one serves with that one for sanctification and blessing. 24. And to this (Jacob and his seed) it was granted that they should always be the blessed and holy ones of the first testimony and law, even as He had sanctified and blessed the Sabbath day on the seventh day. 25. He created heaven and earth and everything that He created in six days, and God made the seventh day holy, for all His works; therefore He commanded on its behalf that, whoever doth any work thereon shall die,[3] and that he who defileth it shall surely die. 26. Wherefore do thou command the children of Israel to observe this day that they may keep it holy [4] and not do thereon any work, and not to defile it, as it is holier than all other days.[5] 27. And whoever profaneth it shall surely die, and whoever doeth thereon any work shall surely die eternally, that the children of Israel may observe this day throughout their generations, and not be rooted out of the land; for it is a holy day and a blessed day. 28. And every one who observeth it and keepeth Sabbath thereon from all his work, will be holy and blessed throughout all days like unto us. 29. Declare and say to the children of Israel the law of this day both that they should keep Sabbath thereon, and that they should not forsake it in the error of their hearts; (and) that it is not lawful to do any work thereon which is unseemly, to do thereon their own pleasure,[6] and that they should not prepare thereon anything to be eaten or drunk,[7] †and (that it is not lawful) to draw water, or bring in or take out thereon through their gates any burden,† [8] which they had not

---

[1] viz. the Sabbath.　　　　　　[2] viz. Jacob.
[3] Cf. Exod. xxxi. 14, 15, xxxv. 2; Num. xv. 32 f.
[4] Cf. Exod. xx. 8.　　　　　　[5] Cf. ii. 30.
[6] Cf. Isa. lviii. 13.　　　[7] Deduced from Exod. xvi. 23, 25.
[8] The obelized words should either be omitted or read *after their own pleasure* above. For the law about " bringing in or taking out . . . any burden " on the Sabbath, cf. ii. 30, l. 8; Jer. xvii. 21 f.; Neh. xiii. 19; John v. 10.

prepared for themselves on the sixth day [1] in their dwellings. 30. And they shall not bring in nor take out from house to house [2] on that day; for that day is more holy and blessed than any jubilee day of the jubilees : on this we kept Sabbath in the heavens before it was made known to any flesh to keep Sabbath thereon on the earth. 31. And the Creator of all things blessed it,[3] but He did not sanctify all peoples and nations to keep Sabbath thereon, but Israel alone : them alone He permitted to eat and drink and to keep Sabbath thereon on the earth. 32. And the Creator of all things blessed this day which He had created for a blessing and a sanctification and a glory above all days. 33. This law and testimony was given to the children of Israel as a law for ever unto their generations.[4]

Paradise and the Fall (iii. 1–35; cf. Gen. ii. 4–iii.).

III. And on the six days of the second week we brought, according to the word of God, unto Adam all the beasts, and all the cattle, and all the birds, and everything that moveth on the earth, and everything that moveth in the water, according to their kinds, and according to their types : the beasts on the first day; the cattle on the second day; the birds on the third day; and all that which moveth on the earth on the fourth day; and that which moveth in the water on the fifth day. 2. And Adam named them all by their respective names, and as he called them, so was their name.[5] 3. And on these five days Adam saw all these, male and female, according to every kind that was on the earth, but he was alone and found no help-

This is in accordance with Rabbinic law which forbids anything being eaten on the Sabbath unless it had been prepared beforehand for that purpose on a week-day.

[2] This was relaxed later by the Rabbinic law of *erub*, which was based on Exod. xvi. 29. See *JE*. v. 203 f. (s.v. Erub).

[3] *i.e.* Israel. [4] Cf. Exod. xxvii. 21, etc., for the phrase. [5] Cf. Gen. ii. 19.

meet for him.[1] 4. And the Lord said unto us : " It is not good that the man should be alone : let us make a helpmeet for him." [2] 5. And the Lord our God caused a deep sleep to fall upon him, and he slept, and He took for the woman one rib from amongst his ribs, and this rib was the origin of the woman from amongst his ribs, and He built up the flesh in its stead, and built the woman. 6. And He awaked Adam out of his sleep and on awaking he rose on the sixth day, and He brought her to him, and he knew her, and said unto her : " This is now bone of my bones and flesh of my flesh; she will be called [my] wife; because she was taken from her husband." [3] 7. Therefore shall man and wife be one, and therefore shall a man leave his father and his mother, and cleave unto his wife, and they shall be one flesh.[4] 8. In the first week was Adam created, and the rib—his wife : in the second week He showed her unto him : and for this reason the commandment was given to keep in their defilement, for a male seven days, and for a female twice seven days.[5] 9. And after Adam had completed forty days in the land where he had been created, we brought him into the Garden of Eden to till and keep it, but his wife they brought in on the eightieth day, and after this she entered into the Garden of Eden. 10. And for this reason the commandment is written on the heavenly tables [6] in

[1] Cf. Gen. ii. 20.

[2] Cf. Gen. ii. 18; LXX and Vulg. have pl. (" let *us* make "), but MT Sam. Syr., " I will make."

[3] Cf. Gen. ii. 21–23. According to the Talmud, Adam was originally (as first created, Gen. i. 27) hermaphroditic.

[4] Cf. Gen. ii. 24.

[5] For these laws cf. Lev. xii. 2–5, according to which in the one case the mother was not to enter the sanctuary till the lapse of forty days, in the other eighty days. The reason for this is given in the following section (9), according to the author of *Jubilees*. This peculiar idea recurs elsewhere (Philo, *Book of Adam and Eve*), but not in Rabbinic literature, except for some slight traces. See Charles, *ad loc.*

[6] Cf. 1 Enoch lxxxi. 1, 2, xciii. 2, ciii. 2; the expression also occurs in *Test. XII. Patriarchs*. In our Book the *heavenly*

regard to her that giveth birth : " if she beareth a male,
she shall remain in her uncleanness seven days according to the first week of days, and thirty and three
days shall she remain in the blood of her purifying,
and she shall not touch any hallowed thing, nor enter
into the sanctuary, until she accomplisheth these days
which (are enjoined) in the case of a male child.
11. But in the case of a female child she shall remain
in her uncleanness two weeks of days, according to
the first two weeks, and sixty-six days in the blood
of her purification, and they will be in all eighty days."
12. And when she had completed these eighty days
we brought her into the Garden of Eden, for it is
holier than all the earth besides, and every tree that
is planted in it is holy. 13. Therefore, there was
ordained regarding her who beareth a male or a female
child the statute of those days that she should touch
no hallowed thing, nor enter into the sanctuary until
these days for the male or female child are accomplished. 14. This is the law and testimony which
was written down for Israel, in order that they should
observe (it) all the days. 15. And in the first week

1 7 A.M. of the first jubilee, Adam and his wife were in the
Garden of Eden for seven [1] years tilling and keeping it,
and we gave him work and we instructed him to do
everything that is suitable for tillage.[2] 16. And he
tilled (the garden), and was naked and knew it not,
and was not ashamed,[3] and he protected the garden
from the birds and beasts and cattle, and gathered

---

tables are conceived of as the divine statute book of which
the Mosaic Law is the earthly reproduction; but they also
contain records of events and predictions. The underlying
idea is predestinarian.

[1] According to *Ber. rabba* xviii., *Sanh.* 38b, Adam was
only six hours in the Garden; cf. *Pirke de R. Eliezer* xviii.
(Adam entered the garden at the seventh hour and was
driven forth at twilight, *i. e.* the twelfth hour on Friday
the eve of the Sabbath).

[2] Agriculture is a divine institution. Here the instruction
is given by angels; contrast Isa. xxviii. 26–29. See also
4 Ezra vi. 42. *Test. XII. Patr.* Issachar iii. 5.

[3] Cf. Gen. ii. 25.

its fruit, and ate, and put aside the residue for himself and for his wife [and put aside that which was being kept].[1] 17.[2] And after the completion of the seven years, which he had completed there, seven years exactly, and in the second month, on the seventeenth day (of the month), the serpent came and approached the woman, and the serpent said to the woman, " Hath God commanded you, saying, Ye shall not eat of every tree of the garden ? " 18. And she said to it, " Of all the fruit of the trees of the garden God hath said unto us, Eat; but of the fruit of the tree which is in the midst of the garden God hath said unto us, Ye shall not eat thereof, neither shall ye touch it, lest ye die." 19. And the serpent said unto the woman, " Ye shall not surely die : for God doth know that on the day ye shall eat thereof, your eyes will be opened, and ye will be as gods, and ye will know good and evil." 20. And the woman saw the tree that it was agreeable and pleasant to the eye, and that its fruit was good for food, and she took thereof and ate. 21. And when she had first covered her shame with fig-leaves, she gave thereof to Adam and he ate, and his eyes were opened, and he saw that he was naked. 22. And he took fig-leaves and sewed (them) together, and made an apron for himself, and covered his shame. 32. And God cursed the serpent, and was wroth with it for ever. . . .[3] 24. And He was wroth with the woman, because she hearkened to the voice of the serpent, and did eat; and He said unto her : [4] " I shall greatly multiply thy sorrow and thy pains : in sorrow thou shalt bring forth children, and thy return [5] shall be unto thy husband, and he will rule over thee." 25.

8 A.M

---

[1] The bracketed words are a dittograph.

[2] For 17–22 cf. Gen. iii. 1–7.

[3] Charles suspects a lacuna here. It may have contained a statement to the effect that the serpent's four feet, which it is supposed to have originally possessed, were cut off. Cf. Targ. Ps.-Jon. on Gen. iii. 14, and Josephus, *Ant.* i. 1, 4.

[4] Cf. Gen. iii. 16.

[5] So LXX and Syr. (ἡ ἀποστραφή σου), MT, " thy desire."

And to Adam also He said, " Because thou hast hearkened unto the voice of thy wife, and hast eaten of the
tree of which I commanded thee that thou shouldst
not eat thereof, cursed be the ground for thy sake :
thorns and thistles shall it bring forth to thee, and
thou shalt eat thy bread in the sweat of thy face, till
thou returnest to the earth from whence thou wast
taken ; for earth thou art, and unto earth shalt thou
return." 26. And He made for them coats of skin,
and clothed them, and sent them forth from the
Garden of Eden.[1] 27. And on that day on which
Adam went forth from the garden, he offered as a
sweet savour an offering, frankincense, galbanum, and
stacte, and spices [2] in the morning with the rising of
the sun from the day when he covered his shame.
28. And on that day was closed the mouth of all
beasts, and of cattle, and of birds, and of whatever
walketh, and of whatever moveth, so that they could
no longer speak : [3] for they had all spoken one with
another with one lip and with one tongue. 29. And
He sent out of the Garden of Eden all flesh that was
in the Garden of Eden, and all flesh was scattered
according to its kinds, and according to its types unto
the places which had been created for them. 30. And
to Adam alone did He give (the wherewithal) to cover
his shame, of all the beasts and cattle. 31. On this
account, it is prescribed on the heavenly tables as
touching all those who know the judgment of the law,
that they should cover their shame, and should not
uncover themselves as the Gentiles uncover them-
8 A.M. selves.[4] 32. And on the new moon of the fourth
month, Adam and his wife went forth from the Garden

---

[1] Cf. Gen. ii. 17–19, 21, 24.

[2] *i. e.* the incense-offering of Exod. xxx. 34.

[3] For this belief cf. Josephus, *Ant.* i. 1, 4. The idea underlying the text here is that up to this time both men and
animals spoke Hebrew, which was the universal language
till the building of the Tower of Babel.

[4] A protest against the Greek custom of exposing the
person in public athletic sports; cf. 1 Macc. i. 13 f.; 2 Macc.
iv. 9–14; Josephus, *Ant.* xii. 5, 1.

of Eden, and they dwelt in the land of 'Eldâ,[1] in the land of their creation. 33. And Adam called the name of his wife Eve. 34. And they had no son till the first jubilee, and after this he knew her. 35. Now he tilled the land as he had been instructed in the Garden of Eden.[2]

Cain and Abel (iv. 1–12; cf. Gen. iv.).

IV. And in the third week in the second jubilee she 64-70 A.M. gave birth to Cain, and in the fourth she gave birth 71-77 A.M. to Abel, and in the fifth she gave birth to her daughter 78-84 A.M. 'Âwân.[3] 2. And in the first (year) of the third jubilee, 99-105 Cain slew Abel because (God) accepted the sacrifice A.M. of Abel, and did not accept the offering of Cain. 3. And he slew him in the field : and his blood cried from the ground to heaven, complaining because he had slain him.[4] 4. And the Lord reproved Cain because of Abel, because he had slain him, and he made him a fugitive on the earth because of the blood of his brother, and he cursed him upon the earth.[5] 5. And on this account it is written on the heavenly tables, " Cursed is he who smiteth his neighbour treacherously, and let all who have seen and heard say, So be it ; and the man who hath seen and not declared (it), let him be accursed as the other." [6] 6. And for this reason we announce when we come before the Lord our God all the sin which is committed in heaven and on earth, and in light and in darkness, and everywhere. 7. And Adam and his wife mourned for Abel four weeks of years, and in the fourth year (99-127) of the fifth week they became joyful, and Adam knew 130 A.M.

[1] Charles suggests that 'Elda may be a corruption of the Hebrew word meaning " nativity " (land of " nativity ").

[2] Cf. iii. 15.

[3] i. e. " iniquity " (Heb. 'āwen). Another daughter, 'Azûrâ (= ? " well guarded "), was born later. Cain married 'Âwân and Seth 'Azûrâ. There is great divergence as to these names in later writers. According to Pirḳe de R. Eliezer, Cain's wife was his twin-sister (xxi.).

[4] Cf. Gen. iv. 4, 5, 8, 10.

[5] Cf. Gen. iv. 11–12.   [6] Cf. Deut. xxvii. 24.

his wife again, and she bare him a son, and he [1] called
his name Seth; for he said "God hath raised up a
second seed unto us on the earth instead of Abel;
for Cain slew him." [2] 8. And in the sixth week he
134-140 begat his daughter 'Azûrâ. 9. And Cain took 'Âwân
A.M. his sister to be his wife and she bare him Enoch [3] at
190-196 the close of the fourth jubilee. And in the first year
A.M. of the first week of the fifth jubilee, houses were built
197 A.M. on the earth, and Cain built a city, and called its
name after the name of his son Enoch. 10. And
Adam knew Eve his wife and she bare yet nine sons. [4]
225-231 11. And in the fifth week of the fifth jubilee Seth
A.M. took 'Azûrâ his sister to be his wife, and in the fourth
235 A.M. (year of the sixth week) she bare him Enos. [5] 12. He [6]
began to call on the name of the Lord on the earth.

The Patriarchs from Adam to Noah (cf. Gen. v.); Life of Enoch ; Death of Adam and Cain (iv. 13–33).

309-315   13. [7] And in the seventh jubilee in the third week
A.M. Enos took Nôâm his sister to be his wife, and she bare
325 A.M. him a son in the third year of the fifth week, and he
called his name Kenan. 14. And at the close of the
386-392 eighth jubilee Kenan took Mûalêlêth [8] his sister to be
A.M. his wife, and she bare him a son in the ninth jubilee,
395 A.M. in the first week in the third year of this week, and
449-455 he called his name Mahalalel. 15. And in the second
A.M. week of the tenth jubilee Mahalalel took unto him to
wife Dînâh, the daughter of Barâkî'êl the daughter of
his father's brother, and she bare him a son in the third
461 A.M. week in the sixth year, and he called his name Jared; [9]
for in his days the angels of the Lord descended on

---

[1] So Sam.; but MT "she." In our Book it is generally
the father who names the child.
[2] Cf. Gen. iv. 25.   [3] Cf. Gen. iv. 17.
[4] Pseudo-Philo, *Bibl. Antiq.*, gives the names of these nine
sons.   [5] Cf. Gen. iv. 26.
[6] So LXX and Vulg.; but MT "then it was begun (men
began)."   [7] For 13–14 cf. Gen. v. 9, 12.
[8] A fem. form = "she who praises God."
[9] Cf. Gen. v. 15.

the earth,[1] those who are named the Watchers,[2] that
they should instruct the children of men,[3] and that
they should do judgment and uprightness on the earth.
16. And in the eleventh jubilee Jared took to himself 512-518
a wife, and her name was Bâraka, the daughter of A.M.
Râsûjâl, a daughter of his father's brother, in the
fourth week of this jubilee, and she bare him a son
in the fifth week, in the fourth year of the jubilee, 522 A.M.
and he called his name Enoch.[4] 17. And he [5] was
the first among men that are born on earth who learnt
writing and knowledge and wisdom [6] and who wrote
down the signs of heaven according to the order of
their months in a book,[7] that men might know the
seasons of the years according to the order of their
separate months. 18. And he was the first to write a
testimony, and he testified to the sons of men among
the generations of the earth, and recounted the weeks
of the jubilees, and made known to them the days
of the years,[8] and set in order the months and re-

---

[1] This last line looks like a quotation from 1 Enoch vi. 6
(" who descended in the days of Jared "). Note the play in
Hebrew on the name *Jared* (*yāred*) and " descended " (Heb.
yārĕdû). The myth of the descent of the angels was based
on Gen. vi. 1–4, but was rejected by the Rabbis, who rendered
" sons of God " (*i. e.* angels) " sons of the judges."

[2] This name is given to angels in Dan. iv. 13, 17, 23; in
1 Enoch it is applied especially to the fallen angels (cf.
1 Enoch i. 5, x. 9, 15 and often).

[3] This statement is interesting. It describes what was
probably the original commission by God to the angelic
watchers, who, however, fell when they descended to the
earth. According to 1 Enoch, Enoch acquired his super-
natural knowledge from the instruction of angels.

[4] Cf. Gen. v. 18.

[5] The passage that follows about Enoch (17–23) implies
knowledge on the part of the author of Enochic writings.
Charles infers that these were 1 Enoch vi.–xvi., xxiii.–xxxvi.,
and lxxii.–xc.

[6] Cf. the phrase " Scribe of righteousness " applied to
Enoch in 1 Enoch xii. 4, xv. 1.

[7] Probably a reference to 1 Enoch lxxii.–lxxxii. (" The
Book of the courses of the Heavenly Luminaries ").

[8] There is nothing in 1 or 2 Enoch about " jubilees," etc.
This statement is probably due solely to the author of *Jubilees*,
who wished to invest the institution with a spurious antiquity.

counted the Sabbaths of the years as we made (them)
known to him.   19. And what was and what will be
he saw in a vision [1] of his sleep, as it will happen to
the children of men throughout their generations
until the day of judgment; he [2] saw and understood
everything, and wrote his testimony, and placed the
testimony on earth for all the children of men and
582-588 for their generations.   20. And in the twelfth jubilee,
A.M. in the seventh week thereof, he took to himself a
wife, and her name was Ednî,[3] the daughter of Dânêl,
587 A.M. the daughter of his father's brother, and in the sixth
year in this week she bare him a son and he called his
name Methuselah.[4]   21. And he was moreover with
the angels of God these six jubilees of years, and they
showed him everything which is on earth [5] and in the
heavens, the rule of the sun, and he wrote down
everything.   22. And he testified to the Watchers,
who had sinned with the daughters of men; for these
had begun to unite themselves, so as to be defiled,
with the daughters of men, and Enoch testified against
(them) all.   23. And he was taken from amongst
the children of men, and we conducted him into the
Garden of Eden [6] in majesty and honour, and behold
there he writeth down the condemnation and judgment
of the world, and all the wickedness of the children
of men.[7]   24. And on account of it (God) brought the
waters of the flood [8] upon all the land of Eden; for
there he was set as a sign and that he should testify
against all the children of men, that he should recount
all the deeds of the generations until the day of con-

---

[1] The reference is probably to the "Dream-Visions"
(1 Enoch lxxxiii.–xc.).

[2] *i. e.* Enoch. The writings of Enoch are mentioned
elsewhere (1 Enoch, *Test. XII. Patriarchs*).

[3] *Edna* in 1 Enoch lxxxv. 3.

[4] Cf. Gen. v. 21.

[5] 1 Enoch xxiii.–xxxvi.

[6] Cf. 1 Enoch lxx. 1–3.

[7] Cf. 1 Enoch xii. 3 f., xiv. 1. The title ("Scribe of the
Knowledge of the Most High") is conferred upon Ezra in
4 Ezra xiv. 50 (Syriac text).

[8] Cf. 2 Enoch xxxiv. 3.

demnation.[1] 25. And he burnt the incense of the sanctuary, (even) sweet spices,[2] acceptable before the Lord on the Mount. 26. For the Lord hath four places[3] on the earth, the Garden of Eden, and the Mount of the East,[4] and this mountain on which thou art this day, Mount Sinai, and Mount Zion (which) will be sanctified in the new creation for a sanctification of the earth; through it will the earth be sanctified from all (its) guilt and its uncleanness throughout the generations of the world.[5] 27. And in the fourteenth 652 A.M. jubilee Methuselah took unto himself a wife, Ednâ the daughter of 'Âzrîâl, the daughter of his father's brother, in the third week, in the first year of this week, and he begat a son and called his name Lamech.[6] 28. And in the fifteenth jubilee in the third week 701-707 Lamech took to himself a wife, and her name was A.M. Bêtênôs the daughter of Bârâkî'îl, the daughter of his father's brother, and in this week she bare him a son and he called his name Noah, saying, "This one will comfort me for my trouble and all my work, and for the ground which the Lord hath cursed." [7] 29. And at the close of the nineteenth jubilee, in the seventh week in the sixth year thereof, Adam died, and all 930 A.M. his sons buried him in the land of his creation,[8] and he was the first to be buried [9] in the earth. 30. And he lacked seventy years of one thousand years; for one thousand years are as one day in the testimony

---

[1] Cf. x. 17.   [2] Cf. Exod. xxx. 7.

[3] Three of these places are connected with critical events in the history of the world; Eden (with Adam), Sinai (with Moses), Zion (with David).

[4] The exact identification is uncertain; possibly the mount above Eden, where the Scthites live, is meant. Other suggestions are Mt. Ephraim, which would imply a Samaritan authorship, and Lubar, on Ararat, which would connect well with the history of Noah.

[5] Cf. i. 29.   [6] Cf. Gen. v. 25.

[7] Cf. Gen. v. 29.   [8] Cf. iii. 32.

[9] This implies the view that Abel's body was not buried before Adam's. According to Pirḳe de R. Eliezer (xxi.), Adam was at first uncertain what to do, but then buried Abel's corpse.

of the heavens and therefore was it written concerning the tree of knowledge : " On the day that ye eat thereof ye will die." [1] For this reason he did not complete the years of this day; for he died during it. 31. At the close of this jubilee Cain was killed after him in the same year; for his house fell upon him and he died in the midst of his house, and he was killed by its stones; for with a stone he had killed Abel, and by a stone was he killed in righteous judgment. 32. For this reason it was ordained on the heavenly tables : " With the instrument with which a man killeth his neighbour with the same shall he be killed; after the manner that he wounded him, in like manner shall they deal with him." [2] 33. And in 1205 A.M. the twenty-fifth jubilee Noah took to himself a wife, and her name was 'Êmzârâ, the daughter of Râkê'êl, the daughter of his father's brother, in the first year 1207 A.M. in the fifth week : and in the third year thereof she 1209 A.M. bare him Shem, in the fifth year thereof she bare him 1212 A.M. Ham, and in the first year in the sixth week she bare him Japheth. [3]

The Fall of the Angels and their Punishment ; the Deluge foretold (v. 1–20; cf. Gen. vi. 1–12).

V. And it came to pass when the children of men began to multiply on the face of the earth and daughters were born unto them, that the angels of God [4] saw them on a certain year of this jubilee, that they were

[1] Cf. Gen. ii. 14. Notice that " day " here is interpreted as = 1000 years—a belief early current among Jews and Christians (cf. *Ber. rabba* xix. on Gen. iii. 8), 2 Pet. iii. 8. Justin Martyr, *Trypho.* lxxxi; cf. also *Pirke de R. Eliezer* xviii.

[2] The *lex talionis ;* cf. Exod. xxi. 24 (" eye for eye, tooth for tooth "); Lev. xxiv. 19. Similar examples are given in 2 Macc. v. 19 f., xv. 32 f. The rigorous application of this " law " was upheld by the Sadducees, as against the Pharisees.

[3] Cf. Gen. v. 22. Note that Shem is represented as the eldest; cf. Gen. x. 21 (R.V.).

[4] This is the LXX rendering of Gen. vi. 2 (R.V. " sons of God ") and represents the older Jewish exegesis, which was later given up.

beautiful to look upon; and they took themselves wives of all whom they chose, and they bare unto them sons and they were giants.[1]   2. And lawlessness increased on the earth and all flesh corrupted its way,[2] alike men and cattle and beasts and birds and everything that walketh on the earth—all of them corrupted their ways and their orders, and they began to devour [3] each other, and lawlessness increased on the earth and every imagination of the thoughts of all men (was) thus evil continually.[4]   3. And God looked upon the earth, and behold it was corrupt, and all flesh had corrupted its orders, and all that were upon the earth [5] had wrought all manner of evil before His eyes.   4. And He said : " I shall destroy man and all flesh upon the face of the earth which I have created."   5. But Noah found grace before the eyes of the Lord.[6]   6. And against the angels whom He had sent upon the earth, He was exceedingly wroth, and He gave commandment to root them out of all their dominion, and He bade us to bind them in the depths of the earth, and behold they are bound in the midst of them, and are (kept) separate.   7. And against their sons went forth a command from before His face that they should be smitten with the sword, and be removed from under heaven.   8. And He said " My spirit will not always abide [7] on man ; for they also are flesh and their days shall be one hundred and twenty years."   9. And He sent His sword into their midst that each should slay his neighbour, and they began to slay each other till they all fell by the sword and were destroyed from the earth. 10. And their fathers were witnesses (of their destruction), and after this they were bound in the depths of the earth for ever, until the day of the great condemnation,[8] when judgment is executed on all those who have corrupted their ways and their works before

---

[1] *Giants, i. e.* " Nephilim."
[2] Cf. Gen. vi. 12.
[3] Cf. 1 Enoch vii. 5.
[4] Cf. Gen. vi. 5.
[5] Cf. Gen. vi. 12.
[6] Cf. Gen. vi. 7, 8.
[7] Cf. Gen. vi. 3, R.V. marg.
[8] Cf. 1 Enoch x. 12.

the Lord.   11. And He †destroyed† all from their places, and there †was† not left one of them whom He judged not according to all their wickedness.   12. And He †made† for all His works a new and righteous nature,[1] so that they should not sin in their whole nature for ever, but thould be all righteous each in his kind alway.   13. And the judgment of all is ordained and written on the heavenly tables in right-eousness—even (the judgment of) all who depart from the path which is ordained for them to walk in ; and if they walk not therein, judgment is written down for every creature and for every kind.   14. And there is nothing in heaven or on earth, or in light or in darkness, or in Sheol or in the depth, or in the place of darkness (which is not judged) ; and all their judgments are ordained and written and engraved. 15. In regard to all He will judge, the great according to his greatness, and the small according to his small-ness, and each according to his way.   16. And He is not one who will regard the person (of any), nor is He one who will receive gifts, if He saith that He will execute judgment on each : if one gave everything that is on the earth, He will not regard the gifts or the person (of any), nor accept anything at his hands, for He is a righteous judge.[2]   [17. And of the children of Israel it hath been written and ordained : If they turn to Him in righteousness, He will forgive all their transgressions and pardon all their sins.   18. It is written and ordained that He will show mercy to all who turn from all their guilt once each year.][3]   19.

---

[1] 10–12, as Charles has shown, describe the *final* judg-ment. The tenses must be altered from past to future. Render : " until the day of the great condemnation, when judgment *shall be* executed. . . . And He *shall* destroy . . . and there *shall not* be left one of them whom He *shall* not have judged. . . . And He *shall* make," etc.

[2] Cf. xl. 8 ; Deut. x. 17 ; 2 Chron. xix. 7.

[3] The bracketed clauses have been either transposed here or interpolated from xxxiv. 18–19. The reference is to the Day of Atonement which takes place on the 10th of the 7th month. For " once each year," cf. Heb. ix. 7.

And as for all those who corrupted their ways and
their thoughts before the flood, no man's person was
accepted save that of Noah alone; for his person was
accepted in behalf of his sons, whom (God) saved from
the waters of the flood on his account; for his heart
was righteous in all his ways, according as it was commanded regarding him, and he had not departed from
aught that was ordained for him.   20. And the Lord
said that He would destroy everything which was upon
the earth, both men and cattle, and beasts, and fowls
of the air, and that which moveth on the earth.[1]

The Building of the Ark ; the Flood (v. 21–32; cf. Gen. vi. 13–viii. 19).

21. And He commanded Noah to make him an
ark, that he might save himself from the waters of
the flood.[2] 22. And Noah made the ark in all respects
as He commanded him, in the twenty-seventh jubilee 1307 A.M.
of years, in the fifth week in the fifth year (on the
new moon of the first month).   23. And he entered
in the sixth (year) thereof, in the second month, on 1308 A.M.
the new moon of the second month, till the sixteenth;
and he entered, and all that we brought to him, into
the ark, and the Lord closed[3] it from without on the
seventeenth[4] evening.

24. And the Lord opened seven flood-gates[5] of heaven,
  And the mouths of the fountains of the great deep,
    seven mouths in number.

25. And the flood-gates began to pour down water
    from the heaven forty days and forty nights,
  And the fountains of the deep also sent up waters,
    until the whole world was full of water.

26. And the waters increased upon the earth :
  Fifteen cubits did the waters rise above all the
    high mountains,

---

[1] Cf. Gen. vi. 7.   [2] Cf. Gen. vi. 14.
[3] Cf. Gen. vii. 16.   [4] Cf. Gen. vii. 11.
[5] Cf. 1 Enoch lxxxix. 2. Note the recurrence of the
number seven in these connexions,

And the ark was lift up above the earth,
And it moved upon the face of the waters.[1]
27. And the water prevailed on the face of the earth
five months—one hundred and fifty days.[2] 28. And
the ark went and rested on the top of Lûbâr, one of
the mountains of Ararat.[3] 29. And (on the new
moon) in the fourth month the fountains of the great
deep were closed and the flood-gates of heaven were
restrained; and on the new moon of the seventh
month all the mouths of the abysses of the earth were
opened, and the water began to descend into the deep
1309 A.M. below.[4] 30. And on the new moon of the tenth month
the tops of the mountains were seen, and on the new
moon of the first month the earth became visible.[5]
31. And the waters disappeared from above the earth
in the fifth week in the seventh year thereof, and on
the seventeenth [6] day in the second month the earth
was dry. 32. And on the twenty-seventh thereof
he opened the ark, and sent forth from it beasts, and
cattle, and birds, and every moving thing.[7]

Noah's Sacrifice ; God's Covenant with him (cf. Gen. viii. 20–ix. 17). Instructions to Moses about eating of Blood, the Feast of Weeks, etc., and Division of the Year (vi. 1–38).

VI. And on the new moon of the third month he
went forth from the ark, and built an altar on that
mountain.[8] 2. And he made atonement for the earth,[9]
and took a kid and made atonement by its blood for

---

[1] For 24–26 cf. Gen. vii. 11, 12, 18, 20.
[2] Cf. Gen. vii. 24, viii. 3.
[3] Cf. Gen. viii. 4.   Lubar is mentioned again in vii. 1, 17.
[4] Cf. Gen. viii. 2 ; 1 Enoch lxxxix. 7.
[5] Cf. Gen. viii. 5, 13.
[6] According to Gen. viii. 14 it was the 27th day of the month.
[7] Cf. Gen. viii. 19.
[8] Cf. Gen. viii. 20. The mountain is Lubar.
[9] The earth needed expiation and cleansing for the vices and crimes that had polluted it.

all the guilt of the earth; for everything that had been on it had been destroyed, save those that were in the ark with Noah. 3. And he placed the fat thereof on the altar, and he took an ox, and a goat, and a sheep and kids, and salt, and a turtle-dove, and the young of a dove, and placed a burnt sacrifice on the altar, and poured thereon an offering mingled with oil, and sprinkled wine and strewed frankincense over everything, and caused a goodly savour to arise, acceptable before the Lord.[1] 4. And the Lord smelt the goodly savour,[2] and He made a covenant with him that there should not be any more a flood to destroy the earth;[3] that all the days of the earth seed-time and harvest should never cease; cold and heat, and summer and winter, and day and night should not change their order, nor cease for ever.[4] 5. "And you, increase ye and multiply upon the earth, and become many upon it, and be a blessing upon it.[5] The fear of you and the dread of you I shall inspire in everything that is on earth and in the sea.[6] 6. And behold I have given unto you all beasts, and all winged things, and everything that moveth on the earth, and the fish in the waters, and all things for food; as the green herbs, I have given you all things to eat.[7] 7. But flesh, with the life thereof, with the blood, ye shall not eat; for the life of all flesh is in the blood, lest your blood of your lives be required. At the hand of every man, at the hand of every (beast), shall I require the blood of man.[8] 8. Whoso sheddeth man's blood by man shall his blood be shed; for in the image of God made He man.[9] 9. And you, increase ye, and multiply on the earth." 10. And Noah and his sons swore that they would not eat

---

[1] The sacrifice is elaborated here to accord with the developed ritual of a later age; cf. Exod. xxix. 40; Lev. ii. 2–5, 15.
[2] Gen. viii. 21. [3] Cf. Gen. ix. 11.
[4] Cf. Gen. viii. 22. [5] Cf. Gen. ix. 7.
[6] Cf. Gen. ix. 2. [7] Cf. Gen. ix. 2, 3.
[8] Cf. Gen. ix. 4, 5. [9] Cf. Gen. ix. 6.

any blood that was in any flesh, and he made a covenant before the Lord God for ever throughout all the
generations of the earth in this month. 11. On this
account He spake to thee [1] that thou shouldst make
a covenant with the children of Israel in this month
upon the mountain with an oath, and that thou
shouldst sprinkle blood [2] upon them because of all
the words of the covenant, which the Lord made with
them for ever. 12. And this testimony is written
concerning you that you should observe it continually,
so that you should not eat on any day any blood of
beasts or birds or cattle during all the days of the
earth, and the man who eateth the blood of beast or
of cattle or of birds during all the days of the earth,
he and his seed shall be rooted out of the land. 13.
And do thou command the children of Israel to eat
no blood, so that their names and their seed may be
before the Lord our God continually.[3] 14. And for
this law there is no limit of days, for it is for ever.
They shall observe it throughout their generations,
so that they may continue supplicating on your behalf
with blood before the altar; [4] every day and at the
time of morning and evening they shall seek forgiveness [5] on your behalf perpetually before the Lord
that they may keep it and not be rooted out. 15
And He gave to Noah [6] and his sons a sign that there
should not again be a flood on the earth. 16. He
set His bow in the cloud for a sign of the eternal
covenant that there should not again be a flood on
the earth to destroy it all the days of the earth.[7]
17. For this reason it is ordained and written on the
heavenly tables, that they should celebrate the feast

[1] *i. e.* Moses.
[2] The proper use of blood in the daily sacrifice is here
referred to; cf. 14 below.
[3] For 12–13 cf. Lev. xvii. 10, 12, 14; Deut. xii. 23.
[4] Cf. Lev. xvii. 11.
[5] Cf. Num. xxviii. 3–8. Note that in our text here 11–14
deal with the Mosaic development of the covenant with Noah.
[6] The text here returns to Noah.
[7] Cf. Gen. ix. 13–15.

of weeks [1] in this month once a year, to renew the covenant every year. 18. And this whole festival was celebrated in heaven from the day of creation till the days of Noah—twenty-six jubilees and five weeks of years : and Noah and his sons observed it for seven jubilees and one week of years, till the day of Noah's death, and from the day of Noah's death his sons did away with (it) until the days of Abraham, and they ate blood.[2] 19. But Abraham observed it, and Isaac and Jacob and his children observed it up to thy days, and in thy days the children of Israel forgot it until ye celebrated it anew on this mountain. 20. And do thou command the children of Israel to observe this festival in all their generations for a commandment unto them : one day [3] in the year in this month they shall celebrate the festival. 21. For it is the feast of weeks and the feast of first-fruits : [4] this feast is twofold and of a double nature : [5] according to what is written and engraven concerning it celebrate it. 22. For I have written in the book of the first law,[6] in that which I have written for thee, that thou shouldst celebrate it in its season, one day [7] in the year, and I explained to thee its sacrifices that the children of Israel should remember and should celebrate it throughout their generations in this month, one day in every year. 23. And on the new moon of the first month, and on the new moon of the fourth

1309-1659
A.M.

[1] The " Feast of Weeks " (cf. Exod. xxxiv. 22) is here only connected with Noah's covenant, the establishment of which it is supposed to commemorate. Later Judaism associated it with the giving of the Law on Sinai. It was celebrated, according to our Book, on the 15th day of the 3rd month.

[2] Notice that the non-observance of the Feast signalizes the breaking of the covenant-condition about eating blood.

[3] Or " the first day (of the week). See 22 below.

[4] It is called " the day of first-fruits " in Num. xxviii. 26.

[5] " Of a double nature " in that (?) it commemorates the covenant with Noah, and also has an agricultural character.

[6] i. e. the Pentateuch.

[7] Or " the first day " (of the week) = Sunday. Consequently, Pentecost would always fall on the same day of the week, Sunday. This accords with the Sadducean view.

month, and on the new moon of the seventh month,
and on the new moon of the tenth month are the days
of remembrance, and the days of the seasons in the
four divisions of the year.[1]   These are written and
ordained as a testimony for ever.   24. And Noah
ordained them for himself as feasts for the generations for ever, so that they have become thereby a
memorial unto him.   25. And on the new moon of
the first month he was bidden to make for himself an
ark, and on that (day) the earth became dry and he
opened (the ark) and saw the earth.   26. And on the
new moon of the fourth month the mouths of the
depths of the abysses beneath were closed.   And on
the new moon of the seventh month all the mouths
of the abysses of the earth were opened, and the waters
began to descend into them.[2]   27. And on the new
moon of the tenth month the tops of the mountains
were seen, and Noah was glad.[3]   28. And on this
account he ordained them for himself as feasts for a
memorial for ever, and thus are they ordained.   29.
And they placed them on the heavenly tables, each
had thirteen weeks; from one to another (passed)
their memorial, from the first to the second, and from
the second to the third, and from the third to the
fourth.   30. And all the days of the commandment
will be two and fifty weeks of days, and (these will
make) the entire year complete.[4]   31. Thus it is engraven and ordained on the heavenly tables.   And

[1] According to Lev. xxiii. 24 only the 1st day of the 7th
month was a " day of memorial." The " four days " here
mentioned correspond to the four intercalary days " which
are not reckoned in the reckoning of the year " mentioned
in 1 Enoch lxxv. 1. They introduce the four quarters of
the year and apparently, according to the scheme of 1 Enoch
and our Book, were intended to be added to the 360 days
(= 12 × 30), which made up the solar year (360 + 4 days).

[2] Cf. 1 Enoch lxxxix. 7, 8.

[3] Cf. Gen. viii. 5.

[4] If the year consists of 52 weeks (= 4 × 13 weeks), how
can it be divided into 12 months of 30 days each, which is
the reckoning implied throughout the Book? For the
solutions proposed see Charles's discussion, *ad loc.*

there is no neglecting (this commandment) for a single year or from year to year. 32. And command thou the children of Israel that they observe the years according to this reckoning—three hundred and sixty-four days, and (these) will constitute a complete year, and they will not disturb its time from its days and from its feasts; for everything will fall out in them according to their testimony, and they will not leave out any day nor disturb any feasts.[1] 33. But if they do neglect and do not observe them according to His commandment, then they will disturb all their seasons, and the years will be dislodged from this (order), [and they will disturb the seasons and the years will be dislodged][2] and they will neglect their ordinances. 34. And all the children of Israel will forget, and will not find the path of the years, and will forget the new moons, and seasons, and sabbaths, and they will go wrong as to all the order of the years.[3] 35. For I know and from henceforth shall I declare it unto thee, and it is not of my own devising; for the book (lieth) written before me, and on the heavenly tables the division of days is ordained, lest they forget the feasts of the covenant and walk according to the feasts of the Gentiles after their error and after their ignorance. 36. For there will be those who will assuredly make observations of the moon—now (it) disturbeth the seasons and cometh in from year to year ten days too soon.[4] 37. For this reason the years will come upon them when they will disturb (the order),

[1] The effect of a solar year reckoned at 364 days would be that the festivals would always be celebrated on the same day of the week. Nisan 14 would always fall on a Sabbath, Nisan 22 (when the wave sheaf was to be offered) on a Sunday, and the Feast of Weeks, Sivan 15, on a Sunday. There is some reason to suppose that this conception of a solar year of 364 days has a dogmatic basis. See Introd., p. xvii.

[2] The bracketed words are a dittograph.

[3] For 33–34 cf. 1 Enoch lxxxii. 4–6.

[4] A lunar year consists of 354 days. Our author wages a polemic against the use of the moon for determining the seasons and feasts. But a lunar year was accepted by the Pharisees.

and make an abominable (day) the day of testimony,
and an unclean day a feast day, and they will confound all the days, the holy with the unclean, and the
unclean day with the holy; for they will go wrong
as to the months and sabbaths and feasts and jubilees.
38. For this reason I command and testify to thee
that thou mayest testify to them; for after thy death
thy children will disturb (them), so that they will
not make the year three hundred and sixty-four days
only, and for this reason they will go wrong as to the
new moons [1] and seasons and sabbaths and festivals,
and they will eat all kinds of blood with all kinds of
flesh.

Noah offers Sacrifice; the Cursing of Canaan (cf. Gen. ix. 20–28): Noah's Sons and Grandsons (cf. Gen. x.) and their Cities. Noah's Admonitions (vii. 1–39).

1317 A.M.   VII. And in the seventh week in the first year
thereof, in this jubilee, Noah planted vines on the
mountain on which the ark had rested, named
Lûbâr,[2] one of the Ararat Mountains, and they pro-
1320 A.M. duced fruit in the fourth year,[3] and he guarded their
fruit, and gathered it in this year in the seventh
month.   2. And he made wine therefrom and put it
1321 A.M. into a vessel, and kept it until the fifth year, until the
first day, on the new moon of the first month.   3. And
he celebrated with joy the day of this feast, and he
made a burnt sacrifice unto the Lord, one young ox
and one ram, and seven sheep, each a year old, and a
kid of the goats, that he might make atonement
thereby for himself and his sons.[4]   4. And he prepared
the kid first, and placed some of its blood on the flesh
that was on the altar which he had made, and all the

---

[1] Render (for " new moons ") " beginnings of the months."
[2] Cf. v. 28.
[3] Cf. Lev. xix. 23–25 (fruit of trees not to be touched
during the first three years after planting).
[4] Cf. Num. xxix. 2, 5.

fat he laid on the altar where he made the burnt sacrifice, and the ox and the ram and the sheep, and he laid all their flesh upon the altar. 5. And he placed all their offerings mingled with oil upon it, and afterwards he sprinkled wine on the fire which he had previously made on the altar, and he placed incense on the altar and caused a sweet savour to ascend acceptable before the Lord his God. 6. And he rejoiced and drank of this wine, he and his children with joy. 7. And it was evening, and he went into his tent, and being drunken he lay down and slept, and was uncovered in his tent as he slept.[1] 8. And Ham saw Noah his father naked, and went forth and told his two brethren without. 9. And Shem took his garment and arose, he and Japheth, and they placed the garment on their shoulders and went backward and covered the shame of their father, and their faces were backward.[2] 10. And Noah awoke from his sleep and knew all that his younger son had done unto him, and he cursed his son and said : " Cursed be Canaan ; an enslaved servant shall he be unto his brethren."[3] 11. And he blessed Shem, and said : " Blessed be the Lord God of Shem, and Canaan shall be his servant. 12. God shall enlarge Japheth, and God shall dwell in the dwelling of Shem, and Canaan shall be his servant."[4] 13. And Ham knew that his father had cursed his younger son, and he was displeased that he had cursed his son, and he parted from his father, he and his sons with him, Cush and Mizraim and Put and Canaan.[5] 14. And he built for himself a city and called its name after the name of his wife Nê'êlâtamâ'ûk. 15. And Japheth saw it, and became envious of his brother, and he too built for himself a city, and he called its name after the name of his wife 'Adâtanêsês. 16. And Shem dwelt with his father Noah, and he built a city close to his father on the mountain, and he too called its name

---

[1] For 6–7 cf. Gen. ix. 21. [2] For 8–9 cf. Gen. ix. 22–23.
[3] Cf. Gen. ix. 24–25. [4] For 11–12 cf. Gen. ix. 26–27.
[5] Cf. Gen. x. 6.

after the name of his wife Sêdêqêtĕlĕbâb.[1] 17. And behold these three cities are near Mount Lûbâr; Sêdêqêtêlĕbâb fronting the mountain on its east; and Na'êlâtamâ'ûk on the south; 'Adatanêsês towards the west. 18. And these are the sons of Shem: Elam, and Asshur, and Arpachshad—this (son) was born two years after the flood—and Lud, and Aram.[2] 19. The sons of Japheth: Gomer and Magog and Madai and Javan, Tubal and Meshech and Tiras: these are the sons of Noah.[3] 20.[4] And in the twenty-eighth jubilee Noah began to enjoin upon his sons' sons the ordinances and commandments, and all the judgments that he knew, and he exhorted his sons to observe righteousness, and to cover the shame [5] of their flesh, and to bless their Creator, and honour father and mother, and love their neighbour, and guard their souls from fornication and uncleanness and all iniquity. 21. For owing to these three things [6] came the flood upon the earth, namely, owing to the fornication wherein the Watchers against the law of their ordinances went a whoring after the daughters of men, and took themselves wives of all which they chose: [7] and they made the beginning of uncleanness. 22. And they begat sons the Nâphîdîm,[8] and †they were all unlike†,[9] and they devoured one another: and the Giants slew the Nâphîl, and the Nâphîl slew the Eljô, and the Eljô mankind, and one man another. 23. And every one sold himself [10] to work iniquity and to

1324-1372
A.M.

---

[1] = "righteousness of the heart."

[2] Cf. Gen. x. 22.   [3] Cf. Gen. x. 2.

[4] From here to the end of the chapter there is incorporated a fragment of the lost Book of Noah.

[5] Cf. iii. 31.

[6] viz. fornication, uncleanness and all iniquity. According to Maimonides (Kings, 89) Adam received six commandments against (1) idolatry; (2) blasphemy; (3) murder; (4) incest; (5) stealing; (6) perverting justice. These were enjoined by Noah, who added a seventh, prohibiting the eating of flesh with blood.

[7] Cf. Gen. vi. 2; 1 Enoch vii. 1.   [8] i. e. the Nephilim.

[9] Text probably corrupt.

[10] Cf. 1 Kings xxi. 20 (phrase).

shed much blood,[1] and the earth was filled with iniquity.[2] 24. And after this they sinned against the beasts and birds, and all that moveth and walketh on the earth :[3] and much blood was shed on the earth, and every imagination and desire of men imagined vanity and evil continually.[4] 25. And the Lord destroyed everything from off the face of the earth;[5] because of the wickedness of their deeds, and because of the blood which they had shed in the midst of the earth He destroyed everything. 26. " And we were left, I[6] and you, my sons, and everything that entered with us into the ark, and behold I see your works before me that ye do not walk in righteousness; for in the path of destruction ye have begun to walk, and ye are parting one from another, and are envious one of another, and (so it cometh) that ye are not in harmony, my sons, each with his brother. 27. For I see, and behold the demons have begun (their) seductions against you and against your children, and now I fear on your behalf, that after my death ye will shed the blood of men upon the earth, and that ye, too, will be destroyed from the face of the earth.[7] 28. For whoso sheddeth man's blood, and whoso eateth the blood of any flesh, will all be destroyed from the earth.[8]

29. And there will not be left any man that eateth blood.

> Or that sheddeth the blood of man on the earth,
> Nor will there be left to him any seed or descendants living under heaven ;
> For into Sheol will they go,
> And into the place of condemnation will they descend.

---

[1] Cf. 1 Enoch ix. 1.
[2] Cf. Gen. vi. 11; 1 Enoch ix. 9.
[3] Cf. 1 Enoch vii. 5.   [4] Cf. Gen. vi. 5.
[5] Cf. Gen. vi. 7, vii. 4.
[6] Noah is the speaker here and to the end of the chapter.
[7] Cf. x. 1 (x. 1–15 is another excerpt from the Noah apocalypse).
[8] Cf. Gen. ix. 4, 6; Lev. vii. 27.

And into the darkness of the deep will they all be removed by a violent death.[1]

30. There shall be no blood seen upon you of all the blood there shall be all the days in which ye have killed any beasts or cattle or whatever flieth upon the earth, and work ye a good work to your souls by covering that which hath been shed [2] on the face of the earth. 31. And ye shall not be like him who eateth with blood, but guard yourselves that none may eat blood before you : [3] cover the blood, for thus have I been commanded to testify to you and your children, together with all flesh. 32. And suffer not the soul to be eaten with the flesh, that your blood, which is your life, may not be required at the hand of any flesh that sheddeth (it) on the earth.[4] 33. For the earth will not be clean from the blood which hath been shed upon it ; [5] for (only) through the blood of him that shed it [6] will the earth be purified throughout all its generations. 34. And now, my children, hearken : work judgment and righteousness that ye may be planted in righteousness [7] over the face of the whole earth, and your glory lifted up before my God, who saved me from the waters of the flood.[8] 35. And behold, ye will go and build for yourselves cities, and plant in them all the plants that are upon the earth, and moreover all fruit-bearing trees. 36. For three years the fruit of everything that is eaten will not be gathered : and in the fourth year its fruit will be accounted holy [and they will offer the first-fruits],[9]

[1] Cf. xxii. 22; 1 Enoch ciii. 7, 8.

[2] Cf. Lev. xvii. 13; Ezek. xxiv. 7 (here the precept is carried back to Noah).

[3] One of the seven Noachic laws (binding on all men) was the prohibition of eating flesh with the blood. Cf. note on 21 above. [4] Cf. Gen. ix. 4; Lev. xvii. 10, 11, 14.

[5] Cf. vi. 2. [6] Cf. Num. xxxv. 33.

[7] A frequent metaphor in the O.T. Israel is " the plant of righteousness " (1 Enoch x. 16, etc.).

[8] Cf. 2 Pet. ii. 5.

[9] These words, if genuine, direct that in the fourth year only the first-fruits (not all the fruit) are to be offered to God. Cf. Lev. xix. 23–24.

acceptable before the Most High God, who created heaven and earth and all things. Let them offer in abundance the first of the wine and oil (as) first-fruits on the altar of the Lord, who receiveth it, and what is left let the servants of the house of the Lord [1] eat before the altar which receiveth (it). 37. And in the fifth year [2]

.   .   .   .

make ye the release so that ye release it [3] in righteousness and uprightness, and ye shall be righteous, and all that you plant will prosper. 38. For thus did Enoch, the father of your father command Methuselah, his son, and Methuselah his son Lamech, and Lamech commanded me all the things which his fathers commanded him. 39. And I also will give you commandment, my sons, as Enoch commanded his son in the first jubilees : whilst still living, the seventh [4] in his generation, he commanded and testified to his son and to his sons' sons until the day of his death."

Genealogy of the Descendants of Shem : Noah and his Sons divide the Earth (viii. 1–30; cf. Gen. x.).

VIII. In the twenty-ninth jubilee, in the first week, 1373 A M. in the beginning thereof Arpachshad took to himself a wife and her name was Râsû'ëjâ, [the daughter of Sûsân,] the daughter of Elam, and she bare him a son in the third year in this week, and he called his name 1375 A.M. Kâinâm.[5] 2. And the son grew, and his father taught

---

[1] *i. e.* the priests. Later Judaism directed that the rest of the fruit should be eaten by the owners within the walls of Jerusalem. The view of the text is supported by the Samaritans, the Ḳaraite Jews and Ibn Ezra.

[2] Charles suspects a lacuna in the text here.

[3] Or render " (In the seventh year) ye will let it (the land) rest and lie fallow " (Charles).

[4] Cf. 1 Enoch lx. 8, xciii. 3; Jude 14.

[5] This name occurs in the LXX of Gen. xi. 13, but not in the MT or other Versions. It also occurs in the genealogy in Luke iii. 36.

him writing, and he went to seek for himself a place
where he might seize for himself a city.   3. And he
found a writing which former (generations) had
carved on the rock, and he read what was thereon,
and he transcribed it and sinned owing to it; for it
contained the teaching of the Watchers in accordance
with which they used to observe the omens of the sun
and moon and stars in all the signs of heaven.[1]   4.
And he wrote it down and said nothing regarding it;
for he was afraid to speak to Noah about it lest he
should be angry with him on account of it.   5. And
in the thirtieth jubilee, in the second week, in the

1429 A.M. first year thereof, he took to himself a wife, and her
name was Mêlkâ, the daughter of Madai, the son of

1432 A.M. Japheth, and in the fourth year he begat a son, and
called his name Shelah;[2] for he said: "Truly I
have been sent."[3]   6. [And in the fourth year he
was born], and Shelah grew up and took to himself
a wife, and her name was Mû'ak, the daughter of
Kêsêd, his father's brother, in the one and thirtieth

1499 A.M. jubilee, in the fifth week, in the first year thereof.
7. And she bare him a son in the fifth year thereof,
and he called his name Eber: and he took unto him-

1503 A.M. self a wife, and her name was 'Azûrâd,[4] the daughter

1564 A.M. of Nêbrôd, in the thirty-second jubilee, in the seventh
week, in the third year thereof.   8. And in the sixth

1567 A.M. year thereof, she bare him a son, and he called his
name Peleg; for in the days when he was born the
children of Noah began to divide the earth amongst
themselves: for this reason he called his name Peleg.[5]
9. And they divided (it) secretly[6] amongst themselves,

---

[1] Cf. Josephus, *Ant.* i. 2, 3, who assigns this wisdom not
to the Watchers, but to the children of Seth.

[2] Cf. Gen. x. 24.

[3] A paronomasia is implied in the original Hebrew here.

[4] Read *'Azûrâ*.

[5] There is a play (in the original Hebrew) on the meaning
of the name *Peleg* he·

[6] The secret division of the earth is followed by an authoritative one by Noah, and made binding on his descendants.
Canaan is included in Shem's lot.   Hence, the Israelite con-

and told it to Noah. 10. And it came to pass in the beginning of the thirty-third jubilee that they divided 1569 A.M. the earth into three parts, for Shem and Ham and Japheth, according to the inheritance of each, in the first year in the first week, when one of us,[1] who had been sent, was with them. 11. And he called his sons, and they drew nigh to him, they and their children, and he divided the earth into the lots, which his three sons were to take in possession, and they reached forth their hands, and took the writing out of the bosom of Noah, their father. 12. And there came forth on the writing as Shem's lot [2] the middle of the earth [3] which he should take as an inheritance for himself and for his sons for the generations of eternity, from the middle of the mountain range of Râfâ,[4] from the mouth of the water from the river Tînâ,[5] and his portion goeth towards the west through the midst of this river, and it extendeth till it reacheth the water of the abysses, out of which this river goeth forth and poureth its waters into the sea Mê'at,[6] and this river floweth into the great sea. And all that is towards the north is Japheth's, and all that is towards the south belongeth to Shem. 13. And it extendeth till it reacheth Kârâsô : [7] this is in the bosom of the tongue [8] which looketh towards the south. 14.

---

quest later is justified. Noah's division of the earth is alluded to in *Pirke de R. Eliezer* xxiii. (end).

[1] *i. e.* one of the angels.

[2] For the countries included in Shem's lot, see 21, ix. 2–6, 13 *b*. According to Epiphanius it extended from Persia and Bactria to India, to Rhinocurura (between Egypt and Palestine).

[3] According to Ezek. xxxviii. 12 (1 Enoch xxvi. 1) Palestine was the " navel " of the earth.

[4] Probably the Rhipaean mountains (identified sometimes with the Ural mountains).

[5] *i. e.* the river Tanais or Don.

[6] *i. e.* the Maeotis or Sea of Azov.

[7] *i. e.* (?) the Rhinocurura (= " the torrent of Egypt ") on the confines of Egypt and Palestine (Charles); cf. Isa. xxvii. 12.

[8] *i. e.* either promontory of land, or bay.

And his portion extendeth along the great sea, and it extendeth in a straight line till it reacheth the west of the tongue which looketh towards the south ;[1] for this sea is named the tongue of the Egyptian Sea.[2] 15. And it turneth from here towards the south towards the mouth of the great sea [3] on the shore of (its) waters, and it extendeth to the west to 'Afrâ,[4] and it extendeth till it reacheth the waters of the river Gihon, and to the south of the waters of Gihon,[5] to the banks of this river. 16. And it extendeth towards the east, till it reacheth the Garden of Eden, to the south thereof, [to the south] and from the east of the whole land of Eden and of the whole east, it turneth to the †east,† [6] and proceedeth till it reacheth the east of the mountain named Râfâ, and it descendeth to the bank of the mouth of the river Tînâ. 17. This portion came forth by lot for Shem and his sons, that they should possess it for ever unto his generations for evermore. 18. And Noah rejoiced that this portion came forth for Shem and for his sons, and he remembered all that he had spoken with his mouth in prophecy ; for he had said :

" Blessed be the Lord God of Shem,
And may the Lord dwell in the dwelling of Shem." [7]

19. And he knew that the Garden of Eden is the holy of holies, and the dwelling of the Lord, and Mount Sinai the centre of the desert, and Mount Zion—the centre of the navel of the earth : these three [8] were created as holy places facing each other. 20. And he blessed the God of gods, who had put the word of the Lord into his mouth, and the Lord for evermore. 21. And he knew that a blessed portion

---

[1] i. e. (?) the promontory on which Mt. Sindi is situated.

[2] i. e. the Gulf of Akaba ; cf. Isa. xi. 15.

[3] ? the northern waters of the Red Sea.

[4] i. e. Africa in the restricted sense of the Roman province which included Egypt and the other northern parts of Africa bordering the Mediterranean.

[5] i. e. the Nile.   [6] ? read " west."   [7] Cf. vii. 11.

[8] These three holy places fall within Shem's lot.

and a blessing had come to Shem and his sons unto the generations for ever—the whole land of Eden and the whole land of the Red Sea, and the whole land of the east, and India, and on the Red Sea and the mountains thereof, and all the land of Bashan, and all the land of Lebanon and the islands of Kaftûr,[1] and all the mountains of Sanîr [2] and 'Amânâ,[3] and the mountains of Asshur in the north, and all the land of Elam, Asshur, and Bâbêl, and Sûsân and Mâ'ĕdâi,[4] and all the mountains of Ararat, and all the region beyond the sea, which is beyond the mountains of Asshur towards the north, a blessed and spacious land, and all that is in it is very good. 22.[5] And for Ham came forth the second portion, beyond the Gihon towards the south to the right [6] of the Garden, and it extendeth towards the south and it extendeth to all the mountains of fire,[7] and it extendeth towards the west to the sea of 'Atêl [8] and it extendeth towards the west till it reacheth the sea of Mâ'ûk [9]— that (sea) into which †everything which is not destroyed descendeth†.[10] 23. And it goeth forth towards the north to the limits of Gâdîr,[11] and it goeth forth to the coast of the waters of the sea to the waters of the great sea till it draweth near to the river Gihon, and goeth along the river Gihon till it reacheth the right of the Garden of Eden. 24. And this is the land which came forth for Ham as the portion which he was to occupy for ever for himself and his sons unto their

[1] ? Crete. The ancient Versions identify Caphtor with Cappadocia.

[2] *i. e.* Senir (Deut. iii. 9; Ezek. xxvii. 5) = Hermon.

[3] ? Mt. Amanus in N. Syria.

[4] *i. e.* Media; cf. x. 35.

[5] 22–24 give details of Ham's portion, which includes all Africa and certain parts of Asia.

[6] *i. e.* to the south.

[7] Cf. 1 Enoch xviii. 6–9, xxiv. 1–3.

[8] *i. e.* the Atlantic.

[9] ? The great ocean stream in the extreme west.

[10] The text may be corrupt. Render, perhaps, " if any-thing descends into it, it perishes " (Charles).

[11] *i. e.* Cadiz.

generations for ever. 25.[1] And for Japheth came
forth the third portion beyond [2] the river Tînâ [3] to the
north of the outflow of its waters, and it extendeth
north-easterly to the whole region of Gog [4] and to
all the country east thereof. 26. And it extendeth
northerly to the north, and it extendeth to the mountains of Qêlt [5] towards the north, and towards the
sea of Mâ'ûk, and it goeth forth to the east of Gâdîr
as far as the region of the waters of the sea. 27. And
it extendeth until it approacheth the west of Fârâ [6]
and it returneth towards 'Afêrâg,[7] and it extendeth
easterly to the waters of the sea of Mê'at.[8] 28. And
it extendeth to the region of the river Tînâ in a north-
easterly direction until it approacheth the boundary
of its waters towards the mountain Râfâ,[9] and it
turneth round towards the north. 29. This is the land
which came forth for Japheth and his sons as the
portion of his inheritance which he should possess
for himself and his sons, for their generations for
ever; five great islands,[10] and a great land in the
north. 30. But it is cold, and the land of Ham is
hot, and the land of Shem is neither hot nor cold, but
it is of blended cold and heat.

Subdivision of the Three Portions amongst the Grandchildren : Oath taken by Noah's Sons (ix. 1–15; cf. Gen. x. partly).

IX. And Ham divided amongst his sons, and the
first portion came forth for Cush [11] towards the east,
and to the west of him for Mizraim,[12] and to the west

---

[1] 25–29a Japheth's portion (N. Asia, Europe, five great
islands); cf. ix. 7–13.

[2] Japheth's portion is elaborately described in Josephus,
Ant. i. 6, 1.

[3] *i. e.* the river Don.

[4] In N. Asia. Josephus identifies Gog with the Scythians.
[5] Qêlt = probably the Celts.   [6] ? Africa.   [7] ? Phrygia.
[8] *i. e.* the Sea of Azov (see viii. 12 above).
[9] ? the Ural mountains (cf. viii. 12 above).
[10] Including, probably, Cyprus, Sicily, Sardinia, Corsica.
[11] = Ethiopia.   [12] *i. e.* Egypt.

of him for Put,[1] and to the west of him [and to the west thereof] on the sea [2] for Canaan.[3]   2. And Shem also divided amongst his sons, and the first portion came forth for Elam and his sons, to the east of the the river Tigris till it approacheth the east, the whole land of India, and on the Red Sea on its coast, and the waters of Dêdân, and all the mountains of Mebrî and 'Êlâ, and all the land of Sûsân and all that is on the side of Pharnâk [4] to the Red Sea and the river Tînâ.   3. And for Asshur came forth the second portion, all the land of Asshur and Nineveh and Shinar and to the border of India, and it ascendeth and skirteth the river.   4. And for Arpachshad came forth the third portion, all the land of the region of the Chaldees to the east of the Euphrates, bordering on the Red Sea, and all the waters of the desert close to the tongue of the sea which looketh towards Egypt, all the land of Lebanon and Sanîr and 'Amânâ [5] to the border of the Euphrates.   5. And for Aram [6] there came forth the fourth portion, all the land of Mesopotamia between the Tigris and the Euphrates to the north of the Chaldees to the border of the mountains of Asshur and the land of 'Arârâ.[7]   6. And there came forth for Lud [8] the fifth portion, the mountains of Asshur and all appertaining to them till it reacheth the Great Sea, and till it reacheth the east of Asshur his brother.   7. And Japheth also divided the land of his inheritance amongst his sons.   8. And the first portion came forth for Gomer to the east from the north side to the river Tînâ; and in the north there came forth for Magog all the inner portions of the north until it reacheth to the sea of Mê'at.   9 And

---

[1] *i. e.* Libya (west of Egypt).

[2] *i. e.* the Atlantic.   For Canaan's portion (from Libya to the Atlantic) cf. x. 28–29.

[3] For 1 cf. Gen. x. 6.

[4] ? Pharnacia on the coast of Pontus (Charles).

[5] Cf. viii. 21.   [6] *i. e.* the Syrians.

[7] Ararat; cf. viii. 21.

[8] According to Josephus the descendants of Lud were the Lydians.

for Madai came forth as his portion that he should possess from the west of his two brothers to the islands,[1] and to the coasts of the islands.   10. And for Javan[2] came forth the fourth portion every island[3] and the islands which are towards the border of Lud. 11. And for Tubal[4] there came forth the fifth portion in the midst of the tongue which approacheth towards the border of the portion of Lud to the second tongue, to the region beyond the second tongue unto the third tongue.[5]   12. And for Meshech came forth the sixth portion, all the region beyond the third tongue[6] till it approacheth the east of Gâdîr.[7]   13. And for Tiras[8] there came forth the seventh portion, four great islands[9] in the midst of the sea, which reach to the portion of Ham [and the islands of Kamâtûrî came out by lot for the sons of Arpachshad as his inheritance].[10]   14. And thus the sons of Noah divided unto their sons in the presence of Noah their father, and he bound them all by an oath, imprecating a curse on every one that sought to seize the portion which had not fallen (to him) by his lot.   15. And they all said, " So be it; so be it," for themselves and their sons for ever throughout their generations till the day of judgment, on which the Lord God shall judge them with a sword and with fire, for all the unclean wickedness of their errors, wherewith they have filled the earth with transgression and uncleanness and fornication and sin.

[1] Including (?) Britain and Ireland.

[2] *i. e.* properly Ionia (so Isa. lxvi. 19; Ezek. xxvii. 13) : but in Daniel (viii. 21, x. 20, xi. 2) it = the Græco-Macedonian Empire.   Here it seems to embrace all the islands off the coast of Asia Minor.

[3] ? coastland.

[4] Tubal's portion apparently extends from Thrace to Italy.

[5] The three tongues of land may be Thrace, Greece and Italy.

[6] *i. e.* probably Italy.   [7] *i. e.* Cadiz.

[8] The descendants of Tiras may have been the Tyrseni, a branch of the Pelasgians.

[9] Cf. viii. 29.

[10] The bracketed words are probably an interpolation (Charles).   Arpachsad was a son of Shem.

Noah's Sons led astray by Evil Spirits ; Noah's Prayer ; Mastêmâ ; Death of Noah (x. 1–17 ; cf. Gen. ix. 28).

X.[1] And in the third week of this jubilee the unclean demons [2] began to lead astray †the children of† [3] the sons of Noah, and to make to err and destroy them. 2. And the sons of Noah came to Noah their father, and they told him concerning the demons which were leading astray and blinding and slaying his sons' sons. 3. And he prayed before the Lord his God, and said :

" God of the spirits of all flesh,[4] who hast shown
    mercy unto me,
And hast saved me and my sons from the waters
    of the flood,
And hast not caused me to perish as Thou didst
    the sons of perdition ; [5]

For Thy grace hath been great towards me,
And great hath been Thy mercy to my soul ;

Let Thy grace be lift up upon my sons,
And let not wicked spirits rule over them
Lest they should destroy them from the earth.

4. But do Thou bless me and my sons, that we may increase and multiply and replenish the earth. 5. And Thou knowest how Thy Watchers, the fathers of these spirits, acted in my day : and as for these spirits which are living, imprison them and hold them fast in the place of condemnation, and let them not bring destruction on the sons of thy servant, my God ; for these are malignant, and created in

[1] Here we have (in x. 1–15) another fragment of the lost Apocalypse of Noah (as in vii. 20–39). The Hebrew original of 1–2 and 9–14 of this section is extant.

[2] i.e. the spirits which issued from the children of the angels and the daughters of men.

[3] Omit *the children of*.

[4] Cf. Num. xvi. 22, xxvii. 16.

[5] Cf. 2 Thess. ii. 3.

order to destroy.   6. And let them not rule over the
spirits of the living; for Thou alone canst exercise
dominion over them.   And let them not have power
over the sons of the righteous from henceforth and for
evermore."   7. And the Lord our God bade us to
bind all.[1]   8. And the chief of the spirits, Mastêmâ,[2]
came and said : " Lord, Creator, let some of them
remain before me, and let them hearken to my voice,
and do all that I shall say unto them; for if some of
them are not left to me, I shall not be able to execute
the power of my will on the sons of men ; for these are
for corruption and leading astray before my judgment, for great is the wickedness of the sons of men."
9. And He said : " Let the tenth part of them
remain before him, and let nine parts descend into
the place of condemnation."[3]   10. And one of us [4]
He commanded that we should teach Noah all their
medicines; for He knew that they would not walk in
uprightness, nor strive in righteousness.   11. And
we did according to all His words : all the malignant
evil ones we bound in the place of condemnation,
and a tenth part of them we left that they might be
subject before Satan [5] on the earth.   12. And we
explained to Noah all the medicines of their diseases,
together with their seductions, how he might heal
them with herbs of the earth.   13. And Noah wrote
down all things in a book as we instructed him concerning every kind of medicine.   Thus the evil

[1] Cf. 1 Enoch x. 4, 12.

[2] The word apparently = *maṣtim* (Hif. part of *Ṣāṭam*),
" to be adverse," " inimical "; the Heb. noun *maṣtêmâ* =
" animosity," in Hos. ix. 7, 8. Thus the word = Satan
(" adversary "). As a proper name it is practically confined
to the Jubilees-literature. The evil spirits under the guidance
of Mastêmâ tempt, accuse and destroy men.

[3] Only one-tenth are permitted to act freely against mankind till the Day of Judgment; but in 1 Enoch xv.–xvi. *all*
the demons are allowed to do this.

[4] The angel Raphael is referred to, as is shown by the
Hebrew Book of Noah. For Raphael in this connection cf.
Tobit iii. 17, xii. 14, 15.

[5] Thus Satan and Mastêmâ are identical.

spirits were precluded from (hurting) the sons of Noah. 14. And he gave all that he had written to Shem, his eldest son; for he loved him exceedingly above all his sons. 15. And Noah slept with his fathers, and was buried on Mount Lûbâr in the land of Ararat. 16. Nine hundred and fifty years he completed in his life, nineteen jubilees and two 1659 A.M. weeks and five years. 17. And in his life on earth he excelled the children of men save Enoch because of the righteousness, wherein he was perfect. For Enoch's office was ordained for a testimony to the generations of the world,[1] so that he should recount all the deeds of generation unto generation, till the day of judgment.

The Tower of Babel and the Confusion of Tongues (x. 18–27; cf. Gen. xi. 1–9).

18. And in the three and thirtieth jubilee, in the first year in the second week, Peleg took to himself a wife, whose name was Lômnâ the daughter of Sînâ'ar, and she bare him a son in the fourth year of this week, and he called his name Reu;[2] for he said: " Behold the children of men have become evil [3] through the wicked purpose of building for themselves a city and a tower in the land of Shinar." 19. For they departed from the land of Ararat eastward to Shinar; for in his days they built the city and the tower, saying, " Go to, let us ascend thereby into heaven."[4] 20. And they began to build, and in the fourth week they made brick with fire, and the bricks served them for stone, and the clay [5] with which they cemented them together was asphalt which cometh out of the sea, and out of the fountains of water in the land of Shinar. 21. And they built it: forty and three years were they building it; its 1645-1688 A.M.

---

[1] Cf. iv. 24.   [2] Cf. Gen. xi. 18.
[3] There is a play on the name Reu in Hebrew here (*re'û
. . . râ'û*).
[4] Cf. Gen. xi. 4.   [5] Cf. Gen. xi. 3.

breadth was 203 bricks, and the height (of a brick)
was the third of one; its height amounted to 5433
cubits and 2 palms, and (the extent of one wall
was) thirteen stades (and of the other thirty stades).
22. And the Lord our God said unto us : " Behold,
they are one people, and (this) they begin to do, and
now nothing will be withholden from them. Go to,
let us go down and confound their language, that
they may not understand one another's speech,[1]
and they may be dispersed into cities and nations,
and one purpose will no longer abide with them till
the day of judgment." 23. And the Lord descended,
and we descended with Him to see the city and the
tower which the children of men had built. 24. And
He confounded their language, and they no longer
understood one another's speech, and they ceased
then to build the city and the tower. 25. For this
reason the whole land of Shinar is called Babel, because the Lord did there confound all the language of
the children of men, and from thence they were dispersed [2] into their cities, each according to his language
and his nation.[3] 26. And the Lord sent a mighty
wind [4] against the tower and overthrew it upon the
earth, and behold it was between Asshur and Babylon
in the land of Shinar, and they called its name " Overthrow." [5] 27. In the fourth week in the first year
in the beginning thereof in the four and thirtieth
jubilee, were they dispersed from the land of Shinar.

1688 A.M

[1] Cf. Gen. xi. 6 f.   [2] Cf. Gen. xi. 9.

[3] According to Jewish tradition seventy nations (under
seventy patron angels) were thus created.

[4] An old tradition ; cf. *Sibyll. Oracles* iii. 98–103 ; Josephus,
Ant. i. 4, 3.

[5] A play on the preceding verb (" overthrew "). But its
real name was Babel.

The Children of Noah enter their Districts ; Canaan seizes Palestine wrongfully ; Madai receives Media (x. 28–36)

28. And Ham and his sons went into the land which he was to occupy, which he acquired as his portion in the land of the south.[1] 29. And Canaan saw the land of Lebanon to the river of Egypt that it was very good, and he went not into the land of his inheritance to the west (that is to) the sea,[2] and he dwelt in the land of Lebanon, eastward and westward from the border of Jordan and from the border of the sea.[3] 30. And Ham, his father, and Cush and Mizraim, his brothers, said unto him : " Thou hast settled in a land which is not thine, and which did not fall to us by lot : do not do so ; for if thou dost do so, thou and thy sons will fall in the land and (be) accursed through sedition ; for by sedition ye have settled, and by sedition will thy children fall, and thou shalt be rooted out for ever. 31. Dwell not in the dwelling of Shem ; for to Shem and to his sons did it come by their lot. 32. Cursed art thou, and cursed shalt thou be beyond all the sons of Noah, by the curse [4] by which we bound ourselves by an oath in the presence of the holy judge,[5] and in the presence of Noah our father." 33. But he did not hearken unto them, and dwelt in the land of Lebanon from Hamath [6] to the entering of Egypt,[7] he and his sons until this day. 34. And for this reason that land is named Canaan. 35. And Japheth and his sons went towards the sea and dwelt in the land of their portion, and Madai saw the land of the sea and it did not please him, and he begged a (portion) from Elam and Asshur and Arpachshad,

---

[1] " South " should be " north " here : N. Africa is meant.

[2] *i. e.* N.-W. Africa (his true inheritance).

[3] Canaan wrongfully seized Palestine, which belonged by right to Arpachshad.

[4] Cf. ix. 14, 15.

[5] *i. e.* the angel who was present at the lot (viii. 10).

[6] Hamath marked the northern boundary of Israel.

[7] The extreme south.

his wife's brother, and he dwelt in the land of Media,
near to his wife's brother until this day. 36. And
he called his dwelling-place, and the dwelling-place
of his sons, Media, after the name of their father
Madai.

The History of the Patriarchs from Reu to Abraham (cf. Gen. xi, 20–30); the Corruption of the Human Race (xi. 1–15).

1681 A.M.   **XI.** And in the thirty-fifth jubilee, in the third
week, in the first year thereof, Reu took to himself a
wife, and her name was 'Ôrâ, the daughter of 'Ûr,
the son of Kêsêd, and she bare him a son, and he
1687 A.M. called his name Sêrôḥ,[1] in the seventh year of this
week in this jubilee. 2.[2] And the sons of Noah began
to war on each other, to take captive and to slay
each other, and to shed the blood of men on the earth,
and to eat blood, and to build strong cities, and walls,
and towers, and individuals (began) to exalt themselves above the nation,[3] and to found the beginnings
of kingdoms, and to go to war people against people,
and nation against nation, and city against city, and
all (began) to do evil, and to acquire arms, and to
teach their sons war, and they began to capture
cities, and to sell male and female slaves. 3. And
'Ûr, the son of Kêsêd,[4] built the city of 'Arâ [5] of the
Chaldees, and called its name after his own name and
the name of his father. 4. And they made for themselves molten images, and they worshipped each the
idol, the molten image which they had made for
themselves, and they began to make graven images
and unclean simulacra, and malignant spirits assisted

---

[1] Cf. Gen. xi. 20 f. (MT. has *Serug* for *Sêrôḥ*).
[2] In 2–6 the corruption of mankind is ascribed to the period of Serug.
[3] A note of hostility to monarchy.
[4] The place name *Ur Kasdîm* (" Ur of the Chaldees ") is here transformed into the names of two persons, after whom the city is named.
[5] *i. e.* Ur.

and seduced (them) into committing transgression and uncleanness. 5. And the prince Mastêmâ exerted himself to do all this, and he sent forth other spirits, those which were put under his hand, to do all manner of wrong and sin, and all manner of transgression, to corrupt and destroy, and to shed blood upon the earth.[1] 6. For this reason he called the name of Sêrôh, Serug, for every one turned to do all manner of sin and transgression. 7. And he grew up, and dwelt in Ur of the Chaldees, near to the father of his wife's mother, and he worshipped idols, and he took to himself a wife in the thirty-sixth jubilee, in the fifth week, in the first year thereof, and her name was Mêlkâ,[2] the daughter of Kâbêr, the daughter of his father's brother. 8. And she bare him Nahor, in the first year of this week, and he grew and dwelt in Ur of the Chaldees, and his father taught him the researches of the Chaldees to divine and augur, according to the signs of heaven. 9. And in the thirty-seventh jubilee, in the sixth week, in the first year thereof, he took to himself a wife, and her name was 'Îjâskâ,[3] the daughter of Nêstâg of the Chaldees. 10. And she bare him Terah [4] in the seventh year of this week. 11. And the prince Mastêmâ sent ravens and birds to devour the seed which was sown in the land, in order to destroy the land, and rob the children of men of their labours. Before they could plough in the seed, the ravens picked (it) from the surface of the ground. 12. And for this reason he called his name Terah, because the ravens and the birds reduced them to destitution and devoured their seed.[5] 13. And the years began to be barren, owing to the birds, and they devoured all the fruit of the

1744 A.M.

1800 A.M.

1806 A.M.

[1] Cf. 1 Enoch xvi.

[2] In Gen. xi. 29 Milcah is the name of the wife of Nahor, Abram's brother.

[3] = Iscah (cf. Gen. xi. 29; but there she is daughter of Haran).

[4] Cf. Gen. xi. 24.

[5] Apparently some play on the name Terah is involved in the original Hebrew; but the explanation is uncertain.

trees from the trees : it was only with great effort that they could save a little of all the fruit of the 1870 A.M. earth in their days. 14. And in this thirty-ninth jubilee, in the second week in the first year, Terah took to himself a wife, and her name was 'Êdnâ,[1] the daughter of 'Abrâm,[2] the daughter of his father's 1876 A.M. sister. 15. And in the seventh year of this week she bare him a son, and he called his name Abram, by the name of the father of his mother ; for he had died before his daughter had conceived a son.[3]

Abram's Knowledge of God and wonderful Deeds (xi. 16–24).

16. And the child began to understand the errors of the earth that all went astray after graven images and after uncleanness, and his father taught him 1890 A.M. writing, and he was two weeks of years old, and he separated himself from his father,[4] that he might not worship idols with him. 17. And he began to pray to the Creator of all things that He might save him from the errors of the children of men, and that his portion should not fall into error after uncleanness and vileness. 18. And the seed time came for the sowing of seed upon the land, and they all went forth together to protect their seed against the ravens, and Abram went forth with those that went, and the child was a lad of fourteen years. 19. And a cloud of ravens came to devour the seed, and Abram ran to meet them before they settled on the ground, and cried to them before they settled on the ground to devour the seed, and said, " Descend not : return to the place

[1] According to the Talmud (*Baba bathra* 91*a*) her name was Amthelai, daughter of Karnebo.

[2] *i. e.* the grandfather of the Biblical Abram.

[3] It was customary to name a child after a grandfather. Here the child's name apparently perpetuates the memory of a grandfather who had died before the child was conceived.

[4] This is the theme of much later Jewish legend. See especially the first part of the *Apocalypse of Abraham*, an edition of which appears in this series. Cf. xii. 1–14 below.

whence ye came," and they proceeded to turn back.
20. And he caused the clouds of ravens to turn back
that day seventy times, and of all the ravens throughout all the land where Abram was there settled there
not so much as one. 21. And all who were with him
throughout all the land saw him cry out, and all
the ravens turn back, and his name became great in
all the land of the Chaldees. 22. And there came
to him this year all those that wished to sow, and he
went with them until the time of sowing ceased :
and they sowed their land, and that year they brought
enough grain home and ate and were satisfied. 23.
And in the first year of the fifth week Abram taught 1891 A.M.
those who made implements for oxen, the artificers
in wood, and they made a vessel above the ground,
facing the frame of the plough,[1] in order to put the
seed thereon, and the seed fell down therefrom upon
the share of the plough, and was hidden in the earth,
and they no longer feared the ravens. 24. And
after this manner they made (vessels) above the
ground on all the frames of the ploughs, and they
sowed and tilled all the land, according as Abram
commanded them, and they no longer feared the
birds.

**Abram seeks to convert Terah from Idolatry ;
the Family of Terah** (cf. Gen. xi. 27–30).
Abram burns the Idols. Death of Haran
(cf. Gen. xi. 28) (xii. 1–14).

XII. And it came to pass in the sixth week, in the 1904 A.M.
seventh year thereof, that Abram said to Terah his
father, saying, " Father ! " And he said, " Behold,
here am I, my son." 2. And he said,

---

[1] An improved method of sowing by means of a seed-
scatterer attached to the plough (Arab. *bûk*) is here described.
This marked an advance on the primitive method of scatter-
ing the seed by hand, and its invention is ascribed to Abraham.
In Rabbinical tradition Noah is the inventor of the plough
and kindred instruments. Cf. Krauss, *Talmudische Archäo-
ogie*, ii. 553 (note 151).

" What help and profit have we from those idols
   which thou dost worship,
And before which thou dost bow thyself? [1]

3. For there is no spirit in them, [2]
   For they are dumb forms, and a misleading of the
     heart.
   Worship them not :

4. Worship the God of heaven,
   Who causeth the rain and the dew to descend on the
     earth, [3]
   And doeth everything upon the earth,

   And hath created everything by His word, [4]
   And all life is from before His face.

5. Why do ye worship things that have no spirit in
     them?
   For they are the work of (men's) hands, [5]

   And on your shoulders do ye bear them, [6]
   And ye have no help from them,

   But they are a great cause of shame to those who
     make them,
   And a misleading of the heart to those who worship
     them :
   Worship them not."

6. And his father said unto him, " I also know it,
my son, but what shall I do with a people who have
made me to serve before them?   7. And if I tell them
the truth, they will slay me; for their soul cleaveth

---

[1] In 1–14 we have an early form of the legend of Abram's
protest against idolatry. This section has remarkable
parallels, both in thought and expression, with chaps. i.–viii.
of the *Apocalypse of Abraham*. In the later (Rabbinic)
forms of the legend Abram's birth excites the alarm of
Nimrod, who endeavours to destroy him in a furnace of
fire.
[2] Cf. Ps. cxxxv. 17.   [3] Cf. xx. 9; Jer. xiv. 22.
[4] Cf. Ps. xxxiii. 6; Heb. xi. 3; 2 Pet. iii. 5; 4 Ezra vi. 38.
[5] Cf. Jer. x. 3, 9.   .
[6] Cf. Isa. xlvi. 7; Jer. x. 5; *Assumpt. Moses*, viii. 4.

to them to worship them and honour them. Keep silent,[1] my son, lest they slay thee." 8. And these words he spake to his two brothers, and they were angry with him and he kept silent. 9. And in the fortieth jubilee, in the second week, in the seventh 1925 A.M. year thereof, Abram took to himself a wife, and her name was Sarai, the daughter of his father, and she became his wife.[2] 10. And Haran, his brother, took to himself a wife in the third year of the third week, and she bare him a son in the seventh year of this 1932 A.M. week and he called his name Lot. 11. And Nahor, his brother, took to himself a wife.[3] 12. And in the sixtieth year of the life of Abram, that is, in the 1936 A.M. fourth week, in the fourth year thereof, Abram arose by night, and burned the house of the idols, and he burned all that was in the house, and no man knew it. 13. And they arose in the night and sought to save their gods from the midst of the fire. 14. And Haran hasted to save them, but the fire flamed over him, and he was burnt in the fire, and he died in Ur of the Chaldees before Terah his father, and they buried him in Ur of the Chaldees.[4]

The Family of Terah in Haran ; Abram's Experiences there ; his Journey to Canaan (xii. 15–31 ; cf. Gen. xi, 31–xii. 3).

15. And Terah went forth from Ur of the Chaldees, he and his sons, to go into the land of Lebanon and into the land of Canaan, and he dwelt in the land of Haran, and Abram, dwelt with Terah his father in

[1] In *Ap. Abraham* Terah is indignant with Abraham for deriding the idols.

[2] Cf. Gen. xx. 12, according to which Sarah was Abraham's half-sister. According to Rabbinic tradition marriage with half-sisters on the father's side was permitted to the descendants of Noah. In Lev. xviii. 9, 11, xx. 17, marriage with a sister or half-sister is strictly forbidden.

[3] According to Gen. xi. 29, Milcah.

[4] In *Ap. Abraham*, viii. the fire descends from heaven and burns the house and all in it (including Terah). Only Abraham escapes.

Haran two weeks of years.[1]   16. And in the sixth
week, in the fifth year thereof, Abram sat up throughout the night on the new moon of the seventh month
to observe the stars from the evening to the morning,
in order to see what would be the character of the
year with regard to the rains, and he was alone as he
sat and observed.   17. And a word came into his
heart and he said : " All the signs of the stars, and the
signs of the moon and of the sun are all in the hand
of the Lord.   Why do I search (them) out ?

18. If He desireth, He causeth it to rain, morning
and evening ;
And if He desireth, He withholdeth it,
And all things are in His hand."

19. And he prayed that night and said
" My God, God Most High, Thou alone art my
God,
And Thee and Thy dominion have I chosen.

And Thou hast created all things,
And all things that are are the work of Thy hands.

20. Deliver me from the hands of evil spirits who have
sway over the thoughts of men's hearts,
And let them not lead me astray from Thee, my
God.
And stablish Thou me and my seed for ever
That we go not astray from henceforth and for
evermore."

21. And he said, " Shall I return unto Ur of the Chaldees who seek my face that I may return to them, or
am I to remain here in this place ?   The right path
before Thee prosper it in the hands of Thy servant
that he may fulfil (it) and that I may not walk in the
deceitfulness of my heart, O my God."   22. And he
made an end of speaking and praying, and behold the
word of the Lord was sent to him through me, saying :
" Get thee up from thy country, and from thy kindred
and from the house of thy father unto a land which
I shall show thee, and I shall make thee a great and
numerous nation.

[1] Cf. Gen. xi. 31.

23. And I shall bless thee
    And I shall make thy name great,

    And thou wilt be blessed in the earth,
    And in thee will all families of the earth be blessed,

    And I shall bless them that bless thee,
    And curse them that curse thee.[1]

24. And I shall be a God to thee and thy son, and to thy son's son, and to all thy seed : fear not, from henceforth and unto all generations of the earth I am thy God." 25. And the Lord God said : " Open his mouth and his ears, that he may hear and speak with his mouth, with the language which hath been revealed " ; [2] for it had ceased from the mouths of all the children of men from the day of the overthrow (of Babel). 26. And I [3] opened his mouth, and his ears and his lips, and I began to speak with him in Hebrew in the tongue of the creation. 27. And he took the books of his fathers, and these were written in Hebrew, and he transcribed them, and he began from henceforth to study them, and I made known to him that which he could not (understand), and he studied them during the six rainy months.[4] 28. And it came to pass in the seventh year of the sixth week 1953 A.M. that he spoke to his father, and informed him that he would leave Haran to go into the land of Canaan to see it and return to him. 29. And Terah his father said unto him ; " Go in peace :

    May the eternal God make thy path straight,
    And the Lord [(be) with thee, and] protect thee from all evil,
    And grant unto thee grace, mercy and favour before those who see thee,
    And may none of the children of men have power over thee to harm thee ;
    Go in peace.

---

[1] Cf. Gen. xii. 1-3 (cf. Acts vii. 3).

[2] *i. e.* the sacred language, Hebrew, knowledge of which had been lost since the overthrow of Babel. According to another tradition Heber alone retained knowledge of Hebrew because he had taken no part in the building of the Tower.

[3] The angel is the speaker.   [4] *i. e.* the winter.

30. And if thou seest a land pleasant to thy eyes to dwell in, then arise and take me to thee and take Lot with thee, the son of Haran thy brother, as thine own son : the Lord be with thee. 31. And Nahor thy brother leave with me till thou returnest in peace, and we go with thee all together."

Abram with Lot in Canaan and Egypt (cf. Gen. xii. 4–20). Abram separates from Lot (cf. Gen. xiii. 11–18) (xiii. 1–21).

XIII. And Abram journeyed from Haran, and he took Sarai, his wife, and Lot, his brother Haran's son, to the land of Canaan, and he came into †Asshur†,[1] and proceeded to Shechem, and dwelt near a lofty oak.[2] 2. And he saw, and, behold, the land was very pleasant from the entering of Hamath to the lofty oak. 3. And the Lord said to him : " To thee and to thy seed will I give this land." 4. And he built an altar there, and he offered thereon a burnt sacrifice to the Lord, who had appeared to him. 5. And he removed from thence unto the mountain . . .[3] Bethel on the west and Ai on the east, and pitched his tent there.[4] 6. And he saw and behold, the land was very wide and good, and everything grew thereon —vines and figs and pomegranates, oaks and ilexes, and terebinths and oil trees, and cedars and cypresses and date trees, and all trees of the field, and there was water on the mountains. 7. And he blessed the Lord who had led him out of Ur of the Chaldees, and had brought him to this land. 8. And it came 1954 A.M. to pass in the first year, in the seventh week, on the new moon of the first month, that he built an altar on this mountain, and called on the name of the Lord : " Thou, the eternal God, art my God."[5] 9. And he offered on the altar a burnt sacrifice unto the Lord

[1] Corrupt. Read probably *Canaan*.
[2] For 1 cf. Gen. xii. 5–6. For " lofty oak " (so LXX) MT has " oak of Moreh."
[3] Supply (?) " to the east of Bethel with " (Charles).
[4] For 3–5 cf. Gen. xii. 7, 8.   [5] Cf. Gen. xii. 8.

that He should be with him and not forsake him all the days of his life. 10. And he removed from thence and went towards the south,[1] and he came to Hebron, and Hebron was built at that time, and he dwelt there two years, and he went (thence) into the land of the south, to Bealoth,[2] and there was a famine in the land. 11. And Abram went into Egypt [3] in the third year of the week, and he dwelt in Egypt five years before his wife was torn away from him. 12. Now Tanais [4] in Egypt was at that time built—seven years after Hebron.[5] 13. And it came to pass when Pharaoh seized Sarai, the wife of Abram, that the Lord plagued Pharaoh and his house with great plagues because of Sarai, Abram's wife. 14. And Abram was very glorious by reason of possessions in sheep, and cattle, and asses, and horses, and camels, and menservants, and maidservants, and in silver and gold exceedingly. And Lot also, his brother's son, was wealthy. 15. And Pharaoh gave back Sarai, the wife of Abram, and he sent him out of the land of Egypt,[6] and he journeyed to the place where he had pitched his tent at the beginning, to the place of the altar, with Ai on the east, and Bethel on the west, and he blessed the Lord his God who had brought him back in peace.[7] 16. And it came to pass in the forty-first jubilee, in the third year of the first week, that he returned to this place and offered thereon a burnt sacrifice, and called on the name of the Lord, and said : " Thou, the most high God, art my God for ever and ever." [8] 17. And in the fourth year of this week Lot parted from him, and Lot dwelt in Sodom, and the men of Sodom were sinners exceedingly.[9] 18. And it grieved him in his heart that his brother's son had parted from him ; for he had no

1956 A.M.

1963 A.M.

1964 A.M.

---

[1] Cf. Gen. xii. 9. [2] A town in S. Judah (Josh. xv. 24).
[3] Cf. Gen. xii. 10. [4] *i. e.* Zoan. [5] Cf. Num. xiii. 22.
[6] For 13–15a cf. Gen. xii. 15–20 (note that Gen. xii. 18 is

children. 19.[1] In that year when Lot was taken
captive, the Lord said unto Abram, after that Lot had
parted from him, in the fourth year of this week :
" Lift up thine eyes from the place where thou art
dwelling, northward and southward, and westward
and eastward. 20. For all the land which thou
seest I shall give to thee and to thy seed for ever, and
I shall make thy seed as the sand of the sea :[2] though
a man may number the dust of the earth, yet thy
seed shall not be numbered.[3] 21. Arise, walk (through
the land) in the length of it and the breadth of it, and
see it all ; for to thy seed shall I give it."   And Abram
went to Hebron, and dwelt there.

The Campaign of Chedorlaomer (xiii. 22–29 ; cf. Gen. xiv.).

22. And in this year came Chedorlaomer, king of
Elam, and Amraphel, king of Shinar, and Arioch,
king of Sêllâsar,[4] and Têrgâl,[5] king of nations, and
slew the king of Gomorrah, and the king of Sodom
fled, and many fell through wounds in the vale of
Siddim, by the Salt Sea. 23. And they took captive
Sodom and Adam [6] and Zeboim, and they took captive Lot also, the son of Abram's brother, and all his
possessions, and they went to Dan.[7] 24. And one
who had escaped came and told Abram that his
brother's son had been taken captive and (Abram)
armed [8] his household servants. 25. . . . . .
. . . . for Abram, and for his seed, a

---

[1] For 19–21 cf. Gen. xiii. 14–18.

[2] Cf. Gen. xxii. 17 (Gen. xiii. 16 has " as the dust of the
earth ").

[3] " So that if a man can number . . . then shall thy seed
also be numbered " (Gen. xiii. 16).

[4] MT *Ellasar*.

[5] MT *Tidal* (for form here cf. LXX Θαργάλ).

[6] *i. e.* Admah.

[7] Cf. Gen. xiv. 14.

[8] R.V. " led forth "; the rendering " armed " has the
support of the Targum Onkelos.

tenth of the first-fruits to the Lord,[1] and the Lord ordained it as an ordinance for ever that they should give it to the priests who served before Him, that they should possess it for ever.[2] 26. And to this law there is no limit of days; for He hath ordained it for the generations for ever that they should give to the Lord the tenth of everything, of the seed and of the wine and of the oil and of the cattle and of the sheep. 27. And He gave (it) unto His priests to eat and to drink with joy before Him. 28. And the king of Sodom came to him and bowed himself before him, and said : " Our Lord Abram, give unto us the souls which thou hast rescued, but let the booty be thine." 29. And Abram said unto him : " I lift up my hands to the Most High God, that from a thread to a shoe-latchet I shall not take aught that is thine, lest thou shouldst say I have made Abram rich; save only what the young men have eaten, and the portion of the men who went with me— Aner, Eschol, and Mamre. These will take their portion." [3]

God's Covenant with Abram (xiv. 1–20; cf. Gen. xv.).

XIV.[4] After these things, in the fourth year of this week, on the new moon of the third month, the word of the Lord came to Abram in a dream, saying : " Fear not, Abram; I am thy defender, and thy reward will be exceeding great." 2. And he said : " Lord, Lord, what wilt thou give me, seeing I go

[1] Charles suspects a lacuna at the beginning of 25. It no doubt contained an account of the pursuit of the kings and told of Melchizedek (cf. Gen. xiv. 15–20). That Abraham should have given tithes to Melchizedek (who was uncircumcised) was a difficulty to later Jews (cf. Justin, *Trypho* xix.). One way of overcoming it was to identify Melchizedek with Shem.

[2] The law about tithes is made to apply for the Levitical priesthood; cf. xxxii. 15.

[3] For 28–29 cf. Gen. xiv. 21–24.

[4] For 1–6 cf. Gen. xv. 1–6.

hence childless, and the son of Mâsêq,[1] the son of my handmaid, is the Dammasek Eliezer : he will be my heir, and to me thou hast given no seed." 3. And He said unto him : " This (man) will not be thy heir, but one that will come out of thine own bowels; he will be thine heir." 4. And He brought him forth abroad, and said unto him : " Look toward heaven and number the stars, if thou art able to number them." 5. And he looked toward heaven, and beheld the stars. And He said unto him : " So shall thy seed be." 6. And he believed in the Lord, and it was counted to him for righteousness. 7. And He said unto him : " I am the Lord that brought thee out of Ur of the Chaldees, to give thee the land of the Canaanites to possess it for ever; and I shall be God unto thee and to thy seed after thee." [2] 8. And he said : " Lord, Lord, whereby shall I know that I shall inherit (it) ? " 9. And he said unto him : " Take Me an heifer of three years, and a goat of three years, and a sheep of three years, and a turtle-dove, and a pigeon." [3] 10. And he took all these in the middle of the month ; and he dwelt at the oak of Mamre, which is near Hebron.[4] 11. And he built there an altar, and sacrificed all these ; and he poured their blood upon the altar, and divided them in the midst, and laid them over against each other ; but the birds divided he not. 12. And birds came down upon the pieces, and Abram drove them away, and did not suffer the birds to touch them.[5] 13. And it came to pass, when the sun had set, that an ecstasy fell upon Abram, and lo ! an horror of great darkness fell upon him, and it was said unto Abram : " Know of a surety that thy seed shall be a stranger in a land (that is) not theirs, and they will bring them into bondage, and afflict them four

[1] Wrongly taken as a proper name (cf. R.V.). So LXX.
[2] Cf. Gen. xv. 7.
[3] For 8–9 cf. Gen. xv. 8–9.
[4] Cf. Gen. xiv. 13.
[5] For 11–12 cf. Gen. xv. 10–11.

hundred years.[1] 14. And the nation also to whom they will be in bondage shall I judge, and after that they will come forth thence with much substance. 15. And thou wilt go to thy fathers in peace, and be buried in a good old age. 16. But in the fourth generation [2] they will return hither; for the iniquity of the Amorites is not yet full." [3] 17. And he awoke from his sleep, and he arose, and the sun had set; and there was a flame, and behold! a furnace was smoking, and a flame of fire passed between the pieces. 18. And on that day the Lord made a covenant with Abram, saying : " To thy seed will I give this land, from the river of Egypt unto the great river, the river Euphrates, the Kenites, the Kenizzites, the Kad-monites, the Perizzites, and the Rephaim, the Phakor-ites,[4] and the Hivites,[5] and the Amorites, and the Canaanites, and the Girgashites, and the Jebusites." [6] 19. And the day passed, and Abram offered the pieces, and the birds, and their fruit-offerings, and their drink-offerings, and the fire devoured them. 20. And on that day [7] we made a covenant with Abram, according as we had covenanted with Noah in this month;[8] and Abram renewed the festival and ordinance for himself for ever.

[1] Cf. Gen. xv. 13, but Exod. xii. 40 gives the number 430. Tradition assumes that the number includes the sojourn of the Patriarchs in Canaan. Our text reckons the period from the birth of Isaac (when Abraham was 100 years old). St. Paul (Gal. iii. 16–17) reckons 430 years from the announce-ment. According to Targ. Ps.-Jon. on Exod. xii. 40 f., the odd 30 years cover the period between the announcement and Isaac's birth.

[2] A generation = 100 years. Isaac was born when Abra-ham was 100 years old (Gen. xxi. 5).

[3] For 13–16 cf. Gen. xv. 12–16.

[4] Absent from MT (which inserts " Hittite " before " Periz-zite ").

[5] So LXX and Sam. here (Gen. xv. 20); but MT, Syr. and Vulg. omit.

[6] For 17–18 cf. Gen. xv. 17–21.

[7] i. e. the 15th of Sivan.

[8] Probably, according to our author, on the same day of the month.

The Birth of Ishmael (xiv. 21–24 ; cf. Gen. xvi. 1–4. 11).

21. And Abram rejoiced, and made all these things known to Sarai his wife ; and he believed that he would have seed, but she did not bear. 22. And Sarai advised her husband Abram, and said unto him : " Go in unto Hagar, my Egyptian maid : it may be that I shall build up seed unto thee by her." 23. And Abram hearkened unto the voice of Sarai his wife, and said unto her, " Do (so)." And Sarai took Hagar, her maid, the Egyptian, and gave her to Abram, her husband, to be his wife. 24. And he went in unto her, and she conceived and bare him a son, and he called his name Ishmael, in the 1965 A.M. fifth year of this week ; and this was the eighty-sixth year in the life of Abram.

The Feast of First-fruits. Circumcision instituted. The Promise of Isaac's Birth. Circumcision ordained for all Israel (xv. 1–34 ; cf. Gen. xvii.).

XV. And in the fifth year of the †fourth†[1] week of this jubilee, in the third month, in the middle of the month,[2] Abram celebrated the feast of the first-fruits[3] of the grain harvest. 2. And he offered new offerings on the altar, the first-fruits of the produce, unto the Lord, an heifer and a goat and a sheep on the altar as a burnt sacrifice unto the Lord ; their fruit-offerings and their drink-offerings he offered upon the altar with frankincense.[4] 3. And the Lord appeared to Abram, and said unto him : " I am God Almighty ; approve thyself before Me and be thou perfect. 4. And I will make My covenant between

---

[1] Read " third."   [2] i. e. the 15th of Sivan.
[3] i. e. the Feast of Weeks. The Pharisees celebrated this feast not on Sivan 15th, but on Sivan 6th. See further Introduction.
[4] Cf. xiv. 9. The offerings prescribed for this festival in Lev. xxiii. 18–20 are different.

Me and thee, and I will multiply thee exceedingly." [1]
5. [2] And Abram fell on his face, and God talked with him, and said :

6. " Behold My ordinance is with thee,
And thou wilt be the father of many nations.

7. Neither will thy name any more be called Abram,
But thy name from henceforth, even for ever,
shall be Abraham.
For the father of many nations have I made thee.

8. And I shall make thee very great,
And I shall make thee into nations,
And kings will come forth from thee.

9. And I shall establish My covenant between Me and thee, and thy seed after thee, throughout their generations, for an eternal covenant, so that I may be a God unto thee, and to thy seed after thee. 10. (And I shall give to thee and to thy seed after thee) [3] the land where thou hast been a sojourner, the land of Canaan, that thou mayst possess it for ever, and I shall be their God." 11. [4] And the Lord said unto Abraham : " And as for thee, do thou keep My Covenant, thou and thy seed after thee ; and circumcise ye every male among you, and circumcise your foreskins, and it will be a token of an eternal covenant between Me and you. 12. And the child on the eighth day [5] ye will circumcise, every male throughout your generations, him that is born in the house, or whom ye have bought with money from any stranger, whom ye have acquired who is not of thy seed. 13. He that is born in thy house will surely be circumcised, and those whom thou hast bought with money will be circumcised, and My covenant will be in your

---

[1] For 3–4 cf. Gen. xvii. 1 f.
[2] For 5–10 cf. Gen. xvii. 3–8.
[3] The bracketed words (lost through homoioteleuton) are restored from Gen. xvii. 8.
[4] For 11–13 cf. Gen. xvii. 9–13.
[5] MT has " and the child of eight days." Our text here may be a deliberate alteration.

flesh for an eternal ordinance. 14.[1] And the uncircumcised male who is not circumcised in the flesh of
his foreskin on the eighth day,[2] that soul will be cut
off from his people, for he hath broken My covenant."
15.[3] And God said unto Abraham : "As for Sarai
thy wife, her name will no more be called Sarai, but
Sarah will be her name. 16. And I shall bless her,
and give thee a son by her, and I shall bless him,[4] and
he will become a nation, and kings of nations will
proceed from him." 17. And Abraham fell on his
face, and rejoiced, and said in his heart : "Shall a
son be born to him that is a hundred years old, and
shall Sarah, who is ninety years old, bring forth?"
18. And Abraham said unto God : "O that Ishmael
might live before thee !" 19. And God said : "Yea,
and Sarah also will bear thee a son, and thou wilt call
his name Isaac, and I shall establish My covenant
with him, an everlasting covenant, and for his seed
after him. 20. And as for Ishmael also have I heard
thee, and behold I shall bless him, and make him great,
and multiply him exceedingly, and he will beget
twelve princes, and I shall make him a great nation.
21. But My covenant shall I establish with Isaac,
whom Sarah will bear to thee, in these days, in the
next year." 22. And He left off speaking with him,
and God went up from Abraham. 23.[5] And Abraham
did according as God had said unto him, and he took
Ishmael his son, and all that were born in his house,
and whom he had bought with his money, every male
in his house, and circumcised the flesh of their fore-

[1] For 14 cf. Gen. xvii. 14.

[2] The words *on the eighth day* are absent from the text of
Gen. xvii. 14, in MT, Syr. and Vulg., but are attested by the
LXX and Sam. The strict rule about the eighth day was
later relaxed among the Jews, but is still practised by the
Samaritans.

[3] For 15–22 cf. Gen. xvii. 15–22.

[4] So LXX, Sam., Syr. and Vulg. of Gen. xvii. 22. But
MT makes the text refer to Sarah ("yea, I will bless her,
[and she shall be a mother of nations : kings of peoples shall
be of her]," R.V.).

[5] For 23–24 cf. Gen. xvii. 23–27.

skin. 24. And on the selfsame day[1] was Abraham circumcised, and all the men of his house, (and those born in the house), and all those, whom he had bought with money from the children of the stranger, were circumcised with him. 25. This law is for all the generations for ever, and there is no circumcision of the days,[2] and no omission of one day out of the eight days;[3] for it is an eternal ordinance, ordained and written on the heavenly tables. 26. And every one that is born, the flesh of whose foreskin is not circumcised on[4] the eighth day, belongeth not to the children of the covenant which the Lord made with Abraham, but to the children of destruction; nor is there, moreover, any sign on him that he is the Lord's, but (he is destined) to be destroyed and slain from the earth, and to be rooted out of the earth, for he hath broken the covenant of the Lord our God. 27. For all the angels of the presence and all the angels of sanctification[5] have been so created[6] from the day of their creation, and before the angels of the presence and the angels of sanctification He hath sanctified Israel, that they should be with Him and with His holy angels. 28. And do thou command the children of Israel and let them observe the sign of this covenant for their generations as an eternal ordinance, and they will not be rooted out of the land. 29. For the command is ordained for a covenant, that they should observe it for ever among all the children of Israel. 30. For Ishmael and his sons and his brothers and Esau, the Lord did not cause to approach Him, and he chose them not because they are the children of Abraham, because He knew them, but He chose Israel to be His people. 31. And He

---

[1] i.e. the 15th of Sivan.

[2] i.e. ? of the days preceding the eighth day.

[3] Only on the eighth day is the rite to be performed.

[4] Ethiop. MSS. and Lat. have " till."

[5] The two highest orders of angels, who share with Israel the privilege of observing the Sabbath (cf. ii. 18–21), and of being circumcised.

[6] i.e. have been created circumcised.

sanctified it, and gathered it from amongst all the children of men[1]; for there are many nations and many peoples, and all are His, and over all hath He placed spirits in authority to lead them astray[2] from Him. 32. But over Israel He did not appoint any angel or spirit, for He alone is their ruler, and He will preserve them and require them at the hand of His angels and His spirits, and at the hand of all His powers in order that He may preserve them and bless them, and that they may be His and He may be theirs from henceforth for ever. 33. And now I announce unto thee that the children of Israel will not keep true to this ordinance, and they will not circumcise their sons according to all this law; for in the flesh of their circumcision they will omit this circumcision of their sons, and all of them, sons of Beliar,[3] will leave their sons uncircumcised as they were born.[4] 34. And there will be great wrath from the Lord against the children of Israel, because they have forsaken His covenant and turned aside from His word, and provoked and blasphemed, inasmuch as they do not observe the ordinance of this law; for they have treated their members like the Gentiles, so that they may be removed and rooted out of the land. And there will no more be pardon or forgiveness unto them [so that there should be forgiveness and pardon] for all the sin of this eternal error.

---

[1] Israel is God's portion; cf. Deut. xxxii. 8–9 in the LXX form of which " angels " is read instead of " children of Israel "; cf. also Ecclus. xvii. 17. The " seventy nations of the earth were placed under the dominion of seventy angels "; but in Dan. x. 13, 20, 21, xii. 1, Michael is referred to as Israel's angel-prince.

[2] This describes the result, not the original purpose of their appointment.

[3] In i. 20 (see note). Beliar is clearly a Satanic being. This meaning may possibly be present in the use of the expression here. " Sons of Belial " is common in the O.T. (cf. *e. g.* 1 Sam. ii. 12).

[4] Apparently such apostasy was widely spread when our author wrote.

Angelic Visitation of Abraham in Hebron ; Promise of Isaac's Birth repeated. The Destruction of Sodom and Lot's Deliverance (xvi. 1–9 ; cf. Gen. xviii.–xix.).

XVI. And on the new moon of the fourth month we [1] appeared unto Abraham, at the oak of Mamre, and we talked with him, and we announced to him that a son would be given to him by Sarah his wife.[2] 2. And Sarah laughed, for she heard that we had spoken these words with Abraham, and we admonished her, and she became afraid, and denied that she had laughed on account of the words.[3] 3. And we told her the name of her son, as his name is ordained and written in the heavenly tables (*i.e.*) Isaac. 4. And (that) when we returned to her at a set time, she would have conceived a son. 5. And in this month the Lord executed his judgments on Sodom, and Gomorrah, and Zeboim,[4] and all the region of the Jordan, and He burned them with fire and brimstone, and destroyed them until this day, even as [lo] I have declared unto thee all their works, that they are wicked and sinners exceedingly, and that they defile themselves and commit fornication in their flesh, and work uncleanness on the earth.[5] 6. And, in like manner, God will execute judgment on the places where they have done according to the uncleanness of the Sodomites, like unto the judgment of Sodom. 7. But Lot we saved ; for God remembered Abraham, and sent him out from the midst of the overthrow. 8. And he and his daughters committed sin upon the earth, such as had not been on the earth since the days of Adam till his time ; for the man lay with his daughters.[6] 9. And, behold, it was commanded and engraven concerning all his seed, on the heavenly tables, to remove them and root them out, and to

---

[1] *i. e.* the angels.
[2] For 1 cf. Gen. xviii. 1, 10 (vers. 2–9 omitted).
[3] Cf. Gen. xviii. 10, 12, 15.   [4] Cf. Gen. xiv. 2, 8.
[5] For 5 cf. Gen. xix. 24.   [6] For 7–8 cf. Gen. xix. 29, 31 ff.

execute judgment upon them like the judgment of
Sodom, and to leave no seed of the man on earth on
the day of condemnation.

Abraham at Beersheba. Birth and Circumcision of Isaac (cf. Gen. xxi. 1–4). Institution of the Feast of Tabernacles (xvi. 10–31).

10. And in this month Abraham moved from
Hebron, and departed and dwelt between Kadesh
and Shur in the mountains [1] of Gerar. 11. And in
the middle of the fifth month he moved from thence,
and dwelt at the Well of the Oath. [2] 12. [3] And in
the middle of the sixth month the Lord visited Sarah
and did unto her as He had spoken, and she conceived.
1980 A.M. 13. And she bare a son in the third month, and in the
middle of the month, [4] at the time of which the Lord
had spoken to Abraham, on the festival of the first-
fruits of the harvest, [5] Isaac was born. 14. And
Abraham circumcised his son on the eighth day : he
was the first that was circumcised according to the
covenant which is ordained for ever. 15. And in
the sixth year of the † fourth † [6] week we came to
Abraham, to the Well of the Oath, and we appeared
unto him [as we had told Sarah that we should return
to her, and she would have conceived a son. 16. And
we returned in the seventh month, and found Sarah
with child before us] [7] and we blessed him, and we
announced to him all the things which had been
decreed concerning him, that he should not die till
he should beget six sons more, [8] and should see (them)
before he died ; but (that) in Isaac should his name
and seed be called : [9] 17. And (that) all the seed of
his sons should be Gentiles, and be reckoned with the
Gentiles ; but from the sons of Isaac one should

---

[1] Or " territories."   [2] i. e. Beersheba; cf. Gen. xxi. 31.
[3] For 12–14 cf. Gen. xxi. 1–4.   [4] i. e. the 15th of Sivan.
[5] i. e. Pentecost.   [6] Read " third " as in xv. 1 (Charles).
[7] The bracketed words are an incorrect gloss, according to
Charles, and should be omitted.
[8] Six sons by Keturah (Gen. xxv. 2).   [9] Cf. Gen. xxi. 12.

become a holy seed, and should not be reckoned among the Gentiles.[1] 18. For he should become the portion of the Most High,[2] and all his seed had fallen into the possession of God, that it should be unto the Lord a people for (His) possession [3] above all nations and that it should become a kingdom and priests and a holy nation.[4] 19. And we went our way, and we announced to Sarah all that we had told him, and they both rejoiced with exceeding great joy. 20. And he built there an altar to the Lord who had delivered him, and who was making him rejoice in the land of his sojourning, and he celebrated a festival of joy in this month seven days,[5] near the altar which he had built at the Well of the Oath. 21. And he built booths for himself and for his servants on this festival, and he was the first to celebrate the feast of tabernacles on the earth. 22. And during these seven days he brought each day to the altar a burnt-offering to the Lord, two oxen,[6] two rams, seven sheep,[7] one he-goat, for a sin-offering, that he might atone thereby for himself and for his seed. 23. And, as a thank-offering, seven rams, seven kids, seven sheep, and seven he-goats, and their fruit-offerings and their drink-offerings; [8] and he burnt all the fat thereof on the altar, a chosen offering unto the Lord for a sweet smelling savour. 24. And morning and evening he burnt fragrant substances,[9] frankincense

[1] All Abraham's descendants, except Jacob and his seed, were to be reckoned among the Gentiles.

[2] Cf. xv. 31 f.

[3] Cf. Deut. vii. 6; Exod. xix. 5.

[4] Cf. Exod. xix. 6 (MT has " a kingdom of priests "); cf. Rev. v. 10, i. 6, which agree with our text substantially, and this may be the original sense. See Introduction, p. xxxii.

[5] In 20–31 we have an account of the Feast of Tabernacles which is marked by peculiar features.

[6] According to Num. xxix. 13–33 thirteen bullocks were sacrificed the first day, and this number was diminished by one each day following.

[7] In Num. xxix. 13 fourteen he-lambs.

[8] Cf. 2 Chron. xxix. 21.

[9] Cf. Exod. xxx. 34; Ecclus. xxiv. 15.

and galbanum, and stacte, and nard, and myrrh,
and spice, and costum; all these seven he offered,
crushed, mixed together in equal parts (and) pure.
25. And he celebrated this feast during seven days,
rejoicing with all his heart and with all his soul, he
and all those who were in his house; and there was
no stranger with him, nor any that was uncircumcised.
26. And he blessed his Creator who had created him
in his generation, for He had created him according
to His good pleasure; for He knew and perceived
that from him would arise the plant of righteousness [1]
for the eternal generations, and from him a holy
seed, so that it should become like Him who had made
all things. 27. And he blessed and rejoiced, and he
called the name of this festival the festival of the
Lord, a joy acceptable to the Most High God. 28.
And we blessed him for ever, and all his seed after him
throughout all the generations of the earth, because
he celebrated this festival in its season, according
to the testimony of the heavenly tables. 29. For
this reason it is ordained on the heavenly tables
concerning Israel, that they shall celebrate the feast of
tabernacles seven days with joy, in the seventh
month, acceptable before the Lord—a statute for
ever throughout their generations every year.[2] 30.
And to this there is no limit of days; for it is ordained
for ever regarding Israel that they should celebrate
it and dwell in booths, and set wreaths upon their
heads,[3] and take leafy boughs, and willows from the
brook.[4] 31. And Abraham took branches of palm
trees, and the fruit of goodly trees, and every day
going round the altar with the branches seven times [5]

[1] Cf. xxi. 24; 1 Enoch x. 16, xciii. 5, 10.

[2] Cf. Lev. xxiii. 41.

[3] This custom in connection with Tabernacles seems to
be unknown to tradition; cf., however, Wisdom ii. 7 f.;
Josephus, *Ant.* xix. 9, 1.   Bridegrooms wore wreaths, but the
custom was later abolished.   See further Introduction, p. xx f.

[4] Cf. Lev. xxiii. 40.

[5] According to later Jewish tradition it was only on the
seventh day that the worshippers went round the altar seven
times.

[a day] in the morning, he praised and gave thanks to his God for all things in joy.

The Expulsion of Hagar and Ishmael (xvii. 1–14; cf. Gen. xxi. 8–21).

XVII. And in the first year of the †fifth† [1] week Isaac was weaned in this jubilee, and Abraham made a great banquet in the third month, on the day his son Isaac was weaned.[2] 2. And Ishmael, the son of Hagar, the Egyptian, was before the face of Abraham, his father, in his place, and Abraham rejoiced and blessed God because he had seen his sons [3] and had not died childless. 3. And he remembered the words which He had spoken to him on the day on which Lot had parted from him, and he rejoiced because the Lord had given him seed upon the earth to inherit the earth, and he blessed with all his mouth the Creator of all things.[4] 4. [5] And Sarah saw Ishmael playing and dancing,[6] and Abraham rejoicing with great joy, and she became jealous of Ishmael and said to Abraham, " Cast out this bondwoman and her son ; for the son of this bondwoman will not be heir with my son, Isaac." 5. And the thing was grievous in Abraham's sight, because of his maid-servant and because of his son, that he should drive them from him. 6. And God said to Abraham " Let it not be grievous in thy sight, because of the child and because of the bondwoman ; in all that Sarah hath said unto thee, hearken to her words and do (them) ; for in Isaac shall thy name and seed be called. 7. But as for the son of this bondwoman I will make him a great [7] nation, because he is of thy seed." 8. And Abraham rose up early in the morning

1982 A.M.

---

[1] Read " fourth " (Charles). [2] Cf. Gen. xxi. 8.
[3] Cf. xvi. 16. [4] Cf. xiii. 19 ff.
[5] For 4–13 cf. Gen. xxi. 9–21.
[6] Possibly *and dancing* is corrupt for *with Isaac,* which is read in LXX and Vulg.; cf. Gen. xxi. 9.
[7] LXX, Sam., Syr. and Vulg. of Gen. xxi. 13, have *great ;* but MT omits.

and took bread and a bottle of water, and placed them on the shoulders of Hagar and the child, and sent her away. 9. And she departed and wandered in the wilderness of Beersheba, and the water in the bottle was spent, and the child thirsted, and was not able to go on, and fell down. 10. And his mother took him and cast him under an olive tree,[1] and went and sat her down over against him, at the distance of a bow-shot; for she said, " Let me not see the death of my child," and as she sat she wept. 11. And an angel of God, one of the holy ones, said unto her, " Why weepest thou, Hagar? Arise, take the child, and hold him in thine hand; for God hath heard thy voice, and hath seen the child." 12. And she [2] opened her eyes, and she saw a well of water, and she went and filled her bottle with water, and she gave her child to drink, and she arose and went towards the wilderness of Paran. 13. And the child grew and became an archer, and God was with him; and his mother took him a wife from among the daughters of Egypt. 14. And she bare him a son, and he called his name Nebaioth; [3] for she said, " The Lord was nigh to me when I called upon him."

Mastêmâ proposes to God that Abraham shall be put to the Proof (xvi. 15–18).

2003 A.M.

15. And it came to pass in the seventh week, in the first year thereof, in the first month in this jubilee,[4] on the twelfth of this month, there were voices in heaven regarding Abraham, that he was faithful in all that He told him, and that he loved the Lord, and that in every affliction he was faithful. 16. And the

---

[1] LXX (Gen. xxi. 15) " under a fir tree "; MT " under one of the shrubs."

[2] Read (?) " He " (God).

[3] Cf. Gen. xxv. 13.

[4] According to the chronology of our Book (cf. xvi. 12 with this passage) Isaac was twenty-three years old when he was offered up; according to the Seder Olam he was thirty-seven.

prince Mastêmâ [1] came and said before God, " Behold, Abraham loveth Isaac his son, and he delighteth in him above all things else ; bid him offer him as a burnt-offering on the altar, and Thou wilt see if he will do this command, and Thou wilt know if he is faithful in everything wherein Thou dost try him. 17. And the Lord knew that Abraham was faithful in all his afflictions ; for He had tried him through his country and with famine, and had tried him with the wealth of kings, and had tried him again through his wife, when she was torn (from him), and with circumcision, and had tried him through Ishmael and Hagar, his maid-servant, when he sent them away.[2] 18. And in everything wherein He had tried him, he was found faithful, and his soul was not impatient, and he was not slow to act ; for he was faithful and a lover of the Lord.

The Sacrifice of Isaac : Abraham returns to Beersheba (xviii. 1-19 ; Cf. Gen. xxii. 1-19).

XVIII. And God said to him, " Abraham, Abraham " ; and he said, " Behold, (here) am I." 2. And He said, " Take thy beloved [3] son whom thou lovest, (even) Isaac, and go unto the high country,[4] and offer him on one of the mountains which I will point out unto thee." 3. And he rose early in the morning and saddled his ass, and took his two young men with him, and Isaac his son, and clave the wood of the burnt-offering, and he went to the place on

---

[1] In Gen. xxii. 1 it is God Himself who directly proves Abraham.

[2] Seven of the traditional ten trials of Abraham are here mentioned : (1) Departure from his country; (2) famine; (3) the wealth of kings; (4) seizure of his wife; (5) circumcision; (6) and (7) expulsion of Hagar and Ishmael [(8) is the unfruitfulness of Sarah; (9) the sacrifice of Isaac, and (10) the burial of Sarah; cf. xiv. 21 and xix. 3, 8]. Slightly different enumerations occur elsewhere (e. g. *Pirke de R. Eliezer*, xxvi.–xxx.).

[3] So LXX (Gen. xxii. 2) : MT *only* (*son*).

[4] So LXX ; but MT " the land of Moriah."

the third day, and he saw the place afar off.   4. And
he came to a well of water, and he said to his young
men, " Abide ye here with the ass, and I and the lad
shall go (yonder), and when we have worshipped
we shall come again to you."   5. And he took the
wood of the burnt-offering and laid it on Isaac his
son, and he took in his hand the fire and the knife,
and they went both of them together to that place.
6. And Isaac said to his father, " Father "; and he
said, " Here am I, my son."   And he said unto him,
" Behold the fire, and the knife, and the wood; but
where is the sheep for the burnt-offering, father ? "
7. And he said, " God will provide for himself a sheep
for a burnt-offering, my son."   And he drew near
to the place of the mount of God.[1] 8. And he built
an altar, and he placed the wood on the altar, and
bound Isaac his son, and placed him on the wood
which was upon the altar, and stretched forth his
hand to take the knife to slay Isaac his son.   9. And
I stood before him, and before the prince of the
Mastêmâ,[2] and the Lord said, " Bid him not to lay
his hand on the lad, nor to do anything to him, for I
have shown that he feareth the Lord."   10. And
I called to him from heaven, and said unto him :
" Abraham, Abraham "; and he was terrified and
said : " Behold, (here) am I."   11. And I said unto
him : " Lay not thy hand upon the lad, neither do
thou anything to him; for now I have shown that
thou fearest the Lord, and hast not 'withheld thy son,
thy first-born son, from me."   12. And the prince of
the Mastêmâ was put to shame; and Abraham
lifted up his eyes and looked, and, behold, a single
ram caught [3] . . . by his horns, and Abraham went
and took the ram and offered it for a burnt-offering
in the stead of his son.   13. And Abraham called

[1] Instead of the words *of the mount of God*, MT (Gen. xxii. 9)
reads, *which God hath told him of*.

[2] Here (cf., also, xviii. 12, xlviii. 9, 12, 15), Mastêmâ is
the name given to the whole class of evil spirits, or Satans;
elsewhere of the prince of these himself.

[3] ? add *in a thicket*.

that place " The Lord hath seen," so that it is said " (in the mount) the Lord hath seen " : [1] that is Mount Sion.   14. And the Lord called Abraham by his name a second time from heaven, as he caused us to appear to speak to him in the name of the Lord. 15. And He said : " By Myself have I sworn, saith the Lord,

Because thou hast done this thing,
And hast not withheld thy son, thy beloved [2] son, from Me,

That in blessing I shall bless thee,
And in multiplying I shall multiply thy seed

As the stars of heaven,
And as the sand which is on the seashore.

And thy seed will inherit the cities [3] of its enemies,
16. And in thy seed will all nations of the earth be blessed ;

Because thou hast obeyed My voice,
And I have shown to all that thou art faithful unto Me in all that I have said unto thee :
Go in peace." [4]

17. And Abraham went to his young men, and they arose and went together to Beersheba, and Abraham dwelt by the Well of the Oath.   18. And he celebrated this festival every year, seven days with joy, and he called it the festival of the Lord according to the seven days during which he went and returned in peace.   19. And accordingly hath it been ordained and written on the heavenly tables regarding Israel and its seed that they should observe this festival seven days with the joy of festival.

---

[1] Syr. and Vulg. render (Gen. xxii. 14) " will see," " seeth." MT " it shall be seen " (provided).

[2] MT " thine only " (Gen. xxii. 16).

[3] So Sam., version, LXX : MT " gate " (Gen. xxii. 17).

[4] Cf. I Sam. i. 17.

The Death and Burial of Sarah (xix. 1–9; cf. Gen. xxiii.).

XIX. And in the first year of the first week in the
forty-second jubilee, Abraham returned and dwelt
opposite Hebron, that is Kirjath Arba, two weeks of
years. 2. And in the first year of the † third † [1]
week of this jubilee the days of the life of Sarah were
accomplished, and she died in Hebron. 3. And
Abraham went to mourn over her and bury her, and
we tried him [to see] if his spirit were patient and he
were not indignant in the words of his mouth; and
he was found patient in this, and was not disturbed.[2]
4. For in patience of spirit he conversed with the
children of Heth, to the intent that they should give
him a place in which to bury his dead. 5. And the
Lord gave him grace before all who saw him, and he
besought in gentleness the sons of Heth, and they gave
him the land of the double cave [3] over against Mamre,
that is Hebron, for four hundred pieces of silver.
6. And they besought him, saying, "We shall give
it to thee for nothing"; but he would not take it
from their hands for nothing, for he gave the price
of the place, the money in full, and he bowed down
before them twice; and after this he buried his dead
in the double cave. 7. And all the days of the life
of Sarah were one hundred and twenty-seven years,
that is, two jubilees and four weeks and one year:
these are the days of the years of the life of Sarah.
8. This is the tenth [2] trial wherewith Abraham was
tried, and he was found faithful, patient in spirit.
9. And he said not a single word regarding the rumour
in the land how that God had said that He would
give it to him and to his seed after him, and he begged
a place there to bury his dead; for he was found faith-

2010 A. M.

[1] Read "second" (Charles).
[2] This is the tenth trial of Abraham; cf. xvii. 17 note.
[3] *i. e.* the cave of Machpelah (LXX, τὸ σπήλαιον τὸ διπλοῦν).

ful, and was recorded on the heavenly tables as the friend of God.[1]

Marriage of Isaac and second Marriage of Abraham (cf. Gen. xxiv. 15, xxv. 1–4); the Birth of Esau and Jacob (cf. Gen. xxv. 19 ff.) (xix. 10–14).

10. And in the fourth year thereof he took a wife 2020 A.M. for his son Isaac and her name was Rebecca [the daughter of Bethuel, the son of Nahor, the brother of Abraham] [2] the sister of Laban and daughter of Bethuel; and Bethuel was the son of Mêlcâ, who was the wife of Nahor, the brother of Abraham. 11. And Abraham took to himself a third wife, and her name was Keturah, from among the daughters of his household servants, for Hagar had died before Sarah.[3] 12. And she bare him six sons, Zimram, and Jokshan, and Medan, and Midian, and Ishbak, and Shuah, in the two weeks of years. 13. And in the sixth week, 2046 A.M. in the second year thereof, Rebecca bare to Isaac two sons, Jacob and Esau, and Jacob was a smooth and upright [4] man, and Esau was fierce, a man of the field, and hairy, and Jacob dwelt in tents. 14. And the youths grew, and Jacob learned to write; [5] but Esau did not learn, for he was a man of the field and a hunter, and he learnt war, and all his deeds were fierce.

[1] A traditional title of Abraham. It goes back to Isa. xli. 8; cf. Jas. ii. 23, *T.B. Men.* 53*b*.

[2] The bracketed words a dittograph.

[3] This explains why Abraham did not take Hagar back. The later tradition (cf. e. g. *Pirḳe de R. Eliezer* xxx.) identifies Hagar with Keturah.

[4] Cf. Gen. xxv. 27 (where " plain " = lit. " upright "), and Gen. xxvii. 11 (combined here).

[5] According to the Targums the " tents " were academies. Jacob is represented as a lifelong student of the Torah (cf. *Ber. rabba* lxiii; *Pirḳe de R. Eliezer* xxxii.).

Abraham loves Jacob and blesses him
(xix. 15–31).

15. And Abraham loved Jacob, but Isaac loved
Esau.   16. And Abraham saw the deeds of Esau, and
he knew that in Jacob [1] should his name and seed be
called; and he called Rebecca and gave commandment regarding Jacob, for he knew that she (too)
loved Jacob much more than Esau.   17. And he said
unto her : " My daughter, watch over my son Jacob,
> For he shall be in my stead on the earth,
> And for a blessing in the midst of the children of
> men,
> And for the glory of the whole seed of Shem.

18. For I know that the Lord will choose him to be a
people for possession unto Himself, above all peoples
that are upon the face of the earth.[2]   19. And behold, Isaac my son loveth Esau more than Jacob, but
I see that thou truly lovest Jacob.

20. Add still further to thy kindness to him,
> And let thine eyes be upon him in love;
> For he will be a blessing unto us on the earth from
> henceforth unto all generations of the earth.

21. Let thy hands be strong
> And let thy heart rejoice in thy son Jacob;
> For I have loved him far beyond all my sons.

> He will be blessed for ever,
> And his seed will fill the whole earth.

22. If a man can number the sand of the earth,
> His seed also will be numbered.[3]

23. And all the blessings wherewith the Lord hath
blessed me and my seed shall belong to Jacob and
his seed alway.   24. And in his seed shall my name
be blessed, and the name of my fathers, Shem, and

---

[1] Jacob was to be the founder of the chosen nation; cf.
ii. 20.

[2] Cf. Deut. vii. 6.

[3] Cf. Gen. xiii. 16 (cf. also xiii. 20 of our Book).

Noah, and Enoch, and Mahalalel, and Enos, and Seth, and Adam.[1] 25. And these shall serve

> To lay the foundations of the heaven,
> And to strengthen the earth,
> And to renew all the luminaries which are in the firmament."

26. And he called Jacob before the eyes of Rebecca his mother, and kissed him, and blessed him, and said : 27. " Jacob, my beloved son, whom my soul loveth, may God bless thee from above the firmament, and may He give thee all the blessings wherewith He blessed Adam, and Enoch, and Noah, and Shem; and all the things of which He told me, and all the things which He promised to give me, may He cause to cleave to thee and to thy seed for ever, according to the days of heaven above the earth.[2] 28. And the spirits of Mastêmâ shall not rule over thee or over thy seed [3] to turn thee from the Lord, who is thy God from henceforth for ever. 29. And may the Lord God be a father to thee and thou the first-born son, and to the people alway. Go in peace, my son." 30. And they both went forth together from Abraham. 31. And Rebecca loved Jacob, with all her heart and with all her soul, very much more than Esau ; but Isaac loved Esau much more than Jacob.

Abraham's Last Words to his Children and Grandchildren (xx. 1–11).

XX. And in the forty-second jubilee, in the first year of the †seventh† [4] week, Abraham called Ishmael, and his twelve sons,[5] and Isaac and his two sons, and the six sons of Keturah, and their sons. 2. And he commanded them that they should observe the way of the Lord ; that they should work righteousness, and love each his neighbour, and act

2052
(?2045)
A.M.

---

[1] Notice that Methuselah is omitted, and Adam is reckoned among the saints (with Noah and Enoch).
[2] Cf. xxii. 13.   [3] As over the Gentiles.
[4] Probably corrupt for " sixth " (Charles).
[5] Cf. Gen. xxv. 13–15.

on this manner amongst all men; that they should each so walk with regard to them as to do judgment and righteousness on the earth. 3. That they should circumcise their sons,[1] according to the covenant which He had made with them, and not deviate to the right hand or the left of all the paths which the Lord had commanded us; and that we should keep ourselves from all fornication and uncleanness, [and renounce from amongst us all fornication and uncleanness].[2] 4. And if any woman or maid commit fornication amongst you, burn her with fire,[3] and let them not commit fornication with her after their eyes and their heart; and let them not take to themselves wives from the daughters of Canaan; for the seed of Canaan will be rooted out of the land. 5. And he told them of the judgment of the giants, and the judgment of the Sodomites, how they had been judged on account of their wickedness, and had died on account of their fornication, and uncleanness, and mutual corruption through fornication.[4]

6. " And guard yourselves from all fornication and
    uncleanness,
    And from all pollution of sin,
    Lest ye make our name a curse,
    And your whole life a hissing,[5]
    And all your sons be destroyed by the sword,
    And ye become accursed like Sodom,
    And all your remnant as the sons of Gomorrah.

7. I implore you, my sons, love the God of
    heaven,
    And cleave ye to all His commandments.

---

[1] Circumcision, according to our author, is binding upon Ishmael's and Keturah's descendants (cf. Gen. xvii. 9 f.). Notice the omission of Esau's descendants. According to *Pirḳe de R. Eliezer* xxix., Esau, though he had been circumcised, " despised circumcision " (his birthright).

[2] Bracketed as a dittograph.

[3] According to the Law only the adulterous priest's daughter was to be burned with fire; others were to be stoned (cf. Lev. xxi. 9, xx. 10).

[4] Cf. vii. 21 (note).   [5] Cf. Isa. lxv. 15; Jer. xxix. 18.

And walk not after their idols, and after their
uncleannesses,

8.[1] And make not for yourselves molten or graven
gods; [2]
For they are vanity,
And there is no spirit in them;
For they are work of (men's) hands,
And all who trust in them, trust in nothing.
Serve them not, nor worship them,[3]

9. But serve ye the Most High God, and worship
Him continually:
And hope for His countenance always,
And work uprightness and righteousness before
Him,
That He may have pleasure in you and grant
you His mercy,
And send rain [4] upon you morning and evening,
And bless all your works which ye have wrought
upon the earth,
And bless thy bread and thy water,[5]
And bless the fruit of thy womb and the fruit
of thy land,
And the herds of thy cattle, and the flocks of
thy sheep.[6]

10. And ye will be for a blessing [7] on the earth,
And all nations of the earth will desire you,
And bless your sons in my name,
That they may be blessed as I am."

11. And he gave to Ishmael and to his sons, and to
the sons of Keturah, gifts, and sent them away from
Isaac his son, and he gave everything to Isaac his
son.[8]

---

[1] For 8 cf. xii. 5, xxii. 18.
[2] Cf. Deut. xxvii. 15.
[3] Cf. Exod. xx. 5.
[4] Cf. xii. 4, 18.
[5] Cf. Exod. xxiii. 25.
[6] Cf. Deut. vii. 13.
[7] Cf. Gen. xii. 2.
[8] Cf. Gen. xxv. 5-6.

The Dwelling-places of the Ishmaelites and of the Sons of Keturah (xx. 12-13).

12. And Ishmael and his sons, and the sons of Keturah and their sons, went together and dwelt from Paran to the entering in of Babylon in all the land which is towards the East facing the desert. 13. And these mingled with each other, and their name was called Arabs, and Ishmaelites.

Abraham's Last Words to Isaac (xxi. 1-25).

2057
(?2050)
A.M.

XXI. And in the sixth year of the †seventh† [1] week of this jubilee Abraham called Isaac his son,[2] and commanded him, saying : " I am become old, and know not the day of my death,[3] and am full of my days.[4] 2. And behold, I am one hundred and seventy-five years old,[5] and throughout all the days of my life I have remembered the Lord, and sought with all my heart to do His will, and to walk uprightly in all His ways. 3. My soul hath hated idols, (and I have despised those that served them, and I have given my heart and spirit) [6] that I might observe to do the will of Him who created me. 4. For He is the living God, and He is holy and faithful, and He is righteous beyond all, and there is with Him no accepting of (men's) persons and no accepting of gifts; [7] for God is righteous, and execut-

---

[1] Read " sixth " (Charles).

[2] The rest of this chapter purports to give Abraham's directions to Isaac regarding certain kinds of sacrifice. It has a remarkable parallel in *Test. XII Patriarchs*, Levi ix., where Isaac instructs Levi in the law of the priesthood, of sacrifices, etc. The latter is much shorter than our chapter, but hardly more original. The two books may have used a common source.

[3] In Gen. xxvii. 2 these words are uttered by Isaac.

[4] Cf. Gen. xxv. 8, where LXX, Sam., Vulg. read " full of days," but MT omits " days."

[5] Cf. Gen. xxv. 7.

[6] The bracketed words are supplied from the Latin.

[7] Cf. Deut. x. 17.

eth judgment on all those who transgress His commandments and despise His covenant. 5. And do
thou, my son, observe His commandments and His
ordinances and His judgments, and walk not after
the abominations and after the graven images and
after the molten images. 6. And eat no blood at
all of animals or cattle, or of any bird which flieth
in the heaven.[1] 7.[2] And if thou dost slay a victim
as an acceptable peace-offering, slay ye it, and pour
out its blood upon the altar, and all the fat of the
offering offer on the altar with fine flour (and the
meat-offering) mingled with oil,[3] with its drink-
offering—offer them all together on the altar of
burnt-offering; it is a sweet savour before the Lord.[4]
8. And thou wilt offer the fat of the sacrifice of
thank-offerings on the fire which is upon the altar,
and the fat which is on the belly, and all the fat
on the inwards and the two kidneys, and all the fat
that is upon them, and upon the loins and liver thou
shalt remove, together with the kidneys.[5] 9. And
offer all these for a sweet savour acceptable before
the Lord, with its meat-offering and with its drink-
offering, for a sweet savour, the bread [6] of the offering unto the Lord, 10. And eat its meat on that day
and on the second day, and let not the sun on the
second day go down upon it till it is eaten, and let
nothing be left over for the third day; for it is not
acceptable [for it is not approved] [7] and let it no
longer be eaten, and all who eat thereof will bring
sin upon themselves; for thus I have found it written
in the books of my forefathers, and in the words of
Enoch, and in the words of Noah.[8] 11. And on all

---

[1] Cf. vii. 28 (note).

[2] For 7–9 cf. the summary in *Test. XII Patr.* Levi ix. 7.

[3] Cf. Lev. ii. 4.   [4] For 7 cf. Lev. iii. 7–10.

[5] Cf. Lev. iii. 9–10.   [6] " Or food "; cf. Lev. iii. 11.

[7] Bracketed words a dittograph.

[8] No trace of such halakic rules exists in the Books of
Enoch or the fragments of the Noah apocalypse that are extant. The statement in the text seems to be original to the
author of *Jubilees.*

thy oblations thou shalt strew salt, and let not the
salt of the covenant be lacking in all thy oblations
before the Lord.[1]   12. And as regards the wood of the
sacrifices, beware lest thou bring (other) wood for
the altar in addition to these :[2] cypress, dêfrân,[3]
sagâd, pine, fir, cedar, savin, palm, olive, myrrh,
laurel, and citron, juniper, and balsam.   13. And of
these kinds of wood lay upon the altar under the
sacrifice, such as have been tested as to their appearance, and do not lay (thereon) any split or dark
wood, (but) hard and clean, without fault, a sound
and new growth ; and do not lay (thereon) old wood,
[for its fragrance is gone] for there is no longer
fragrance in it as before.[4]   14. Besides these kinds
of wood there is none other that thou shalt place
(on the altar), for the fragrance is dispersed, and the
smell of its fragrance goeth not up to heaven.   15. Observe this commandment and do it, my son, that
thou mayst be upright in all thy deeds.   16. And at
all times be clean in thy body, and wash thyself
with water before thou approachest to offer on the
altar, and wash thy hands and thy feet before thou
drawest near to the altar ; and when thou art done
sacrificing, wash again thy hands and thy feet.[5]
17. And let no blood appear upon you nor upon
your clothes ; be on thy guard, my son, against
blood, be on thy guard exceedingly ; cover it with
dust.[6]   18. And do not eat any blood, for it is the
soul ; eat no blood whatever.[7]   19. And take no
gifts for the blood of man, lest it be shed with impunity, without judgment ; for it is the blood that

---

[1] Cf. Lev. ii. 13 ; *Test. Levi* ix. 14.

[2] In *Test. Levi* ix. 12 " twelve " evergreen trees are mentioned ; here fourteen, and this number is probably correct.

[3] Probably a kind of fir.

[4] This may be the old halaka ; the Mishna has no trace of
it.   The Mishna (*Tamid* ii. 3) allows all kinds of wood except
that of the olive and vine ; cf., also, *Sifra* on Lev. i. 8.

[5] Cf. Exod. xxx. 19–21 ; cf. Test. Levi ix. 11.

[6] Cf. Lev. xvii. 13.

[7] Cf. Lev. xvii. 14 ; Deut. xii. 23.

is shed that causeth the earth to sin, and the earth cannot be cleansed from the blood of man save by the blood of him who shed it.[1] 20. And take no present or gift for the blood of man : blood for blood, that thou mayest be accepted before the Lord, the Most High God ; for He is the defence of the good : and that thou mayest be preserved from all evil, and that He may save thee from every kind of death.

21. I see, my son,

That all the works of the children of men are sin and wickedness,

And all their deeds are uncleanness and an abomination and a pollution,

And there is no righteousness with them.

22. Beware, lest thou shouldest walk in their ways And tread in their paths,

And sin a sin unto death [2] before the Most High God.

Else He will [hide His face from thee,

And] [3] give thee back into the hands [4] of thy transgression,

And root thee out of the land, and thy seed likewise from under heaven,

And thy name and thy seed will perish from the whole earth.

23. Turn away from all their deeds and all their uncleanness,

And observe the ordinance of the Most High God, And do His will and be upright in all things.

24. And He will bless thee in all thy deeds,

And will raise up from thee the plant of righteousness [5] through all the earth, throughout all generations of the earth,

And my name and thy name will not be forgotten under heaven for ever.

[1] Cf. vii. 33 ; Num. xxxv. 33.   [2] Cf. xxxiii. 18.
[3] Bracketed by Charles as an interpolation.
[4] *i. e.* into the power of.
[5] Cf. xvi. 26.

25. Go, my son, in peace.

May the Most High God, my God and thy God, strengthen thee to do His will,

And may He bless all thy seed and the residue of thy seed for the generations for ever, with all righteous blessings,

That thou mayest be a blessing on all the earth." [1]

26. And he went out from him rejoicing.

Isaac, Ishmael and Jacob join in Festival with Abraham for the Last Time. Abraham's Prayer (xxii. 1–9).

XXII. And it came to pass in the †first† [2] week in the †forty-fourth† [3] jubilee, in the †second† year, that is, the year in which Abraham died, that Isaac and Ishmael came from the Well of the Oath to celebrate the feast of weeks—that is, the feast of the first-fruits of the harvest—to Abraham, their father, and Abraham rejoiced because his two sons had come. 2. For Isaac had many possessions in Beersheba, and Isaac was wont to go and see his possessions and to return to his father. 3. And in those days Ishmael came to see his father, and they both came together, and Isaac offered a sacrifice for a burnt-offering, and presented it on the altar of his father which he had made in Hebron. 4. And he offered a thank-offering and made a feast of joy before Ishmael, his brother : and Rebecca made new cakes from the new grain, and gave them to Jacob, her son, to take them to Abraham, his father, from the first-fruits of the land, that he might eat and bless the Creator of all things before he died. 5. And Isaac, too, sent by the hand of Jacob to Abraham a best thank-offering, that he might eat and drink. 6. And he ate and drank, and blessed the Most High God,

[1] Cf. xx. 10.
[2] Read " sixth " (Charles).
[3] Read " forty-second " (Charles).

Who hath created heaven and earth,
Who hath made all the fat things of the earth,
And given them to the children of men
That they might eat and drink and bless their
   Creator.

7. "And now I give thanks unto Thee, my God,
because Thou hast caused me to see this day : behold,
I am one hundred three score and fifteen years, an
old man and full of days,[1] and all my days have
been unto me peace. 8. The sword of the adversary [2] hath not overcome me in all that Thou hast
given me and my children all the days of my life
until this day. 9. My God, may Thy mercy and
Thy peace be upon Thy servant, and upon the seed
of his sons, that they may be to Thee a chosen
nation and an inheritance [3] from amongst all the
nations of the earth from henceforth unto all the days
of the generations of the earth, unto all the ages."

Abraham's Last Words to and Blessings of Jacob (xxii. 10–30).

10. And he called Jacob and said : " My son
Jacob, may the God of all [4] bless thee and strengthen
thee to do righteousness, and His will before Him,
and may He choose thee and thy seed that ye may
become a people for His inheritance according to His
will alway. And do thou, my son, Jacob, draw near
and kiss me." 11. And he drew near and kissed
him, and he said :
" Blessed be my son Jacob
And all the sons of God Most High, unto all the
   ages :
May God give unto thee a seed of righteousness ;
And some of thy sons may He sanctify in the
   midst of the whole earth ;
May nations serve thee,

[1] Cf. xxi. 1.   [2] Cf. Jer. vi. 25.
[3] Israel is God's inheritance ; cf. Deut. iv. 20.
[4] i. e. of the universe ; this idea often recurs in our author.

And all the nations bow themselves before thy
    seed.[1]

12. Be strong in the presence of men,
    And exercise authority over all the seed of Seth.[2]
    Then thy ways and the ways of thy sons will be
        justified,
    So that they shall become a holy nation.

13. May the Most High God give thee all the blessings
        Wherewith he hath blessed me
    And wherewith He blessed Noah and Adam; [3]
    May they rest on the sacred head of thy seed
        from generation to generation for ever.

14. And may He cleanse thee from all unrighteous-
        ness and impurity,
    That thou mayest be forgiven all (thy) trans-
        gressions; (and) thy sins of ignorance.
    And may He strengthen thee,
    And bless thee.
    And mayest thou inherit the whole earth,

15. And may He renew His covenant with thee,
    That thou mayest be to Him a nation for His
        inheritance [4] for all the ages,
    And that He may be to thee and to thy seed a
        God in truth and righteousness throughout all
        the days of the earth.

16. And do thou, my son Jacob, remember my words,
    And observe the commandments of Abraham, thy
        father :
    Separate thyself from the nations,
    And eat not with them : [5]
    And do not according to their works,
    And become not their associate ;
    For their works are unclean,

[1] Verbally from Gen. xxvii. 29 (Isaac's blessing of Jacob).
[2] *i. e.* all mankind (Charles).
[3] Cf. xix. 27.
[4] Cf. xxii. 9.
[5] A strict observance of the dietary laws would make this
practically impossible; cf. Dan. i. 8; Matt. ix. 11. The
question was one of crucial importance in the early Maccabean
period; cf. *e. g.* 1 Macc. i. 62.

And all their ways are a pollution and an abomination and uncleanness.

17. They offer their sacrifices to the dead [1]
And they worship evil spirits,[2]
And they eat over the graves,[3]
And all their works are vanity and nothingness.

18. They have no heart to understand
And their eyes do not see what their works are,
And how they err in saying to a piece of wood :
' Thou art my God,'
And to a stone : ' Thou art my Lord and thou
art my deliverer.' [4]
[And they have no heart.] [5]

19. And as for thee, my son Jacob,
May the Most High God help thee
And the God of heaven bless thee
And remove thee from their uncleanness and from
all their error.

20. Be thou ware, my son Jacob, of taking a wife
from any seed of the daughters of Canaan ;
For all his seed is to be rooted out of the earth.[6]

21. For, owing to the transgression of Ham,[7] Canaan
erred,[8]
And all his seed will be destroyed from off the
earth and all the residue thereof,
And none springing from him will be saved on
the day of judgment.

22. And as for all the worshippers of idols and the
profane
[9](b) There will be no hope for them in the land of
the living ;

---

[1] Cf. Deut. xxvi. 14 ; Ecclus. xxx. 18, 19, etc.
[2] Cf. 1 Cor. x. 20 (1 Enoch xix. 1).
[3] i. e. Partake of the sacrifices offered to the dead ; cf.
Deut. xxvi. 14 (according to one interpretation).
[4] Cf. Jer. ii. 27.   [5] Bracketed words a dittograph.
[6] Cf. Gen. xxviii. 1 ; Test. Levi ix. 10.
[7] Cf. vii. 8.
[8] Canaan wrongfully seized Palestine ; cf. x. 29–34.
[9] The four following lines have been transposed by Charles
for the sake of parallelism.

(e) And there will be no remembrance of them on
the earth;
(c) For they will descend into Sheol,
(d) And into the place of condemnation will they go,[1]
As the children of Sodom were taken away from
the earth
So will all those who worship idols be taken
away.

23. Fear not, my son Jacob,
And be not dismayed, O son of Abraham :
May the Most High God preserve thee from
destruction,
And from all the paths of error may He deliver
thee.

24. This house have I built for myself that I might
put my name upon it in the earth : [it is given to
thee and to thy seed for ever],[2] and it will be named
the house of Abraham; it is given to thee and to
thy seed for ever; for thou wilt build my house[3] and
establish my name before God for ever: thy seed
and thy name will stand throughout all generations
of the earth."

25. And he ceased commanding[4] him and blessing
him.   26. And the two lay together on one bed, and
Jacob slept in the bosom of Abraham, his father's
father and he kissed him seven times, and his affection and his heart rejoiced over him.   27.[5] And he
blessed him with all his heart and said : " The Most
High God, the God of all, and Creator of all, who
brought me forth from Ur of the Chaldees, that He
might give me this land to inherit[6] it for ever, and
that I might establish a holy seed—blessed be the
Most High for ever."   28. And he blessed Jacob and
said : " My son, over whom with all my heart and
my affection I rejoice, may Thy grace and Thy mercy

---

[1] Cf. vii. 29.   [2] Bracketed words a dittograph.
[3] " House " throughout this passage = " family."
[4] i. e. giving the last commands; cf. Gen. xlix. 33 and often.
[5] Charles suspects 27 may be an interpolation.
[6] Cf. Gen. xv. 7; Neh. ix. 7.

be lift up[1] upon him and upon his seed alway. 29. And do not forsake him, nor set him at nought from henceforth unto the days of eternity, and may Thine eyes be opened upon him and upon his seed,[2] that Thou mayest preserve him, and bless him, and mayest sanctify him as a nation for Thine inheritance; 30. And bless him with all Thy blessings from henceforth unto all the days of eternity, and renew Thy covenant and Thy grace with him and with his seed according to all Thy good pleasure unto all the generations of the earth."

The Death and Burial of Abraham (xxiii. 1–8; cf. Gen. xxv. 7–10).

XXIII. And he placed two fingers of Jacob on his eyes,[3] and he blessed the God of gods, and he covered his face and stretched out his feet[4] and slept the sleep of eternity,[5] and was gathered to his fathers. 2. And notwithstanding all this Jacob was lying in his bosom, and knew not that Abraham, his father's father, was dead. 3. And Jacob awoke from his sleep, and behold Abraham was cold as ice, and he said: " Father, father!"; but there was none that spake, and he knew that he was dead. 4. And he arose from his bosom and ran and told Rebecca, his mother; and Rebecca went to Isaac in the night and told him; and they went together, and Jacob with them, and a lamp was in his hand, and when they had gone in they found Abraham lying dead. 5. And Isaac fell on the face of his father, and wept and kissed him.[6] 6. And the voices were heard in the house of Abraham, and Ishmael his son arose, and went to Abraham his father, and wept over

---

[1] Cf. Num. vi. 26.

[2] Cf. 1 Kings viii. 29, 52; Dan. ix. 18.

[3] Cf. Gen. xlvi. 4. The closing of the eyes (by the eldest son) should strictly only be done after death, according to Jewish tradition.

[4] Cf. Gen. xlix. 33 (of the death of Jacob).

[5] Cf. Jer. li. 39, 57. [6] Cf. Gen. l. 1.

Abraham his father, he and all the house of Abraham, and they wept with a great weeping. 7. And his sons Isaac and Ishmael buried him in the double cave,[1] near Sarah his wife, and they wept for him forty days, all the men of his house, and Isaac and Ishmael, and all their sons, and all the sons of Keturah in their places; and the days of weeping for Abraham were ended. 8. And he lived three jubilees and four weeks of years, one hundred and seventy-five years, and completed the days of his life, being old and full of days.

The decreasing Years and increasing Corruption of Mankind (xxiii. 9–17).

9. For the days of the forefathers, of their life, were nineteen jubilees; and after the Flood they began to grow less than nineteen jubilees, and to decrease in jubilees, and to grow old quickly, and to be full of their days by reason of manifold tribulation and the wickedness of their ways, with the exception of Abraham.[2] 10. For Abraham was perfect in all his deeds with the Lord, and well-pleasing in righteousness all the days of his life; and behold, he did not complete four jubilees in his life, when he had grown old by reason of the wickedness,[3] and was full of his days. 11. And all the generations which will arise from this time until the day of the great judgment will grow old quickly, before they complete two jubilees, and their knowledge will forsake them by reason of their old age [and all their knowledge will vanish away].[4] 12. And in those days, if a man live a jubilee and a half of years, they will say regarding him: " He hath lived long, and the greater part of his days are pain and sorrow and

---

[1] i. e. Machpelah; cf. Gen. xxv. 9.

[2] Man's years grow less as mankind grows more corrupt; cf. for a similar idea 4 Ezra v. 50–55.

[3] Even Abraham grew prematurely old owing to the universal wickedness.

[4] Bracketed words a dittograph.

tribulation,[1] and there is no peace : 13. For calamity followeth on calamity, and wound on wound, and tribulation on tribulation, and evil tidings on evil tidings, and illness on illness, and all evil judgments such as these, one with another, illness and over-throw, and snow and frost and ice, and fever, and chills, and torpor, and famine, and death, and sword, and captivity, and all kinds of calamities and pains." [2] 14. And all these will come on an evil generation, which transgresseth on the earth : their works are uncleanness and fornication, and pollution and abominations.[3] 15. Then they will say : " The days of the forefathers were many (even), unto a thousand years, and were good ; but, behold, the days of our life, if a man hath lived many, are three score years and ten, and, if he is strong, four score years, and those evil,[4] and there is no peace in the days of this evil generation." 16. And in that generation the sons will convict their fathers and their elders of sin and unrighteousness,[5] and of the words of their mouth and the great wickednesses which they per-petrate, and concerning their forsaking the covenant [6] which the Lord made between them and Him, that they should observe and do all His commandments and His ordinances and all His laws, without depart-ing either to the right hand or to the left.[7] 17. For all have done evil,[8] and every mouth speaketh iniquity[9] and all their works are an uncleanness and an abom-ination, and all their ways are pollution, uncleanness and destruction.

---

[1] Cf. Ps. xc. 10.

[2] ? a picture of contemporary misfortunes (200 B.C. and following years).

[3] Cf. vii. 21, xx. 5, xxii. 16.

[4] Cf. Ps. xc. 10.

[5] ? the protest of the Hasidim (" the pious ") against the Hellenizers; cf. 1 Macc. ii. 42 ff.

[6] Cf. 1 Macc. i. 15.

[7] Cf. 1 Macc. ii. 21 f. (Deut. v. 31–32, xxviii. 14).

[8] Cf. 1 Macc. i. 52–53. [9] Cf. 1 Macc. ii. 6.

The Messianic Woes (xxiii. 18–25).
[Eschatological partly.]

18. Behold the earth will be destroyed on account
of all their works, and there will be no seed of the
vine, and no oil; for their works are altogether
faithless, and they will all perish together, beasts
and cattle and birds, and all the fish of the sea,[1]
on account of the children of men.   19. And they
will strive one with another, the young with the old,
and the old with the young, the poor with the rich,
and the lowly with the great, and the beggar with
the prince,[2] on account of the law and the covenant;[3] for they have forgotten commandment, and
covenant, and feasts, and months, and Sabbaths,
and jubilees, and all judgments.   20. And they will
stand (with bows and) swords and war to turn them
back into the way;[4] but they will not return until
much blood hath been shed on the earth, one by
another.[5]   21. And those who have escaped will not
return from their wickedness to the way of righteousness, but they will all exalt themselves to deceit
and wealth, that they may each take all that is his
neighbour's, and they will name the great name, but
not in truth and not in righteousness, and they will
defile the holy of holies with their uncleanness and
the corruption of their pollution.[6]   22. And a great
punishment will befall the deeds of this generation

[1] Cf. 4 Ezra v. 7 (Ezek. xxxviii. 20).

[2] Internecine strife is a standing feature in such eschato-
logical passages; cf. 4 Ezra vi. 24; Matt. xxiv. 10; *Ap.
Bar.*, lxx. 3–4.

[3] Here the writer passes to a description of what is
happening in his own time.

[4] " Way " here = the true path of religion; cf. Isa. xxx.
21; Acts ix. 2, etc.

[5] The conflicts between the early Maccabeans (at the
head of the national party in Judah) and the Hellenizers
seem to be referred to.

[6] Probably the machinations of the Hellenizing party
under the High Priest Alcimus are referred to; cf. 1 Macc.
ix. 54.

from the Lord, and He will give them over to the
sword and to judgment and to captivity, and to be
plundered and devoured.   23. And He will wake up
against them the sinners of the Gentiles, who have
neither mercy nor compassion, and who will respect
the person of none, neither old nor young, nor any
one, for they are more wicked and strong to do evil
than all the children of men.

> And they will use violence against Israel and
>   transgression against Jacob,
> And much blood will be shed upon the earth,
> And there will be none to gather and none to
>   bury.[1]

24. In those days they will cry aloud,
> And call and pray that they may be saved from
>   the hand of the sinners, the Gentiles;[2]
> But none will be saved.

25. And the heads of the children will be white with
>   grey hair,[3]
> And a child of three weeks will appear old like a
>   man of one hundred years,
> And their stature will be destroyed by tribulation
>   and oppression.

**Renewed Study of the Law followed by a Re-
newal of Mankind.   The Messianic Kingdom and the Blessedness of the Righteous
(xxiii. 26–32; cf. Isa. lxv. 17ff). [Eschatological.]**

26. And in those days the children will begin to
>   study the laws,
> And to seek the commandments,
> And to return to the path of righteousness.

27. And the days will begin to grow many and
>   increase amongst those children of men,

---

[1] The sufferings of the nation up to (but not including)
Simon's High Priesthood (142–135 B.C.) may be referred to.
For the last line cf. Jer. viii. 2.   [2] Cf. Gal. ii. 15.
[3] Cf. *Sibylline Oracles*, ii. 155 (" children with grey hair
on their temples born ")—one of the signs of the coming in
of the Messianic age.

Till their days draw nigh to one thousand years,[1]
And to a greater number of years than (before)
   was the number of the days.

28. And there will be no old man
Nor one who is not satisfied with his days,
For all will be (as) children and youths.[2]

29. And all their days they will complete and live
   in peace and in joy,[3]
And there will be no Satan [4] nor any evil
   destroyer;
For all their days will be days of blessing and
   healing.[5]

30. And at that time the Lord will heal His servants,
And they will rise up [6] and see [7] great peace,
And drive out their adversaries.
And the righteous will see and be thankful,
And rejoice with joy for ever and ever,
And will see all their judgments and all their
   curses on their enemies.

31. And their bones will rest in the earth,
And their spirits will have much joy,[8]
And they will know that it is the Lord who
   executeth judgment,
And showeth mercy to hundreds and thousands
   and to all that love Him.[9]

32. And do thou, Moses, write down these words;
for thus are they written, and they record (them) on
the heavenly tables for a testimony for the generations
for ever.

[1] The span of life originally designed for mankind.   Adam
fell short of this because of his sin.

[2] Cf. Isa. lxv. 20.   [3] Cf. Isa. lxv. 14.

[4] Cf. *Assumpt. Moses* x. 1.   .   [5] Cf. i. 29.

[6] Probably there is no reference here to a resurrection.
Apparently the Messianic kingdom depicted is a temporary
one. The eschatology harmonizes with that of 1 Enoch
xci.–civ.

[7] *i. e.* enjoy.

[8] *i. e.* they will enjoy a blessed immortality (with no
bodily resurrection); cf. 1 Enoch ciii. 3–4.

[9] Cf. 4 Ezra vii. 132 ff.

Isaac at the Well of Vision : Esau sells his Birthright (xxiv. 1–7; cf. Gen. xxv. 11, 29–34).

XXIV. And it came to pass after the death of Abraham, that the Lord blessed Isaac his son, and he arose from Hebron and went and dwelt at the Well of the Vision [1] in the first year of the third week of this jubilee, seven years. 2. And in the first year of the fourth week a famine began in the land, besides the first famine, which had been in the days of Abraham.[2] 3. And Jacob sod lentil pottage, and Esau came from the field hungry. And he said to Jacob his brother : " Give me of this red pottage." [3] And Jacob said to him : " Sell to me thy [primogeniture, this] birthright and I will give thee bread, and also some of this lentil pottage." 4. And Esau said in his heart : " I shall die; of what profit to me is this birthright ? " And he said to Jacob : " I give it to thee." 5. And Jacob said : " Swear to me, this day," and he sware unto him. 6. And Jacob gave his brother Esau bread and pottage, and he ate till he was satisfied, and Esau despised his birthright; for this reason was Esau's name called Edom,[4] on account of the red pottage which Jacob gave him for his birthright. 7. And Jacob became the elder, and Esau was brought down from his dignity.

2073 A.M.
2080 A.M.

Isaac's Sojourn in Gerar and Dealings with Abimelech (xxiv. 8–27; cf. Gen. xxvi.).

8. And the famine was over the land, and Isaac departed to go down into Egypt in the second year of this week, and went to the king of the Philistines to Gerar, unto Abimelech. 9.[5] And the Lord appeared unto him and said unto him : " Go not down into Egypt; dwell in the land that I shall tell thee of, and sojourn in this land, and I shall be

---

[1] *i. e. Beer-lahai-roi* ("the well of the Living One that seeth me "); Gen. xxv. 11.

[2] Cf. Gen. xxvi. 1. [3] Cf. Gen. xxv. 30.

[4] *Edom* = " red." [5] For 9–12 cf. Gen. xxvi. 2–6.

with thee and bless thee. 10. For to thee and to thy seed shall I give all this land, and I shall establish My oath which I sware unto Abraham thy father, and I shall multiply thy seed as the stars of heaven, and shall give unto thy seed all this land. 11. And in thy seed will all the nations of the earth be blessed, because thy father obeyed My voice, and kept My charge and My commandments, and My laws, and My ordinances, and My covenant; and now obey My voice and dwell in this land."

2080-2101 A.M. 12. And he dwelt in Gerar three weeks of years. 13. And Abimelech charged concerning him, and concerning all that was his, saying : " Any man that shall touch him or aught that is his shall surely die." [1] 14. And Isaac waxed strong among the Philistines, and he got many possessions, oxen and sheep and camels and asses and a great household. 15. And he sowed in the land of the Philistines and brought in a hundred-fold, and Isaac became exceedingly great, and the Philistines envied him. 16. Now all the wells which the servants of Abraham had dug during the life of Abraham, the Philistines had stopped them after the death of Abraham, and filled them with earth. 17. And Abimelech said unto Isaac : " Go from us, for thou art much mightier than we "; and Isaac departed thence in 2101 A.M. the first year of the seventh week, and sojourned in the valleys of Gerar. 18. And they digged again the wells of water which the servants of Abraham, his father, had digged, and which the Philistines had closed after the death of Abraham his father, and he called their names as Abraham his father had named them. 19. And the servants of Isaac dug a well in the valley, and found living water, and the shepherds of Gerar strove with the shepherds of Isaac, saying : " The water is ours "; and Isaac called the name of the well " Perversity," [2] because

[1] Cf. Gen. xxvi. 11. Notice that no reference is made in our text to Isaac's deception about Rebecca.

[2] = Esek; cf. Gen. xxvi. 20.

they had been perverse with us.   20. And they dug
a second well, and they strove for that also, and
he called its name " Enmity." [1]   And he arose from
thence and they digged another well, and for that
they strove not, and he called the name of it " Room," [2]
and Isaac said : " Now the Lord hath made room
for us, and we have increased in the land."   21. And
he went up from thence to the Well of the Oath,[3]
in the first year of the first week in the forty-fourth 2108 A.M.
jubilee.   22. And the Lord appeared to him that
night, on the new moon of the first month, and
said unto him : " I am the God of Abraham thy
father ; fear not, for I am with thee, and shall bless
thee and shall surely multiply thy seed as the sand
of the earth, for the sake of Abraham my servant."
23. And he built an altar there, which Abraham his
father had first built, and he called upon the name
of the Lord, and he offered sacrifice to the God of
Abraham his father.   24. And they digged a well
and they found living water.   25. And the servants
of Isaac digged another well and did not [4] find
water, and they went and told Isaac that they had
not found water, and Isaac said : " I have sworn
this day to the Philistines and this thing hath been
announced to us."   26. And he called the name of
that place the " Well of the Oath " ; for there he
had sworn to Abimelech and Ahuzzath his friend and
Phicol the prefect of his host.[5]   27. And Isaac knew
that day that under constraint he had sworn to
them to make peace with them.

---

[1] = Sitnah ; cf. Gen. xxvi. 21.
[2] = Rehoboth ; cf. Gen. xxvi. 22.
[3] *i. e.* Beersheba.
[4] In Gen. xxvi. 32 the MT does not read *not ;* but LXX
agrees with our text in so reading.   It is implied here that
their failure to find water was due to the covenant made with
Abimelech.
[5] Cf. Gen. xxvi. 31, 33.

Isaac curses the Philistines (xxiv. 28–33).

28. And Isaac on that day cursed the Philistines [1] and said : " Cursed be the Philistines unto the day of wrath and indignation from the midst of all nations; may God make them a derision and a curse and an object of wrath and indignation in the hands of the sinners the Gentiles and in the hands of the Kittim.[2] 29. And whoever escapeth the sword of the enemy and the Kittim, may the righteous nation [3] root out in judgment from under heaven ; for they will be the enemies and foes of my children throughout their generations upon the earth.
30. And no remnant will be left to them,

    Nor one that will be saved on the day of the wrath of judgment;

    For for destruction and rooting out and expulsion from the earth is the whole seed of the Philistines (reserved),

    And there will no longer be left for these Caphtorim [4] a name or a seed on the earth.

31.[5] For though he ascend unto heaven,

    Thence will he be brought down,

    And though he make himself strong on earth,

    Thence will he be dragged forth;

    And though he hide himself amongst the nations,

    Even from thence will he be rooted out ;

    And though he descend into Sheol,

    There also will his condemnation be great,

    And there also he will have no peace.

32. And if he go into captivity,

    By the hands of those that seek his life will they slay him on the way,

---

[1] The text reflects the bitter feeling towards the Philistines existing among the Jews in Maccabean times.   The Philistine cities were either destroyed or captured by the Maccabees.

[2] *i. e.* the Macedonians; cf. 1 Macc. i. 1, viii. 5.

[3] *i. e.* Judah under the Maccabees.

[4] The Philistines came originally from Caphtor according to Amos ix. 7 (Deut. ii. 23; Jer. xlvii. 4).

[5] The basis of 31–32 seems to be Amos ix. 2–4.

And neither name nor seed will be left to him
    on all the earth;
For into eternal malediction will he depart."
33. And thus is it written and engraved concerning
him on the heavenly tables, to do unto him on the
day of judgment, so that he may be rooted out of
the earth.

Rebecca admonishes Jacob not to marry a Canaanitish Woman. Rebecca's Blessing
(xxv. 1–23; cf. Gen. xxviii. 1–4).[1]

XXV. And in the second year of this week in this 2109 A.M.
jubilee, Rebecca called Jacob her son, and spake
unto him, saying : " My son, do not take thee a
wife of the daughters of Canaan, as Esau, thy brother,
who took him two wives of the daughters of Canaan,[2]
and they have embittered my soul[3] with all their
unclean deeds : for all their deeds are fornication
and lust, and there is no righteousness with them,
for (their deeds) are evil. 2. And I, my son, love
thee exceedingly, and my heart and my affection
bless thee every hour of the day and watch of the
night. 3. And now, my son, hearken to my voice,
and do the will of thy mother, and do not take thee
a wife of the daughters of this land, but only of the
house of my father, and of my father's kindred.
Thou wilt take thee a wife of the house of my father,
and the Most High God will bless thee, and thy
children will be a righteous generation and a holy
seed." 4. And then spake Jacob to Rebecca, his
mother, and said unto her : " Behold, mother, I am
nine weeks[4] of years old, and I neither know nor
have I touched any woman, nor have I betrothed
myself to any, nor even think of taking me a wife
of the daughters of Canaan. 5. For I remember,

---

[1] With this section also compare xxvii. of our Book.
[2] Cf. Gen. xxvi. 34.
[3] Cf. Gen. xxvii. 46, xxvi. 35.   [4] i. e. 63.

mother, the words of Abraham, our father, for he commanded me not to take a wife of the daughters of Canaan, but to take me a wife from the seed of my father's house and from my kindred. 6. I have heard before that daughters have been born to Laban, thy brother, and I have set my heart on them to take a wife from amongst them. 7. And for this reason I have guarded myself in my spirit against sinning or being corrupted in all my ways throughout all the days of my life; for with regard to lust and fornication, Abraham, my father, gave me many commands.[1] 8. And, despite all that he hath commanded me, these two and twenty years my brother hath striven with me, and spoken frequently to me and said : ' My brother, take to wife a sister of my two wives'; but I refuse to do as he hath done. 9. I swear before thee, mother, that all the days of my life I will not take me a wife from the daughters of the seed of Canaan, and I will not act wickedly as my brother hath done.   19. Fear not, mother; be assured that I shall do thy will and walk in uprightness, and not corrupt my ways for ever."   11. And thereupon she lifted up her face to heaven and extended the fingers of her hands, and opened her mouth and blessed the Most High God, who had created the heaven and the earth, and she gave Him thanks and praise.   12. And she said : " Blessed be the Lord God, and may His holy name be blessed for ever and ever, who hath given me Jacob as a pure son and a holy seed; for He is Thine, and Thine shall his seed be continually and throughout all the generations for evermore.   13. Bless him, O Lord, and place in my mouth the blessing of righteousness, that I may bless him."   14. And at that hour, when the spirit of righteousness [2] descended into her mouth, she placed both her hands on the head of Jacob, and said :

[1] Cf. xx. 4, xxxix. 6.
[2] Cf. John xiv. 17, xv. 26, xvi. 13 (τὸ πνεῦμα τῆς ἀληθείας) : a variant reading here is " Holy Spirit."

15. " Blessed art thou, Lord of righteousness and
        God of the ages ;
      And may He bless thee beyond all the generations
        of men.
      May He give thee, my son, the path of righteous-
        ness,
      And reveal righteousness to thy seed.
16. And may He make thy sons many during thy
        life,
      And may they arise according to the number of
        the months of the year.
      And may their sons become many and great
        beyond the stars of heaven,
      And their numbers be more than the sand of
        the sea.
17. And may He give them this goodly land—as He
        said He would give it to Abraham and to his
        seed after him alway [1]—
      And may they hold it as a possession for ever.
18. And may I see (born) unto thee, my son, blessed
        children during my life,
      And a blessed and holy seed may all thy seed be.
19. And as thou hast refreshed thy mother's spirit
        during †my† [2] life,
      The womb of her that bare thee blesseth thee,
      [My affection] and my breasts bless thee
      And my mouth and my tongue praise thee greatly.
20. Increase and spread over the earth,
      And may thy seed be perfect in the joy of heaven
        and earth for ever ;
      And may thy seed rejoice,
      And on the great day of peace may it have
        peace.
21. And may thy name and thy seed endure to all
        the ages,
      And may the Most High God be their God,
      And may the God of righteousness dwell with
        them,

---

[1] Cf. Luke i. 55.
[2] Read " thy " (Charles).

And by them may His sanctuary be built unto
all the ages.[1]

22. Blessed be he that blesseth thee,
And all flesh that curseth thee falsely may it be
cursed." [2]

23. And she kissed him, and said to him :
" May the Lord of the world love thee
As the heart of thy mother and her affection
rejoice in thee and bless thee."
And she ceased from blessing.

Jacob obtains the Blessing of the Firstborn
(xxvi. 1–35 ; cf. Gen. xxvii.).

2114 A.M. XXVI. And in the seventh year of this week
Isaac called Esau, his elder son, and said unto him :
" I am old, my son, and behold my eyes are dim in
seeing, and I know not the day of my death. 2. And
now take thy hunting weapons, thy quiver and thy
bow, and go out to the field, and hunt and catch me
(venison), my son, and make me savoury meat, such
as my soul loveth, and bring it to me that I may
eat, and that my soul may bless thee before I die."
3. But Rebecca heard Isaac speaking to Esau.
4. And Esau went forth early to the field to hunt
and catch and bring home to his father. 5. And
Rebecca called Jacob, her son, and said unto him :
" Behold, I heard Isaac, thy father, speak unto
Esau, thy brother, saying : ' Hunt for me, and make
me savoury meat, and bring (it) to me that I may
eat and bless thee before the Lord before I die.'
6. And now, my son, obey my voice in that which
I command thee : Go to thy flock and fetch me two
good kids of the goats, and I will make them savoury
meat for thy father, such as he loveth, and thou
shalt bring (it) to thy father that he may eat and
bless thee before the Lord before he die, and that
thou mayst be blessed." 7. And Jacob said to
Rebecca his mother : " Mother, I shall not withhold

[1] Cf. i. 29. [2] Cf. Gen. xxvii. 29.

anything which my father would eat, and which would please him : only I fear, my mother, that he will recognise my voice and wish to touch me. 8. And thou knowest that I am smooth, and Esau, my brother, is hairy, and I shall appear before his eyes as an evildoer, and shall do a deed which he had not commanded me, and he will be wroth with me, and I shall bring upon myself a curse, and not a blessing." 9. And Rebecca, his mother, said unto him : " Upon me be thy curse, my son, only obey my voice." 10. And Jacob obeyed the voice of Rebecca, his mother, and went and fetched two good and fat kids of the goats, and brought them to his mother, and his mother made them (savoury meat) such as he loved. 11. And Rebecca took the goodly raiment of Esau, her elder son, which was with her in the house, and she clothed Jacob, her younger son, (with them), and she put the skins of the kids upon his hands and on the exposed parts of his neck. 12. And she gave the meat and the bread which she had prepared into the hand of her son Jacob. 13. And Jacob went in to his father and said : " I am thy son : I have done according as thou badest me : arise and sit and eat of that which I have caught, father, that thy soul may bless me." 14. And Isaac said to his son : " How hast thou found so quickly, my son ? " 15. And Jacob said : " Because (the Lord) thy God caused me to find." 16. And Isaac said unto him : " Come near, that I may feel thee, my son, if thou art my son Esau or not." 17. And Jacob went near to Isaac, his father, and he felt him and said : 18. " The voice is Jacob's voice, but the hands are the hands of Esau," and he discerned him not, because it was a dispensation from heaven [1] to remove his power of perception and Isaac discerned not, for his hands were hairy as (his brother) Esau's, so that he blessed him. 19. And he said : " Art thou my son Esau ? " and he said : " I am thy son " : and he said, " Bring

[1] Cf. 1 Kings xii. 15.

near to me that I may eat of that which thou hast caught, my son, that my soul may bless thee."
20. And he brought near to him, and he did eat, and he brought him wine and he drank. 21. And Isaac, his father, said unto him : " Come near and kiss me, my son." And he came near and kissed him. 22. And he smelled the smell of his raiment, and he blessed him and said : " Behold, the smell of my son is as the smell of a (full)[1] field which the Lord hath blessed.

23. And may the Lord give thee of the dew of heaven
     And of the dew [2] of the earth, and plenty of corn
          and oil : [3]
     Let nations serve thee,
     And peoples bow down to thee.
24. Be lord over thy brethren,
     And let thy mother's sons bow down to thee ;
     And may all the blessings wherewith the Lord
          hath blessed me and blessed Abraham, my
          father,[4]
     Be imparted to thee and to thy seed for ever :
     Cursed be he that curseth thee,
     And blessed be he that blesseth thee."

25. And it came to pass as soon as Isaac had made an end of blessing his son Jacob, and Jacob had gone forth from Isaac his father †he hid himself and†[5] Esau, his brother, came in from his hunting. 26. And he also made savoury meat, and brought (it) to his father, and said unto his father : " Let my father arise, and eat of my venison that thy soul may bless me." 27. And Isaac, his father, said unto him : " Who art thou ? " And he said unto him : " I am thy first born, thy son Esau : I have done as thou hast commanded me." 28. And Isaac was very

---

[1] So Latin here, and Sam. LXX and Vulg. in Gen. xxvii. 27 : MT omits.

[2] Text of Gen. xxvii. 28 has " fatness."

[3] Text of Genesis has " wine."

[4] Cf. Gen. xxviii. 4.

[5] Charles suspects this to be an addition to the text : read " that."

greatly astonished, and said : " Who is he that hath
hunted and caught and brought (it) to me, and I
have eaten of all before thou camest, and have
blessed him : (and) he shall be blessed, and all his
seed for ever." 29. And it came to pass when Esau
heard the words of his father Isaac that he cried
with an exceeding great and bitter cry, and said
unto his father: " Bless me, (even) me also, father."
30. And he said unto him: " Thy brother came with
guile, and hath taken away thy blessing." And
he said : " Now I know why his name is named
Jacob : behold, he hath supplanted me these two
times : he took away my birth-right, and now he
hath taken away my blessing." 31. And he said :
" Hast thou not reserved a blessing for me, father? "
and Isaac answered and said unto Esau :

> " Behold, I have made him thy lord,
> And all his brethren have I given to him for
> servants,
> And with plenty of corn and wine and oil have I
> strengthened him :
> And what now shall I do for thee, my son? "

32. And Esau said to Isaac, his father :

> " Hast thou but one blessing, O father?
> Bless me, (even) me also, father " :

And Esau lifted up his voice and wept. 33. And
Isaac answered and said unto him :

> " Behold, far from the dew of the earth shall be
> thy dwelling,
> And far from the dew of heaven from above.

34. And by thy sword wilt thou live,

> And thou wilt serve thy brother.
> And it shall come to pass when thou becomest great,[1]
> And dost shake his yoke from off thy neck,
> Thou wilt sin a complete sin unto death,[2]

[1] So Sam. of Gen. xxvii. 40 : MT " when Thou shalt
break loose."

[2] This line is a complete departure from the original text,
which has : " thou shalt shake his yoke from off thy neck."
The interpretation here given in the text has no support
elsewhere.

> And thy seed will be rooted out from under
> heaven."

35. And Esau kept threatening Jacob because of the blessing wherewith his father blessed him, and he said in his heart : " May the days of mourning for my father now come, so that I may slay my brother Jacob."

Rebecca induces Isaac to send Jacob to Mesopotamia. Jacob's Dream and View at Bethel (xxvii. 1–27 ; cf. Gen. xxviii.).

XXVII. And the words of Esau, her elder son, were told to Rebecca in a dream, and Rebecca sent and called Jacob her younger son, and said unto him : 2. " Behold Esau thy brother will take vengeance on thee so as to kill thee. 3. Now, therefore, my son, obey my voice, and arise and flee thou to Laban, my brother, to Haran, and tarry with him a few days until thy brother's anger turneth away, and he remove his anger from thee, and forget all that thou hast done ; then I will send and fetch thee from thence." 4. And Jacob said : " I am not afraid ; if he wisheth to kill me, I will kill him." 5. But she said unto him : " Let me not be bereft of both my sons on one day." 6. And Jacob said to Rebecca his mother : " Behold, thou knowest that my father hath become old, and doth not see because his eyes are dull, and if I leave him it will be evil in his eyes, because I leave him and go away from you, and my father will be angry, and will curse me. I will not go ; [1] when he sendeth me, then only will I go." 7. And Rebecca said to Jacob : " I will go in and speak to him, and he will send thee away." 8. And Rebecca went in and said to Isaac : " I loathe my life because of the two daughters of Heth, whom Esau hath taken him as wives ; and if Jacob take a wife from among the daughters of the land such as these, for what purpose

---

[1] The author desires to relieve Jacob of the reproach of leaving his father in his old age.

do I further live; for the daughters of Canaan are evil." [1] 9. And Isaac called Jacob and blessed him, and admonished him and said unto him : 10. " Do not take thee a wife of any of the daughters of Canaan ; arise and go to Mesopotamia, to the house of Bethuel, thy mother's father, and take thee a wife from thence of the daughters of Laban, thy mother's brother. 11. And God Almighty bless thee and increase and multiply thee that thou mayest become a company of nations, and give thee the blessings of my father Abraham, to thee and to thy seed after thee, that thou mayest inherit the land of thy sojournings and all the land which God gave to Abraham : go, my son, in peace." 12. And Isaac sent Jacob away, and he went to Mesopotamia, to Laban the son of Bethuel the Syrian, the brother of Rebecca, Jacob's mother. 13. And it came to pass after Jacob had arisen to go to Mesopotamia that the spirit of Rebecca was grieved after her son, and she wept. 14. And Isaac said to Rebecca : " My sister,[2] weep not on account of Jacob, my son ; for he goeth in peace, and in peace will he return. 15. The Most High God will preserve him from all evil, and will be with him; for He will not forsake him all his days; 16. For I know that his ways will be prospered in all things wherever he goeth, until he return in peace to us, and we see him in peace. 17. Fear not on his acount, my sister, for he is on the upright path and he is a perfect man : and he is faithful and will not perish. Weep not." 18. And Isaac comforted Rebecca on account of her son Jacob, and blessed him. 19. And Jacob went from the Well of the Oath to go to Haran on the first year of the second week in the forty-fourth jubilee, and he came to Luz on the mountains, that is, Bethel, on the new moon of the first month of this 2115 A.M.

---

[1] Cf. Gen. xxvii. 46.

[2] The use of " sister " as a term of endearment (to a wife) may be illustrated from Tobit v. 20, vii. 16; Canticles iv. 9, etc., but appears to be unknown to Rabbinic literature. Its use here may be designed to justify Isaac's having called Rebecca his sister at Abimelech's court.

week, and he came to the place at even and turned
from the way to the west of the road that night :
and he slept there; for the sun had set.   20. And
he took one of the stones of that place and laid it
(at his head) under the tree,[1] and he was journeying
alone, and he slept.   21. And he dreamt that night,
and behold a ladder set up on the earth, and the top
of it reached to heaven, and behold, the angels of the
Lord ascended and descended on it : and behold, the
Lord stood upon it.   22. And He spake to Jacob and
said : " I am the Lord God of Abraham, thy father,
and the God of Isaac; the land whereon thou art
sleeping, to thee shall I give it, and to thy seed after
thee.   23. And thy seed will be as the dust of the
earth, and thou wilt increase to the west and to the
east, to the north and the south, and in thee and in
thy seed will all the families of the nations be blessed.
24. And behold, I shall be with thee, and shall keep
thee whithersoever thou goest, and I shall bring thee
again into this land in peace; for I shall not leave
thee until I do everything that I told thee of."
25. And Jacob awoke from his sleep, and said,
" Truly this place is the house of the Lord, and I
knew it not."   And he was afraid and said : " Dread-
ful is this place which is none other than the house of
God, and this is the gate of heaven."   26. And
Jacob arose early in the morning, and took the stone
which he had put under his head and set it up as a
pillar for a sign, and he poured oil upon the top of it.
And he called the name of that place Bethel; but
the name of the place was Luz at the first.   27. And
Jacob vowed a vow unto the Lord, saying : " If the
Lord will be with me, and will keep me in this way
that I go, and give me bread to eat and raiment to
put on, so that I come again to my father's house in
peace, then shall the Lord be my God, and this stone
which I have set up as a pillar for a sign in this place,
shall be the Lord's house, and of all that thou givest
me, I shall give the tenth to thee, my God."

---

[1] ? which marked a shrine.

Jacob's Marriage to Leah and Rachel; his Children and Riches (xxviii. 1–30; cf. Gen. xxix., xxx., xxxi. 1–2).

XXVIII. And he went on his journey, and came to the land of the east, to Laban, the brother of Rebecca, and he was with him, and served him for Rachel his daughter one week.[1] 2.[2] And in the first year of the third week he said unto him : " Give me my wife, for whom I have served thee seven years;" and Laban said unto Jacob. " I will give thee thy wife." 3. And Laban made a feast, and took Leah his elder daughter, and gave (her) to Jacob as a wife, and gave her Zilpah his handmaid for an handmaid; and Jacob did not know, for he thought that she was Rachel. 4. And he went in unto her, and behold, she was Leah; and Jacob was angry with Laban, and said unto him : " Why hast thou dealt thus with me ? Did not I serve thee for Rachel and not for Leah ? Why hast thou wronged me ? Take thy daughter, and I will go ; for thou hast done evil to me." 5. For Jacob loved Rachel more than Leah ; for Leah's eyes were weak, but her form was very handsome ; but Rachel had beautiful eyes and a beautiful and very handsome form.[3] 6. And Laban said to Jacob : " It is not so done in our country, to give the younger before the elder." [4] And it is not right to do this; for thus it is ordained and written in the heavenly tables,[5] that no one should give his younger daughter before the elder— but the elder one giveth first and after her the younger —and the man who doeth so, they set down guilt against him in heaven, and none is righteous that doeth this thing, for this deed is evil before the Lord.

2122 A.M.

---

[1] *i. e.* seven years. For 1 cf. Gen. xxix. 1, 20.
[2] For 2–4 cf. Gen. xxix. 21–25.
[3] Cf. Gen. xxix. 17–18*a.*
[4] Cf. Gen. xxix. 26.
[5] The comment of the angels. This rule seems to be unknown to tradition.

7. And command thou the children of Israel that they
do not this thing; let them neither take nor give the
younger before they have given the elder, for it is
very wicked. 8.[1] And Laban said to Jacob : " Let
the seven days of the feast of this one pass by, and
I shall give thee Rachel,[2] that thou mayest serve me
another seven years, that thou mayest pasture my
sheep as thou didst in the former week." 9. And on
the day when the seven days of the feast of Leah
had passed, Laban gave Rachel to Jacob, that he
might serve him another seven years, and he gave to
Rachel Bilhah, the sister of Zilpah,[3] as a handmaid.
10. And he served yet other seven years for Rachel,
for Leah had been given to him for nothing. 11. And
the Lord opened the womb of Leah, and she conceived and bare Jacob a son, and he [4] called his name
2122 A.M.   Reuben,[5] on the fourteenth day of the ninth month,
in the first year of the third week. 12. But the
womb of Rachel was closed, for the Lord saw that
Leah was hated and Rachel loved. 13. And again
Jacob went in unto Leah, and she conceived, and
bare Jacob a second son, and he called his name
2124 A.M.   Simeon, on the twenty-first of the tenth month, and
in the third year of this week. 14. And again Jacob
went in unto Leah, and she conceived, and bare him
a third son, and he called his name Levi, in the new
2127 A.M.   moon of the first month in the sixth year of this week. .

[1] For 8–10 cf. Gen. xxix. 27–29.

[2] The marriage of two living sisters to the same man is
expressly forbidden in the Mosaic Law ; cf. Lev. xviii. 18.

[3] According to *Test. Naphtali* i. also, Bilhah and Zilpah
were sisters. In later Jewish tradition they are represented
as daughters of Laban; cf. e. g. *Pirḳe de R. Eliezer*, xxxvi.

[4] Gen. xxix. 32 has " she called."

[5] The twelve sons of Jacob appear in our text in the same
order as in Gen. xxix. 32–34, xxx. 1–24, xxxv. 17–18, viz.
(1) Reuben ; (2) Simeon ; (3) Levi ; (4) Judah ; (5) Dan ;
(6) Naphtali ; (7) Gad ; (8) Asher ; (9) Issachar ; (10)
Zebulon ; (11) Joseph ; (12) Benjamin. A different order is
given in Gen. xlix. and in the *Test. XII Patriarchs*. The
order of birth, as given in *Jubilees*, is complicated by textual
difficulties ; see Charles *ad loc.*

15. And again Jacob went in unto her, and she conceived, and bare him a fourth son, and he called his name Judah, on the fifteenth of the third month, 2129 A.M. in the †first† year of the †fourth† week.   16. And on account of all this Rachel envied Leah, for she did not bear, and she said to Jacob : " Give me children " ; and Jacob said : " Have I withheld from thee the fruits of thy womb?   Have I forsaken thee? "   17. And when Rachel saw that Leah had borne four sons to Jacob, Reuben and Simeon and Levi and Judah, she said unto him : " Go in unto Bilhah my handmaid, and she will conceive, and bear a son unto me." 18. (And she gave (him) Bilhah her handmaid to wife.) And he went in unto her, and she conceived, and bare him a son, and he called his name Dan, on the ninth of 2127 A.M. the sixth month, in the †sixth† year of the †third† week.   19. And Jacob went in again unto Bilhah a second time, and she conceived, and bare Jacob another son, and Rachel called his name Naphtali, on the fifth of the seventh month, in the second year 2130 A.M. of the fourth week.   20. And when Leah saw that she had become sterile and did not bear, she envied (Rachel) and she also gave her handmaid Zilpah to Jacob to wife, and she conceived, and bare a son, and Leah called his name Gad, on the twelfth of the eighth month, in the third year of the fourth week.   21. And 2131 A.M. he went in again unto her, and she conceived, and bare him a second son, and Leah called his name Asher, on the second of the eleventh month, in the †fifth† 2133 A.M. year of the fourth week.   22. And Jacob went in unto Leah, and she conceived, and bare a son, and she called his name Issachar, on the fourth of the fifth month, in the †fourth† year of the fourth week, 2132 A.M. and she gave him to a nurse.   23. And Jacob went in again unto her, and she conceived, and bare two (children), a son and a daughter, and she called the name of the son Zebulon, and the name of the daughter Dinah, in the seventh of the seventh month, in the 2134 A.M. sixth year of the fourth week.   24. And the Lord was gracious to Rachel, and opened her womb, and she

conceived, and bare a son, and she called his name Joseph, on the new moon of the fourth month, in the †sixth† year in this fourth week. 25. And in the days when Joseph was born, Jacob said to Laban: "Give me my wives and sons, and let me go to my father Isaac, and let me make me an house; for I have completed the years in which I have served thee for thy two daughters, and I will go to the house of my father." 26. And Laban said to Jacob: "†Tarry with me for thy wages†[1], and pasture my flock for me again, and take thy wages." 27. And they agreed with one another that he should give him as his wages those of the lambs and kids which were born black and spotted and white,[2] (these) were to be his wages. 28. And all the sheep brought forth spotted and speckled and black, variously marked,[3] and they brought forth again lambs like themselves, and all that were spotted were Jacob's and those which were not were Laban's. 29. And Jacob's possessions multiplied exceedingly, and he possessed oxen and sheep[4] and asses and camels, and menservants and maidservants. 30. And Laban and his sons envied Jacob, and Laban took back his sheep from him, and he observed him with evil intent.

2134 A.M.

Jacob's Flight with his Family : his Covenant with Laban (xxix. 1–12; cf. Gen. xxxi.).

XXIX. And it came to pass when Rachel had borne Joseph, that Laban went to shear his sheep; for they were distant from him a three days' journey. 2. And Jacob saw that Laban was going to shear his

---

[1] Gen. xxx. 28 has "appoint me thy wages."

[2] A wrong rendering of the Hebrew (Gen. xxx. 32), which means "speckled" (nāḳōd).

[3] *Speckled and black, variously marked* = LXX ποικίλα καὶ σποδοειδῆ ῥαντά : MT does not represent σποδοειδῆ.

[4] *And sheep* : so LXX (Gen. xxx. 43); but MT and other versions omit.

sheep, and Jacob called Leah and Rachel, and spake kindly unto them that they should come with him to the land of Canaan. 3. For he told them how he had seen everything in a dream, even all that He had spoken unto him that he should return to his father's house; and they said: "To every place whither thou goest we will go with thee." 4. And Jacob blessed the God of Isaac his father, and the God of Abraham his father's father, and he arose and mounted his wives and his children, and took all his possessions and crossed the river, and came to the land of Gilead, and Jacob hid[1] his intention from 2135 A.M. Laban and told him not. 5. And in the seventh year of the fourth week ·Jacob turned (his face) toward Gilead in the first month, on the twenty-first thereof. And Laban pursued after him and overtook Jacob in the mountain of Gilead in the third month, on the thirteenth thereof. 6. And the Lord did not suffer him to injure Jacob; for He appeared to him in a dream by night. And Laban spake to Jacob. 7. And on the fifteenth of those days Jacob made a feast for Laban, and for all who came with him, and Jacob sware to Laban that day, and Laban also to Jacob, that neither should cross the mountain of Gilead to the other with evil purpose. 8. And he made there a heap for a witness; wherefore the name of that place is called: "The Heap of Witness," after this heap.[2] 9. But before they used to call the land of Gilead the land of the Rephaim;[3] for it was the land of the Rephaim, and the Rephaim were born (there), giants whose height was ten, nine, eight down to seven cubits. 10.[4] And their habitation was from the land of the children of Ammon to Mount Hermon, and the seats of their kingdom were Karnaim and

---

[1] So LXX (Gen. xxxi. 20) and Targ. Onkelos; but MT Sam., Vulg., "stole" (the heart of Laban).

[2] Cf. Gen. xxxi. 47 ("Galeed" = "Heap of Witness").

[3] Cf. Gen. xiv. 5.

[4] The places here mentioned were, perhaps, associated with Maccabean victories in the mind of our author (Charles).

Ashtaroth,[1] and Edrei, and Mîsûr,[2] and Beon.[3]
11. And the Lord destroyed them because of the evil
of their deeds ; for they were very malignant, and the
Amorites dwelt in their stead, wicked and sinful, and
there is no people to-day which hath wrought to the
full all their sins, and they have no longer length of
life on the earth.[4] 12. And Jacob sent away Laban,
and he departed into Mesopotamia, the land of the
East, and Jacob returned to the land of Gilead.

Jacob, reconciled with Esau, dwells in Canaan and supports his Parents (xxix. 13-20; cf. Gen. xxxii., xxxiii.).

13. And he passed over the Jabbok [5] in the ninth
month, on the eleventh thereof. And on that day
Esau, his brother, came to him, and he was reconciled
to him, and departed from him unto the land of
Seir, but Jacob dwelt in tents. 14. And in the first
year of the fifth week in this jubilee he crossed the
Jordan, and dwelt beyond the Jordan, and he pas-
tured his sheep from the sea †of the heap† [6] unto
Bethshan,[7] and unto Dothan and unto the †forest† [8]
of Akrabbim. 15. And he sent to his father Isaac
of all his substance, clothing, and food, and meat,
and drink, and milk, and butter, and cheese, and some
dates of the valley, 16. And to his mother Rebecca
also four times a year, between the times of the
months, between ploughing and reaping, and between
autumn and the rain (season) and between winter

2136 A.M

[1] In MT of Gen. xiv. 5, Asheroth-karnaim is one place;
but Syr. and some MSS. of LXX support our text. Karnaim
was captured by Judas Maccabæus (1 Macc. v. 43 f.).

[2] In Deut. iii. 10 " plain " = *mishôr*.

[3] = probably the *Bæan* of 1 Macc. v. 4 f., which was
destroyed by Judas.

[4] Judas " must have nearly annihilated " the Amorites
(Charles).

[5] Cf. Gen. xxxii. 22.

[6] Text corrupt. Latin has " from the Salt Sea."

[7] Cf. 1 Macc. v. 52, xii. 40.

[8] ? read " ascent " (cf. Num. xxxiv. 4; Josh. xv. 3). Judas
fought in this district (of Idumea); cf. 1 Macc. v. 3.

and spring, to the tower of Abraham. 17. For Isaac had returned from the Well of the Oath and gone up to the tower of his father Abraham, and he dwelt there apart from his son Esau. 18. For in the days when Jacob went to Mesopotamia, Esau took to himself a wife Mahalath, the daughter of Ishmael, and he gathered together all the flocks of his father and his wives, and went up and dwelt on Mount Seir, and left Isaac his father at the Well of the Oath alone.[1] 19. And Isaac went up from the Well of the Oath and dwelt in the tower of Abraham his father on the mountains of Hebron, 20. And thither Jacob sent all that he did send to his father and his mother from time to time, all they needed, and they blessed Jacob with all their heart and with all their soul.

Dinah ravished. Slaughter of the Shechemites. Laws against Intermarriage between Israel and the Heathen. The Choice of Levi (xxx. 1–26; cf. Gen. xxxiv.).

XXX. And in the first year of the sixth week he went up to Salem, to the east of Shechem, in peace,[2] in the fourth month. 2. And there they carried off Dinah, the daughter of Jacob, into the house of Shechem, the son of Hamor, the Hivite, the prince of the land, and he lay with her and defiled her, and she was a little girl, a child of twelve years. 3. And he besought his father and her brothers that she might be given to him to wife. And Jacob and his sons were wroth because of the men of Shechem;[3] 2143 A.M.

[1] Cf. Gen. xxviii. 9, xxxvi. 6, 8. In contrast with Jacob's conduct to his parents, Esau's is unfilial.

[2] Based upon xxxiii. 18 (cf. R.V. marg.). Our text combines two readings (" Shalem," the name of a city, and *shālōm*, " peace ").

[3] Our author omits all reference to the circumcision of the Shechemites, because he approves of the conduct of Simeon and Levi, and extols it. On the other hand, their conduct in the matter is severely reprobated in Gen. xlix. 5–7. Our author's view seems to reflect a bitter feeling against the people of Shechem which prevailed in his time.

for they had defiled Dinah, their sister, and they spake
to them with evil intent and dealt deceitfully with
them and beguiled them.   4. And Simeon and
Levi came unexpectedly to Shechem and executed
judgment on all the men of Shechem, and slew all the
men whom they found in it, and left not a single one
remaining in it : they slew all in torments because
they had dishonoured their sister Dinah.   5. And
thus let it not again be done from henceforth that a
daughter of Israel be defiled ; for judgment is ordained
in heaven against them that they should destroy with
the sword all the men of the Shechemites because
they had wrought shame in Israel.   6. And the Lord
delivered them into the hands of the sons of Jacob
that they might exterminate them with the sword and
execute judgment upon them, and that it might not
thus again be done in Israel that a virgin of Israel
should be defiled.   7. And if there is any man who
wisheth in Israel to give his daughter or his sister to
any man who is of the seed of the Gentiles he shall
surely die, and they shall stone him with stones ; for
he hath wrought shame in Israel ; and they shall burn
the woman with fire, because she hath dishonoured
the name of the house of her father, and she shall be
rooted out of Israel.[1]   8. And let not an adulteress
and no uncleanness be found in Israel throughout
all the days of the generations of the earth ; for Israel
is holy unto the Lord, and every man who hath defiled
(it) shall surely die : they shall stone him with stones.
9. For thus hath it been ordained and written in the
heavenly tables regarding all the seed of Israel : he
who defileth (it) shall surely die, and he shall be
stoned with stones.   10. And to this law there is no
limit of days, and no remission, nor any atonement :
but the man who hath defiled his daughter shall be
rooted out in the midst of all Israel, because he hath

[1] Notice the passionate denunciation of mixed marriages.
The burning of the woman with fire, according to the Mosaic
Law (Lev. xxi. 9), was reserved for the priest's daughter who
played the harlot.

given of his seed to Moloch,[1] and wrought impiously so as to defile it. 11. And do thou, Moses, command the children of Israel and exhort them not to give their daughters to the Gentiles, and not to take for their sons any of the daughters of the Gentiles, for this is abominable before the Lord. 12. For this reason I have written for thee in the words of the Law all the deeds of the Shechemites, which they wrought against Dinah, and how the sons of Jacob spake, saying : " We shall not give our daughter to a man who is uncircumcised; for that were a reproach unto us." 13. And it is a reproach to Israel, to those who give, and to those who take the daughters of the Gentiles; for this is unclean and abominable to Israel. 14.[2] And Israel will not be free from this uncleanness if it hath a wife of the daughters of the Gentiles, or hath given any of its daughters to a man who is of any of the Gentiles. 15. For there will be plague upon plague, and curse upon curse, and every judgment and plague and curse will come (upon him) : if he do this thing, or hide his eyes from [3] those who commit uncleanness, or those who defile the sanctuary of the Lord, or those who profane His holy name,[4] (then) will the whole nation [5] together be judged for all the uncleanness and profanation of this (man). 16. And there will be no respect of persons [and no consideration of persons],[6] and no receiving at his hands of fruits and offerings and burnt-offerings and fat, nor the fragrance of sweet savour, so as to accept it: and so fare every man or woman in Israel who defileth the sanctuary. 17. For

---

[1] Cf. Lev. xviii. 21 : here the prohibition in Lev. against making " any of thy seed pass through the fire to Molech " is interpreted as = to give one's child in marriage to a Gentile; so, also, Targ. Ps.-Jonathan on this verse. In later times the rule has not always been strictly enjoined.

[2] 14–15 are based upon Lev. xx. 2–4.

[3] *i. e.* " ignore "; cf. Lev. xx. 4.

[4] Cf. Lev. xx. 3.

[5] In Lev. xx. 5, only the guilty man's family is involved.

[6] Bracketed as a dittograph.

this reason I have commanded thee, saying : " Testify this testimony to Israel : see how the Shechemites fared and their sons : how they were delivered into the hands of two sons of Jacob, and they slew them under tortures, and it was (reckoned) unto them for righteousness, and it is written down to them for righteousness. 18. And the seed of Levi was chosen for the priesthood, and to be Levites, that they might minister before the Lord, as we, continually, and that Levi and his sons may be blessed for ever ; for he was zealous to execute righteousness and judgment and vengeance on all those who arose against Israel.[1] 19. And so they inscribe as a testimony in his favour on the heavenly tables blessing and righteousness before the God of all : 20. And we remember the righteousness which the man fulfilled during his life, at all periods of the year; until a thousand generations they will record it, and it will come to him and to his descendants after him, and he hath been recorded on the heavenly tables as a friend [2] and a righteous man. 21. All this account I have written for thee, and have commanded thee to say to the children of Israel, that they should not commit sin nor transgress the ordinances nor break the covenant which hath been ordained for them, (but) that they should fulfil it and be recorded as friends.[2] 22. But if they transgress and work uncleanness in every way, they will be recorded on the heavenly tables as adversaries, and they will be destroyed out of the book of life,[3] and they will be recorded in the book of those who will be destroyed and with those who will be rooted out of the earth. 23. And on the

[1] A different reason for Levi's choice for the priesthood is given in xxxii. 3 ; cf. also *Test. Levi* iv. 2.

[2] *sc.* of God.

[3] This expression, derived from the O.T. (cf. Ps. lxix. 28; Exod. xxxii. 32) had reference originally to the temporal blessings of the theocracy, and this may be its meaning here; but later the meaning was extended to eternal life. It occurs frequently in the N.T. (cf. Rev. iii. 5, xiii. 8, etc.); cf. also 1 Enoch xlvii. 3.

day when the sons of Jacob slew Shechem a writing was recorded in their favour in heaven that they had executed righteousness and uprightness and vengeance on the sinners, and it was written for a blessing. 24. And they brought Dinah, their sister, out of the house of Shechem, and they took captive everything that was in Shechem, their sheep and their oxen and their asses, and all their wealth, and all their flocks, and brought them all to Jacob their father. 25. And he reproached them because they had put the city to the sword; [1] for he feared those who dwelt in the land, the Canaanites and the Perizzites. 26. And the dread of the Lord was upon all the cities which are around about Shechem, and they did not rise to pursue after the sons of Jacob; for terror had fallen upon them. [2]

Jacob's Journey to Bethel and Hebron. Isaac blesses Levi and Judah (xxxi. 1–25; cf. Gen. xxxv.).

XXXI. And on the new moon of the month Jacob spake to all the people of his house, saying : " Purify yourselves and change your garments, and let us arise and go up to Bethel, where I vowed a vow to Him on the day when I fled from the face of Esau my brother, because He hath been with me and brought me into this land in peace, and put ye away the strange gods that are among you." 2. And they gave up the strange gods and that which was in their ears and which was †on their necks,†[3] and the idols which Rachel stole from Laban her brother she gave wholly to Jacob. And he burnt and brake them to pieces and destroyed them, and hid them under an oak which is in the land of Shechem. 3. And he went up on the new moon of the seventh month to Bethel. And he built an altar at the place where he had slept, and he set up a pillar there, and he sent word to his father Isaac to come to him to his sacrifice, and to his mother Rebecca.

---

[1] Cf. *Test. Levi* vi.　　[2] Cf. Gen. xxxv. 5.　　[3] Corrupt.

4. And Isaac said: "Let my son Jacob come, and let me see him before I die."[1]   5. And Jacob went to his father Isaac and to his mother Rebecca, to the house of his father Abraham,[2] and he took two of his sons with him, Levi and Judah, and he came to his father Isaac and to his mother Rebecca.[3]   6. And Rebecca came forth from the tower to the front of it to kiss Jacob and embrace him; for her spirit had revived when she heard: "Behold Jacob thy son hath come"; and she kissed him.   7. And she saw his two sons, and she recognised them, and said unto him: "Are these thy sons, my son?" and she embraced them and kissed them, and blessed them, saying: "In you shall the seed of Abraham become illustrious, and ye will prove a blessing on the earth."   8. And Jacob went in to Isaac his father, to the chamber where he lay, and his two sons were with him, and he took the hand of his father, and stooping down he kissed him, and Isaac clung to the neck of Jacob his son, and wept upon his neck.   9. And the darkness left the eyes of Isaac, and he saw the two sons of Jacob, Levi and Judah, and he said: "Are these thy sons, my son? for they are like thee."   10. And he said unto him that they were truly his sons: "And thou hast truly seen that they are truly my sons."   11. And they came near to him, and he turned and kissed them and embraced them both together.   12. And the spirit of prophecy came down into his mouth, and he took Levi by his right hand and Judah by his left.   13. And he turned to Levi first,[4] and began to bless him first, and said unto him: "May the God of all, the very Lord of all the ages, bless thee and thy children throughout all the ages.   14. And may the Lord give to thee and to thy seed †greatness and great

---

[1] Isaac refused to go to Bethel; cf. *Test. Levi* ix. 2.

[2] *i. e.* to Hebron.

[3] This last meeting of Jacob with Isaac is not referred to in the Rabbinical Haggada.

[4] Cf. *Test. Levi* ix. 1 f.   The primacy of Levi is here marked.

glory†, and cause thee and thy seed, from among all flesh, to approach Him to serve in His sanctuary as the angels of the presence and as the holy ones.[1] (Even) as they, will the seed of thy sons be for glory and greatness and holiness, and may He make them great unto all the ages. 15. And they will be princes and judges, and chiefs [2] of all the seed of the sons of Jacob;

> They will speak the word of the Lord in righteousness,
> And they will judge all His judgments in righteousness.
> And they will declare My ways to Jacob
> And My paths to Israel.
> The blessing of the Lord will be given in their mouths [3]
> To bless all the seed of the beloved.[4]

16. Thy mother hath called thy name Levi,
> And justly hath she called thy name;
> Thou wilt be joined [5] to the Lord
> And be the companion of all the sons of Jacob;
> Let His table be thine,[6]
> And do thou and thy sons eat thereof;
> And may thy table be full unto all generations,
> And thy food fail not unto all the ages.

17. And let all who hate thee fall down before thee,
> And let all thy adversaries be rooted out and perish;
> And blessed be he that blesseth thee,
> And cursed be every nation that curseth thee.

---

[1] Levi is to serve in the sanctuary as the two highest orders of angels serve in the highest heaven.

[2] Levi's descendants are not only to be priests but also rulers of the nation. This double function was exercised by the Maccabean priest-princes: cf. *Test. Levi* viii. 11 ff.

[3] *i. e.* the priestly blessing; cf. Ecclus. l. 20.

[4] *i. e.* of Abraham.

[5] A play on the name " Levi " (= *attaché*); cf. Gen. xxix. 34 (R.V. marg.); also Num. xviii. 2, 4.

[6] Cf. *Test. Levi* viii. 16 (" and the table of the Lord shall thy seed apportion ").

18. And to Judah he said :

    May the Lord give thee strength and power
    To tread down all that hate thee ;
    A prince shalt thou be, thou and one of thy sons,[1]
      over the sons of Jacob;
    May thy name and the name of thy sons [2] go
      forth and traverse every land and region.
    Then will the Gentiles fear before thy face,
    And all the nations will quake
    [And all the peoples will quake].[3]

19. In thee shall be the help of Jacob,
    And in thee be found the salvation of Israel.

20. And when thou sittest on the throne of the
      honour of thy righteousness,
    There will be great peace for all the seed of the
      sons of the beloved,[4]
    And blessed will he be that blesseth thee ;
    And all that hate thee and afflict thee and curse thee
    Shall be rooted out and destroyed from the earth
      and accursed."

21. And turning he kissed him again and embraced him, and rejoiced greatly ; for he had seen the sons of Jacob his son in very truth. 22. And he went forth from between his feet and fell down and worshipped him. And he blessed them. And (Jacob) rested there with Isaac his father that night, and they ate and drank with joy. 23. And he made the two sons of Jacob sleep, the one on his right hand and the other on his left, and it was counted to him for righteousness. 24. And Jacob told his father everything during the night, how the Lord had shown him great mercy, and how He had prospered (him in) all his ways, and protected him from all evil. 25. And Isaac blessed the God of his father Abraham, who had not withdrawn His mercy and His righteousness from the sons of His servant Isaac.

---

[1] i. e. ? the Messiah who is to spring from Judah : but if so the expression of the hope is somewhat vague.   More probably the reference is to the historical David.

[2] i. e. the name of the Jewish people.

[3] Bracketed as a dittograph.   [4] i. e. of Abraham.

Rebecca journeys with Jacob to Bethel
(xxxi. 26–32).

26. And in the morning Jacob told his father Isaac the vow which he had vowed to the Lord, and the vision which he had seen, and that he had built an altar,[1] and that everything was ready for the sacrifice to be made before the Lord as he had vowed, and that he had come to set him on an ass. 27. And Isaac said unto Jacob his son : " I am not able to go with thee ; for I am old, and not able to bear the way : go, my son, in peace ; for I am one hundred and sixty-five years this day ; I am no longer able to journey ; set thy mother (on an ass) and let her go with thee. 28. And I know, my son, that thou hast come on my account, and may this day be blessed on which thou hast seen me alive, and I also have seen thee, my son. 29. Mayest thou prosper and fulfil the vow which thou hast vowed ; and put not off thy vow ; for thou wilt be called to account as touching the vow ;[2] now therefore make haste to perform it, and may He be pleased who hath made all things, to whom thou hast vowed the vow." 30. And he said to Rebecca : " Go with Jacob thy son " ; and Rebecca went with Jacob her son, and Deborah with her, and they came to Bethel. 31. And Jacob remembered the prayer with which his father had blessed him and his two sons, Levi and Judah, and he rejoiced and blessed the God of his fathers, Abraham and Isaac. 32. And he said : " Now I know that I have an eternal hope, and my sons also, before the God of all ; " and thus is it ordained concerning the two ; and they record it as an eternal testimony unto them on the heavenly tables how Isaac blessed them.

---

[1] At Bethel ; cf. Gen. xxviii. 18–22.
[2] Note the emphasis on the obligation to keep a vow.

Levi's Dream at Bethel ; he is appointed to the Priesthood.   Jacob celebrates the Feast of Tabernacles and offers Tithes.   The Institution of Tithes (xxxii. 1–15 ; cf. Gen. xxxv.).

XXXII. And he abode that night at Bethel, and Levi dreamed [1] that they had ordained and made him the priest of the Most High God,[2] him and his sons for ever ; and he awoke from his sleep and blessed the Lord.   2. And Jacob rose early in the morning, on the fourteenth of this month, and he gave a tithe of all that came with him, both of men and cattle, both of gold and every vessel and garment, yea, he gave tithes of all.   3. And in those days Rachel became pregnant with her son Benjamin.   And Jacob counted his sons from him [3] upwards and Levi fell to the portion of the Lord,[4] and his father clothed him in the garments of the priesthood and filled his hands.[5] 4. And on the fifteenth of this month, he brought to the altar fourteen oxen from amongst the cattle, and twenty-eight rams, and forty-nine sheep, and seven lambs, and twenty-one kids of the goats as a burnt-offering on the altar of sacrifice, well pleasing for a sweet savour before God.[6]   5. This was his offering,

[1] Cf. *Test. Levi* viii. (which describes Levi's dream-vision of seven men in white as having taken place at Bethel); also v. of the same work (in ix. 3 Jacob has this dream also).

[2] Cf. Gen. xiv. 18–20 (Melchizedek).   The title, " Priest of the Most High God," was appropriated by the Maccabean priest-kings.   Apparently it was expected in certain quarters that the Messiah would spring from this priestly ruling house; cf. Ps. cx., especially ver. 4.

[3] *i.e.* from Benjamin.

[4] Levi, as the tenth son (counting backwards from Benjamin), fell, under the law of tithe, to the Lord, and was consecrated to the priesthood; cf. also *Pirḳe de R. Eliezer* xxxvii., where Levi is counted (by a different method) as tenth " and was reckoned as the tithe, holy to God " (cf. Lev. xxvii. 32).

[5] A technical expression meaning appointment to the priesthood; cf. Exod. xxviii. 41 (R.V. marg.) ; xxix. 9.

[6] The number of victims does not agree with the prescriptions of the Mosaic Law regarding the Feast of Tabernacles; cf. Num. xxix. 12–40; Lev. xxiii. 34–36, 39–44.

in consequence of the vow which he had vowed that
he would give a tenth,[1] with their fruit-offerings and
their drink-offerings. 6. And when the fire had con-
sumed it, he burnt incense on the fire over the fire,
and for a thank-offering two oxen and four rams and
four sheep, four he-goats, and two sheep of a year old,
and two kids of the goats; and thus he did daily for
seven days. 7. And he and all his sons and his men
were eating (this) with joy there during seven days
and blessing and thanking the Lord, who had delivered
him out of all his tribulation and had given him his
vow. 8. And he tithed all the clean animals, and
made a burnt sacrifice, but the unclean animals he
gave (not) to Levi his son, and he gave him all the
souls of the men.[2] 9. And Levi discharged the priestly
office at Bethel before Jacob his father in preference
to his ten brothers, and he was a priest there, and
Jacob gave his vow : thus he tithed again the tithe [3]
to the Lord and sanctified it, and it became holy unto
Him. 10. And for this reason it is ordained on the
heavenly tables as a law for the tithing again the
tithe to eat before the Lord from year to year,[4] in
the place where it is chosen that His name should
dwell, and to this law there is no limit of days for ever.
11. This ordinance is written that it may be fulfilled
from year to year in eating the second tithe before
the Lord in the place where it hath been chosen, and
nothing shall remain over from it from this year to
the year following. 12. For in its year shall the seed
be eaten till the days of the gathering of the seed of
the year, and the wine till the days of the wine, and
the oil till the days of its season. 13. And all that is
left thereof and becometh old, let it be regarded as
polluted : let it be burnt with fire, for it is unclean.
14. And thus let them eat it together in the

---

[1] Cf. Gen. xxviii. 22.

[2] Cf. *Test. Levi* ix. 3 (" And he [Jacob] paid tithes of all
to the Lord through me ").

[3] *i. e.* the second tithe; cf. Num. xviii. 26.

[4] Cf. Deut. xiv. 23 (Tobit i. 7).

sanctuary, and let them not suffer it to become old. 15. And all the tithes of the oxen and sheep shall be holy unto the Lord,[1] and shall belong to His priests, which they will eat before Him from year to year; for thus is it ordained and engraven regarding the tithe on the heavenly tables.

Jacob's Visions. He celebrates the eighth day of Tabernacles. The Birth of Benjamin and Death of Rachel (xxxii. 16–34; cf. Gen. xxxv.).

16. And on the following night, on the twenty-second day of this month, Jacob resolved to build that place, and to surround the court with a wall, and to sanctify it and make it holy for ever, for himself and his children after him. 17. And the Lord appeared to him by night and blessed him and said unto him: " Thy name shall not be called Jacob, but Israel shall they name thy name." 18. And He said unto him again : " I am the Lord who created the heaven and the earth, and I shall increase thee and multiply thee exceedingly, and kings will come forth from thee, and they will judge everywhere wherever the foot of the sons of men hath trodden. 19. And I shall give to thy seed all the earth [2] which is under heaven, and they will judge all the nations according to their desires, and after that they will get possession of the whole earth and inherit it for ever." 20. And He finished speaking with him, and He went up from him, and Jacob looked till He had ascended into heaven.[3] 21. And he saw in a vision of the night, and behold an angel descended from heaven with seven tablets [4] in his hands, and he gave them to Jacob, and he read them and knew all that was written therein which would befall him and his sons through-

---

[1] Cf. Lev. xxvii. 32; 2 Chron. xxxi. 6. These tithes are not otherwise attested in the O.T.

[2] For 17–18 cf. Gen. xxxv. 10–12. Notice that the whole inhabited earth (not merely Palestine, as in Gen. xxxv. 12) is here promised to Israel.

[3] Cf. Gen. xxxv. 13.   [4] Cf. 4 Ezra xiv. 24.

out all the ages.[1] 22. And he showed him all that was written on the tablets, and said unto him : " Do not build this place, and do not make it an eternal sanctuary,[2] and do not dwell here ; for this is not the place. Go to the house of Abraham thy father and dwell with Isaac thy father until the day of the death of thy father. 23. For in Eygpt thou wilt die in peace, and in this land thou wilt be buried with honour in the sepulchre of thy fathers, with Abraham and Isaac. 24. Fear not, for as thou hast seen and read it, thus will it all be ; and do thou write down everything as thou hast seen and read." 25. And Jacob said : " Lord, how can I remember all that I have read and seen ? " And he said unto him : " I will bring all things to thy remembrance." [3] 26. And he went up from him, and he awoke from his sleep, and he remembered everything which he had read and seen, and he wrote down all the words which he had read and seen. 27. And he celebrated there yet another day,[4] and he sacrificed thereon according to all that he sacrificed on the former days, and called its name †" Addition,"† [5] for †this day was added,† [5] and the former days he called " The Feast." [6] 28. And thus it was manifested that it should be, and it is written on the heavenly tables : wherefore it was revealed to him that he should celebrate it, and add it to the seven days of the feast. 29.[7] And its name

[1] Cf. xlv. 4.

[2] The sanctuary at Bethel was not to be the one central shrine, where alone acceptable worship was to be offered.

[3] In 4 Ezra xiv. 40, Ezra's memory is said to have been miraculously strengthened after he had received the cup of inspiration; cf. also John xiv. 26.

[4] i. e. the eighth day of the Feast of Tabernacles.

[5] The Hebrew name is ʾa ṣereth (ʿaṣarta), from a root meaning " detain " (ʿāṣar). Hence, perhaps, we may emend here " keeping back," for on that day he was kept back (Charles).

[6] So in Rabbinic the Feast of Tabernacles was called, par excellence, " the Feast."

[7] 29 is very corrupt. Charles suggests that it should be read : " And its name was called ' a keeping back ' (i. e. ʾaṣereth) when it was recorded amongst the days of the feast days in the number of the days of the year."

was called †" Addition,"† †because that† it was
recorded amongst the days of the feast days, †accord-
ing to† the number of the days of the year.   30. And
in the night, on the twenty-third of this month,
Deborah Rebecca's nurse died, and they buried her
beneath the city under the oak of the river, and he
called the name of this place, " The river of Deborah,"
and the oak, " The oak of the mourning of Deborah."[1]
31. And Rebecca went and returned to her house to
his father Isaac, and Jacob sent by her hand rams and
sheep and he-goats that she should prepare a meal
for his father such as he desired.   32. And he went
after his mother till he came to the land of Kabrâtân,[2]
and he dwelt there.   33. And Rachel bare a son in
the night, and called his name " Son of my sorrow ";
for she suffered in giving him birth : but his father
called his name Benjamin, on the eleventh of the
eighth month in the first of the sixth week of this
jubilee.   34. And Rachel died there and she was
buried in the land [3] of Ephrath, the same is Bethlehem,
and Jacob built a pillar on the grave of Rachel, on the
road above her grave.

2143 A.M.

Reuben's Sin with Bilhah. Laws regarding Incest. Jacob's Children (xxxiii. 1–23; cf. Gen. xxxv. 21–27).

XXXIII. And Jacob went and dwelt to the south
of Magdalâdrâ'êf.[4]   And he went to his father Isaac,
he and Leah his wife, on the new moon of the tenth
month.   2. And Reuben saw Bilhah, Rachel's maid,
the concubine of his father, bathing in water in a

---

[1] Cf. Gen. xxxv. 8 (R.V. marg.).

[2] Due to a misunderstanding of the words rendered " some
distance " (*kibrath hā'areṣ*) in Gen. xxxv. 16. The LXX
also took *kibrath* to be a proper name (Χιβραθα).

[3] " On the way to " in the text of Gen. xxxv. 19.

[4] A compound of *migdal 'eder 'ephrāth* (" the tower of
Eder of Ephrath "); cf. Gen. xxxv. 21, also *Test. Reuben* iii.
9–15, where the same incident is narrated. In later Jewish
tradition an explanation is given which exculpates Reuben
(cf. Targ. Ps.-Jon. on Gen. xxxv. 22).

secret place, and he loved her. 3. And he hid himself
at night, and he entered the house of Bilhah [at night],
and he found her sleeping alone on a bed in her house.
4. And he lay with her, and she awoke and saw, and
behold Reuben was lying with her in the bed, and
she uncovered the border of her covering and seized
him, and cried out, and discovered that it was Reuben.
5. And she was ashamed because of him, and released
her hand from him, and he fled. 6. And she lamented
because of this thing exceedingly, and did not tell it
to any one. 7. And when Jacob returned and sought
her, she said unto him : " I am not clean for thee,
for I have been defiled as regards thee; for Reuben
hath defiled me, and hath lain with me in the night,
and I was asleep, and did not discover until he
uncovered my skirt and slept with me." 8. And
Jacob was exceedingly wroth with Reuben because
he had lain with Bilhah, because he had uncovered
his father's skirt.[1] 9. And Jacob did not approach
her again because Reuben had defiled her. And as
for any man who uncovereth his father's skirt his deed
is wicked exceedingly, for he is abominable before the
Lord. 10. For this reason it is written and ordained
on the heavenly tables that a man should not lie
with his father's wife, and should not uncover his
father's skirt, for this is unclean : they shall surely
die together,[2] the man who lieth with his father's wife
and the woman also, for they have wrought uncleanness on the earth. 11. And there shall be nothing
unclean before our God in the nation which He hath
chosen for Himself as a possession. 12. And again,
it is written a second time : " Cursed he be who lieth
with the wife of his father, for he hath uncovered
his father's shame "; and all the holy ones of the
Lord said " So be it ; so be it." [3] 13. And do thou,
Moses, command the children of Israel that they
observe this word; for it (entaileth) a punishment of
death ; and it is unclean, and there is no atonement

[1] Cf. Deut. xxii. 30.   [2] Cf. Lev. xx. 11.
[3] Cf. Deut. xxvii. 20.

for ever to atone for the man who hath committed this, but he is to be put to death and slain, and stoned with stones, and rooted out from the midst of the people of our God.   14. For to no man who doeth so in Israel is it permitted to remain alive a single day on the earth, for he is abominable and unclean.   15. And let them not say : to Reuben was granted life and forgiveness after he had lain with his father's concubine, and to her also though she had a husband, and her husband Jacob, his father, was still alive. 16. For until that time there had not been revealed the ordinance and judgment and law in its complete-ness for all, but in thy days (it hath been revealed) as a law of seasons and of days, and an everlasting law for the everlasting generations.[1]   17. And for this law there is no consummation of days, and no atone-ment for it, but they must both be rooted out in the midst of the nation : on the day whereon they com-mitted it they shall slay them.   18. And do thou, Moses, write (it) down for Israel that they may observe it, and do according to these words, and not commit a sin unto death ; [2] for the Lord our God is judge, who respecteth not persons and accepteth not gifts.[3]   19. And tell them these words of the covenant, that they may hear and observe, and be on their guard with respect to them, and not be destroyed and rooted out of the land ; for an uncleanness, and an abomination, and a contamination, and a pollution are all they who commit it on the earth before our God.   20. And there is no greater sin than the forni-cation which they commit on earth ; for Israel is a holy nation unto the Lord its God, and a nation of inheritance, and a priestly and royal nation and for (His own) possession ; [4] and there shall no such un-cleanness appear in the midst of the holy nation. 2145 A.M.   21. And in the third year of this sixth week Jacob and all his sons went and dwelt in the house of Abra-

---

[1] " Where there is no law there is no transgression " (Rom. iv. 15).
[2] Cf. xxi. 22.   [3] Cf. v. 16, xl. 8.
[4] Cf. xvi. 18 (note).

ham, near Isaac his father and Rebecca his mother.
22.[1] And these were the names of the sons of Jacob :
the first-born Reuben, Simeon, Levi, Judah, Issachar,
Zebulon, the sons of Leah; and the sons of Rachel,
Joseph and Benjamin; and the sons of Bilhah, Dan
and Naphtali; and the sons of Zilpah, Gad and Asher;
and Dinah, the daughter of Leah, the only daughter
of Jacob. 23. And they came and bowed themselves
to Isaac and Rebecca, and when they saw them they
blessed Jacob and all his sons, and Isaac rejoiced
exceedingly, for he saw the sons of Jacob, his younger
son, and he blessed them.

War of the Amorite Kings against Jacob and his Sons. Joseph sold into Egypt (cf. Gen. xxxvii.). The Death of Bilhah and Dinah (xxxiv. 1–19).

XXXIV. And in the sixth year of this week of this 2148 A.M.
forty-fourth jubilee Jacob sent his sons to pasture
their sheep, and his servants with them, to the pastures of Shechem. 2.[2] And the seven kings of the
Amorites assembled themselves together against
them, to slay them, hiding themselves under the trees,
and to take their cattle as a prey. 3. And Jacob and
Levi and Judah and Joseph were in the house with
Isaac their father; for his spirit was sorrowful, and
they could not leave him : and Benjamin was the
youngest, and for this reason remained with his
father. 4. And there came the king[s][3] of Tâphû,[4]

[1] For 22 cf. Gen. xxxv. 23–27.

[2] The account given in 2–8 of the conquest of Shechem
is given in a fuller form in the *Test. Judah* iii.–vii., and in
the Midrash Wajjissau (cf. Gaster, *Chronicles of Jerahmeel*,
pp. 80–87). The legend evidently has an old basis, for it
harmonizes with the statement given in Gen. xlviii. 22,
which refers to Jacob's conquest of Shechem (cf. R.V. margin).
This form of the story is obviously independent of, and
possibly older than, that given in Gen. xxxiv.

[3] Read " king."

[4] = Tappuah (Josh. xv. 53, xvi. 8). It is the Tephon
mentioned in 1 Macc. ix. 50. This and the following places
mentioned may have been specially interesting to our author
because of events connected with them in Maccabean times.

and the king[s] [1] of †'Arêsa,† [2] and the king[s] [1] of Sêrâgân,[3] and the king[s] [1] of Sêlô,[4] and the king[s] [1] of Gâ'as,[5] and the king of Bêthô.ôn,[6] and the king of †Ma'anîsâkîr,† [7] and all those who dwell in these mountains (and) who dwell in the woods in the land of Canaan. 5. And they announced this to Jacob saying: "Behold, the kings of the Amorites have surrounded thy sons, and plundered their herds." 6. And he arose from his house, he and his three sons and all the servants of his father, and his own servants, and he went against them with six thousand [8] men, who carried swords. 7. And he slew them in the pastures of Shechem, and pursued those who fled, and he slew them with the edge of the sword, and he slew [9] †'Arêsa† and Tâphû and Sarêgân and Sêlô and †'Amânîsakîr† and Gâ[gâ]'as, and he recovered his herds. 8. And he prevailed over them, and imposed tribute on them that they should pay him tribute, five fruit products of their land, and he built Rôbêl [10] and Tamnâtârês.[11] 9. And he returned in peace, and made peace with them, and they became his servants, until the day that he and his sons went down into

2149 A.M. Egypt. 10.[12] And in the seventh year of this week he sent Joseph to learn about the welfare of his brothers from his house to the land of Shechem, and he found them in the land of Dothan. 11. And they dealt treacherously with him, and formed a plot against him to slay him, but changing their minds,

[1] Read "king."
[2] Read "Asor," i.e. Hazor, the scene of a great victory by Jonathan, 1 Macc. xi. 67 ff.
[3] Unknown.   [4] i.e. Shiloh.
[5] = ? Gaash (Josh. xxiv. 30).
[6] The scene of more than one Maccabean victory; cf. 1 Macc. iii. 13 ff., vii. 39 ff.
[7] Corrupt for "Shakir-Maani."
[8] Another reading is "800."
[9] Six out of the seven kings are slain; so Test. Judah iv. [For the names see notes on 4 above.]
[10] Perhaps corrupt for "Arbael" = Arbela (1 Macc. ix. 2).
[11] = Timnath-heres (Jud. ii. 9); cf. 1 Macc. ix. 50.
[12] For 10-11 cf. Gen. xxxvii. 12 ff.

they sold him to Ishmaelite merchants, and they brought him down into Egypt, and they sold him to Potiphar, the eunuch [1] of Pharaoh, the chief of the cooks,[2] priest of the city of 'Êlêw.[3] 12. And the sons of Jacob slaughtered a kid, and dipped the coat of Joseph in the blood, and sent (it) to Jacob their father on the tenth of the seventh month. 13. And he mourned all that night, for they had brought it to him in the evening, and he became feverish with mourning for his death, and he said : " An evil beast hath devoured Joseph " ; and all the members of his house [mourned with him that day, and they] [4] were grieving and mourning with him all that day. 14. And his sons and his daughter rose up to comfort him, but he refused to be comforted for his son. 15. And on that day Bilhah heard that Joseph had perished, and she died mourning him, and she was living in †Qafrâtêf,† [5] and Dinah also, his daughter, died after Joseph had perished. And there came these three mournings upon Israel in one month. 16. And they buried Bilhah over against the tomb of Rachel, and Dinah also, his daughter, they buried there. 17. And he mourned for Joseph one year, and did not cease, for he said " Let me go down to the grave mourning for my son." [6] 18. For this reason [7] it is ordained for the children of Israel that they should afflict themselves [8] on the tenth of the seventh month —on the day that the news which made him weep for Joseph came to Jacob his father—that they should make atonement for themselves thereon with a young goat on the tenth of the seventh month,

[1] Or " court official."

[2] So LXX of Gen. xxxvii. 36 (ἀρχιμάγειρος), misunderstanding the Hebrew (= " captain of the guard").

[3] i. e. Heliopolis (LXX Ἡλίου πόλεως, Gen. xli. 45, 50), i. e. " On."

[4] Bracketed as a dittograph.

[5] ? = " Kabrâtân," xxxii. 32.   [6] Cf. Gen. xxxvii. 35.

[7] The reason here given for the institution of the Day of Atonement (cf. Lev. xvi.) seems to be peculiar to our Book.

[8] = " fast," cf. Lev. xvi. 31, etc.

once a year, for their sins; for they had grieved the
affection of their father regarding Joseph his son.
19. And this day hath been ordained that they should
grieve thereon for their sins, and for all their transgressions and for all their errors, so that they might
cleanse themselves on that day once a year.

The Wives of Jacob's Sons (xxxiv. 20–21).

20. And after Joseph perished, the sons of Jacob
took unto themselves wives. The name of Reuben's
wife is 'Adâ; and the name of Simeon's wife is 'Adîbâ'a,
a Canaanite;[1] and the name of Levi's wife is Mêlkâ,[2]
of the daughters of Aram, of the seed of the sons of
Terah; and the name of Judah's wife, Bêtasû'êl,[3] a
Canaanite; and the name of Issachar's wife, Hêzaqâ;
and the name of Zebulon's wife, †Nî'îmân†;[4] and
the name of Dan's wife, 'Êglâ; and the name of
Naphtali's wife, Rasû'û, of Mesopotamia; and the
name of Gad's wife, Mâka; and the name of Asher's
wife, 'Îjônâ; and the name of Joseph's wife, Asenath,[5]
the Egyptian; and the name of Benjamin's wife,
'Îjasaka. 21. And Simeon repented, and took a
second wife from Mesopotamia as his brothers.

Rebecca's Last Admonitions and Death
(xxxv. 1–27).

2157 A.M. XXXV. And in the first year of the first week of
the forty-fifth jubilee Rebecca called Jacob, her son,
and commanded him regarding his father and regarding his brother, that he should honour them all the
days of his life. 2. And Jacob said: "I will do

---

[1] Cf. Gen. xlvi. 10. According to xxx. 7 ff. such a marriage
(with a Canaanitish woman) was punishable with death.

[2] Cf. *Test. Levi* xi. 1.

[3] Cf. xli. 7. The name goes back to "Bath-shua" (*i. e.*
"daughter of Shua"); cf. *Test. Judah* viii. 2, etc.; cf. Gen.
xxxviii. 2.

[4] The name is doubtful. Some Ethiopic MSS. omit it.

[5] Cf. Gen. xli. 45.

everything as thou hast commanded me ; for this thing will be honour and greatness to me, and righteousness before the Lord, that I should honour them. 3. And thou too, mother, knowest from the time I was born until this day, all my deeds and all that is in my heart, that I always think good concerning all. 4. And how should I not do this thing which thou hast commanded me, that I should honour my father and my brother ! 5. Tell me, mother, what perversity hast thou seen in me and I shall turn away from it, and mercy will be upon me." 6. And she said unto him : " My son, I have not seen in thee all my days any perverse but (only) upright deeds. And yet I shall tell thee the truth, my son : I shall die this year, and I shall not survive this year in my life ; for I have seen in a dream the day of my death, that I should not live beyond a hundred and fifty-five years : and behold I have completed all the days of my life which I am to live." 7. And Jacob laughed at the words of his mother, because his mother had said unto him that she should die ; and she was sitting opposite to him in possession of her strength, and she was not infirm in her strength ; for she went in and out and saw, and her teeth were strong, and no ailment had touched her all the days of her life. 8. And Jacob said unto her : " Blessed am I, mother, if my days approach the days of thy life, and my strength remain with me thus as thy strength : and thou wilt not die, for thou art jesting idly with me regarding thy death." 9. And she went in to Isaac and said unto him : " One petition I make unto thee : make Esau swear that he will not injure Jacob, nor pursue him with enmity ; for thou knowest Esau's thoughts that they are perverse from his youth, and there is no goodness in him ; for he desireth after thy death to kill him. 10. And thou knowest all that he hath done since the day Jacob his brother went to Haran until this day ; how he hath forsaken us with his whole heart, and hath done evil to us ; thy flocks he hath taken to himself, and carried off all thy possessions from before thy face. 11. And when we implored and besought him for what was our own, he did as a man who was taking pity on us. 12. And he is bitter against thee because thou didst bless Jacob thy perfect and upright son ; for there is no evil but only goodness in him, and since he came from Haran unto this day he hath not robbed us of aught, for he bringeth us everything in its season always, and rejoiceth with all his heart when we take at his hands, and he blesseth us, and hath not parted from us since he came from Haran until this day, and he remaineth with us continually at home honouring us." 13. And Isaac said unto her : " I, too, know and see the deeds of Jacob who is with us, how that with all his heart he honoureth us ; but I loved Esau formerly more than Jacob, because he was the first-born ; but now I love Jacob more than Esau, for he hath done manifold evil deeds, and there is no righteousness in him, for all his ways are unrighteousness and violence, [and there is no righteousness around him].¹ 14. And now my heart is troubled because of all his deeds, and neither he nor his seed is to be saved, for they are those who will be destroyed from the earth, and who will be rooted out from under heaven, for he hath forsaken the God of Abraham and gone after his wives and after their uncleanness and after their error, he and his children. 15. And thou dost bid me make him swear that he will not slay Jacob, his brother ; even if he swear he will not abide by his oath, and he will not do good but evil only. 16. But if he desireth to slay Jacob, his brother, into Jacob's hands will he be given, and he will not escape from his hands, [for he will descend into his hands.] ² 17. And fear thou not on account of Jacob; for the guardian ³ of Jacob is great and powerful and honoured, and praised more than the guardian of Esau." 18. And Rebecca sent

---

¹ ? a dittograph.
² ? bracketed words a gloss; cf. xxxvi. 9.
³ ? the guardian-angel; cf. Matt. xviii. 10; Acts xii. 15; Heb. i. 14.

and called Esau, and he came to her, and she said
unto him : " I have a petition, my son, to make
unto thee, and do thou promise to do it, my son."
19. And he said : " I will do everything that thou
sayest unto me, and I will not refuse thy petition."
20. And she said unto him : " I ask you that the day
I die, thou wilt take me in and bury me near Sarah,
thy father's mother, and that thou and Jacob will
love each other, and that neither will desire evil
against the other, but mutual love only, and (so) ye
will prosper, my sons, and be honoured in the midst
of the land, and no enemy will rejoice over you, and
ye will be a blessing and a mercy in the eyes of all
those that love you." 21. And he said : " I will do
all that thou hast told me, and I shall bury thee on
the day thou diest near Sarah, my father's mother,
as thou hast desired that her bones may be near thy
bones. 22. And Jacob, my brother, also, I shall
love above all flesh ; for I have not a brother in all the
earth but him only : and this is no great merit for
me if I love him ; for he is my brother, and we were
sown together in thy body, and together came we
forth from thy womb, and if I do not love my brother,
whom shall I love ? 23. And I, myself, beg thee to
exhort Jacob concerning me and concerning my sons,
for I know that he will assuredly be king over me and
my sons, for on the day my father blessed him he
made him the higher and me the lower. 24. And I
swear unto thee that I shall love him, and not desire
evil against him all the days of my life but good only."
And he sware unto her regarding all this matter.
25. And she called Jacob before the eyes of Esau,
and gave him commandment according to the words
which she had spoken to Esau. 26. And he said :
" I shall do thy pleasure ; believe me that no evil
will proceed from me or from my sons against Esau,
and I shall be first in naught save in love only." 27.
And they ate and drank, she and her sons that night,
and she died, three jubilees and one week and one
year old, on that night, and her two sons, Esau and

Jacob, buried her in the double cave [1] near Sarah, their father's mother.

Isaac's Last Words and Admonitions : his Death. The Death of Leah (xxxvi. 1–24).

2162 A.M.   XXXVI. And in the sixth year of this week Isaac called his two sons, Esau and Jacob, and they came to him, and he said unto them : " My sons, I am going the way of my fathers, to the eternal house [2] where my fathers are.   2. Wherefore bury me near Abraham my father, in the double cave in the field of Ephron the Hittite, where Abraham purchased a sepulchre to bury in ; in the sepulchre which I digged for myself, there bury me.   3. And this I command you, my sons, that ye practise righteousness and uprightness on the earth, so that the Lord may bring upon you all that the Lord said that he would do to Abraham and to his seed.   4. And love one another, my sons, your brothers [3] as a man who loveth his own soul, and let each seek in what he may benefit his brother, and act together on the earth; and let them love each other as their own souls.   5. And concerning the question of idols, I command and admonish you to reject them and hate them, and love them not ; for they are full of deception for those that worship them and for those that bow down to them.   6. Remember ye, my sons, the Lord God of Abraham your father, and how I too worshipped Him and served Him in righteousness and in joy, that He might multiply you and increase your seed as the stars of heaven in multitude, and establish you on the earth as the plant of righteousness [4] which will not be rooted out unto all the generations for ever.   7. And now I shall make you swear a great oath—for there is no oath which is greater than it by the name glorious and honoured

---

[1] *i. e.* Machpelah.

[2] Cf. Eccles. xii. 5 (" man goeth to his long home," lit. " to his eternal house ").

[3] " Your brothers " probably a gloss.

[4] Cf. i. 16, xvi. 26, xxi. 24.

and great and splendid and wonderful and mighty, which created the heavens and the earth and all things together—that ye will fear Him and worship Him. 8. And that each will love his brother with affection and righteousness, and that neither will desire evil against his brother from henceforth for ever all the days of your life, so that ye may prosper in all your deeds and not be destroyed. 9. And if either of you deviseth evil against his brother, know that from henceforth every one that deviseth evil against his brother will fall into his hand, and will be rooted out of the land of the living, and his seed will be destroyed from under heaven. 10. But on the day of turbulence and execration and indignation and anger, with flaming devouring fire as He burnt Sodom, so likewise will He burn his land and his city and all that is his, and he will be blotted out of the book of the discipline of the children of men, and not be recorded in the book of life,[1] but in that which is appointed to destruction, and he will depart into eternal execration; so that their condemnation may be always renewed in hate and in execration and in wrath and in torment and in indignation and in plagues and in disease for ever. 11. I say and testify to you, my sons, according to the judgment which will come upon the man who wisheth to injure his brother." 12. And he divided all his possessions between the two on that day, and he gave the larger portion to him that was the first-born, and the tower and all that was about it, and all that Abraham possessed at the Well of the Oath. 13. And he said, " This larger portion I shall give to the first-born." 14. And Esau said, " I have sold to Jacob and given my birthright to Jacob; to him let it be given, and I have not a single word to say regarding it, for it is his." 15. And Isaac said, " May a blessing rest upon you, my sons, and upon your seed this day, for ye have given me rest, and my heart is not pained concerning the birthright, lest thou shouldest work wickedness on account

---

[1] Cf. xxx. 22.

of it. 16. May the Most High God [1] bless the man
that worketh righteousness, him and his seed for
ever." 17. And he ended commanding them and
blessing them, and they ate and drank together before
him, and he rejoiced because there was one mind
between them, and they went forth from him and
rested that day and slept. 18. And Isaac slept on
his bed that day rejoicing; and he slept the eternal
sleep, and died one hundred and eighty years old.
He completed twenty-five weeks and five years; and
his two sons Esau and Jacob buried him.[2] 19. And
Esau went to the land of Edom, to the mountains of
Seir, and dwelt there. 20. And Jacob dwelt in the
mountains of Hebron, in the tower of the land of the
sojournings of his father Abraham, and he worshipped
the Lord with all his heart and according to the
visible commands according as He had divided the
days of his generations.[3] 21. And Leah his wife died
2167 A.M. in the fourth year of the second week of the forty-
fifth jubilee, and he buried her in the double cave near
Rebecca his mother, to the left of the grave of Sarah,
his father's mother. 22. And all her sons and his
sons came to mourn over Leah his wife with him, and
to comfort him regarding her, for he was lamenting
her. 23. For he loved her exceedingly after Rachel
her sister died; for she was perfect and upright in all
her ways and honoured Jacob, and all the days that
she lived with him he did not hear from her mouth a
harsh word, for she was gentle and peaceable and
upright and honourable. 24. And he remembered
all her deeds which she had done during her life, and
he lamented her exceedingly; for he loved her with
all his heart and with all his soul.

---

[1] This divine title occurs frequently in our Book, and in
Ecclus. (48 times), and Daniel (13 times). In the Pentateuch,
outside Gen. xiv. (where it occurs four times), it is only found
twice. Its use was revived in *Ap. Bar.* (23 times), and in 4 Ezra.

[2] Cf. Gen. xxxv. 29.

[3] These commands had been made visible to Jacob on the
seven tables which the angel had shown him in a vision;
cf. xxxii. 21.

Esau and his Sons wage War with Jacob
(xxxvii. 1–25).

XXXVII.[1] And on the day that Isaac the father 2162 A.M. of Jacob and Esau died, the sons of Esau heard that Isaac had given the portion of the elder to his younger son Jacob and they were very angry. 2. And they strove with their father, saying : " Why hath thy father given Jacob the portion of the elder and passed over thee, although thou art the elder and Jacob the younger ? " 3. And he said unto them " Because I sold my birthright to Jacob for a small mess of lentils ; and on the day my father sent me to hunt and catch and bring him something that he should eat and bless me, he came with guile and brought my father food and drink, and my father blessed him and put me under his hand. 4. And now our father hath caused us to swear, me and him, that we shall not mutually devise evil, either against his brother, and that we shall continue in love and in peace each with his brother and not make our ways corrupt." [2] 5. And they said unto him, " We shall not hearken unto thee to make peace with him ; for our strength is greater than his strength, and we are more powerful than he ; we shall go against him and slay him, and destroy him and his sons. And if thou wilt not go with us, we shall do hurt to thee also. 6. And now hearken unto us : Let us send to Aram [3] and Philistia [4] and Moab

[1] The legend of the wars between the sons of Jacob and Esau contained in chaps. xxxvii.–xxxviii. here seems to be ancient. It is also found in *Test. Judah* ix. and in the Jewish Midrashic literature. Our text contains the oldest form.

[2] This representation gives a favourable view of Esau's own attitude. In the later form of the legend (in the *Yalḳut*) this is altered to Esau's disadvantage.

[3] The peoples mentioned here and in the context nearly all played a prominent part in the campaigns of the Maccabees. " Aram," *i. e.* Syria, was, of course, the suzerain power in their day, who sought to oppress the Jews, and whose yoke was ultimately entirely thrown off.

[4] Cf. xxiv. 28 (note).

and Ammon,[1] and let us choose for ourselves chosen men who are ardent for battle, and let us go against him and do battle with him, and let us exterminate him from the earth before he groweth strong." 7. And their father said unto them, " Do not go and do not make war with him lest ye fall before him." 8. And they said unto him, " This too, is exactly thy mode of action from thy youth until this day, and thou art putting thy neck under his yoke. We shall not hearken to these words." 9. And they sent to Aram, and to 'Adurâm [2] to the friend of their father, and they hired along with them one thousand fighting men, chosen men of war. 10. And there came to them from Moab and from the children of Ammon, those who were hired, one thousand chosen men, and from Philistia, one thousand chosen men of war, and from Edom [3] and from the Horites one thousand chosen fighting men, and from the Kittim [4] mighty men of war. 11. And they said unto their father : " Go forth with them and lead them, else we shall slay thee." 12. And he was filled with wrath and indignation on seeing that his sons were forcing him to go before (them) to lead them against Jacob his brother. 13. But afterward he remembered all the evil which lay hidden in his heart against Jacob his brother; and he remembered not the oath which he had sworn to his father and to his mother that he would devise no evil all his days against Jacob his brother. 14. And notwithstanding all this, Jacob knew not that they were coming against him to battle, and he was mourning for Leah, his wife, until they approached very near to the tower with four thousand warriors and chosen men of war. 15. And the men of Hebron sent to him saying, " Behold thy brother hath come against thee, to fight thee, with four thousand girt with the sword, and they carry shields and weapons " ; for they loved Jacob more than Esau. So they told him ; for Jacob was a more liberal and merciful man

---

[1] Cf. 1 Macc. v. 6–8. [2] An Aramaean; cf. xxxviii. 3.
[3] Cf. 1 Macc. v. 3, 65 (also iv. 29, 61). [4] Cf. xxiv. 28.

than Esau. 16. But Jacob would not believe until they came very near to the tower. 17. And he closed the gates of the tower; and he stood on the battlements and spake to his brother Esau and said, " Noble is the comfort wherewith thou hast come to comfort me for my wife who hath died. Is this the oath that thou didst swear to thy father and again to thy mother before they died? Thou hast broken the oath, and on the moment that thou didst swear to thy father wast thou condemned." 18. And then Esau answered and said unto him, " Neither the children of men nor the beasts of the earth have any oath of righteousness which in swearing they have sworn (an oath valid) for ever; but every day they devise evil one against another, and how each may slay his adversary and foe. 19. And thou dost hate me and my children for ever. And there is no observing the tie of brotherhood with thee. 20. Hear these words which I declare unto thee,

> If the boar can change its skin and make its bristles as soft as wool,
> Or if it can cause horns to sprout forth on its head like the horns of a stag or of a sheep,
> Then shall I observe the tie of brotherhood with thee.[1]

[And if the breasts separated themselves from their mother; for thou hast not been a brother to me.] [2]

21. And if the wolves make peace with the lambs so as not to devour or do them violence,
> And if their hearts are towards them for good,
> Then there will be peace in my heart towards thee.

22. And if the lion becometh the friend of the ox and maketh peace with him,

[1] For the construction of such sayings cf. the rebuke administered to Aḳiba (when the latter recognized Bar-Kokba as the Messiah) by Jochanan ben Torta: " Sooner shall grass grow from thy beard, Aḳiba, than that Messiah should appear." The " boar " may symbolize Esau.

[2] Charles thinks the bracketed words may be out of place or corrupt.

And if he is bound under one yoke with him and
  plougheth with him,
Then shall I make peace with thee.

23. And when the raven becometh white as the râzâ,[1]
Then know that I have loved thee
And shall make peace with thee.
Thou shalt be rooted out,
And thy sons shall be rooted out,
And there shall be no peace for thee."

24. And when Jacob saw that he was (so) evilly dis-
posed towards him with his heart, and with all his soul
as to slay him, and that he had come springing like the
wild boar which cometh upon the spear that pierceth
and killeth it, and recoileth not from it; 25. Then he
spake to his own and to his servants that they should
attack him and all his companions.

The War between Jacob and Esau at the Tower of Hebron. The Death of Esau and Over-throw of his Forces (xxxviii. 1–14).

XXXVIII. And after that Judah spake to Jacob,
his father, and said unto him : " Bend thy bow,
father, and send forth thy arrows and cast down the
adversary and slay the enemy ; and mayest thou have
the power, for we shall not slay thy brother, for he is
such as thou, and he is like thee : let us give him
(this) honour." 2. Then Jacob bent his bow and sent
forth the arrow and struck Esau, his brother, (on his
right breast) and slew him.[2] 3. And again he sent
forth an arrow and struck 'Adôrân the Aramaean,[3]
on the left breast, and drove him backward and slew
him. 4. And then went forth the sons of Jacob,
they and their servants, dividing themselves into
companies on the four sides of the tower. 5. And

---

[1] " A large white bird which eats grasshoppers " (Isenberg,
quoted by Charles).

[2] According to later Jewish tradition Esau was killed by
Chushim, son of Dan, at the cave of Machpelah when Jacob's
corpse had arrived there for burial; cf. *Pirḳe de R. Eliezer*
xxxix. (towards end).

[3] Cf. xxxvii. 9.

Judah went forth in front, and Naphtali and Gad with him and fifty servants with him on the south side of the tower, and they slew all they found before them, and not one individual of them escaped. 6. And Levi and Dan and Asher went forth on the east side of the tower, and fifty (men) with them, and they slew the fighting men of Moab and Ammon. 7. And Reuben and Issachar and Zebulon went forth on the north side of the tower, and fifty men with them, and they slew the fighting men of the Philistines. 8. And Simeon and Benjamin and Enoch, Reuben's son, went forth on the west side of the tower, and fifty (men) with them, and they slew of Edom and of the Horites four hundred men, stout warriors; and six hundred fled, and four of the sons of Esau fled with them, and left their father lying slain, as he had fallen on the hill which is in 'Adûrâm.[1] 9. And the sons of Jacob pursued after them to the mountains of Seir. And Jacob buried his brother on the hill which is in 'Adûrâm, and he returned to his house. 10. And the sons of Jacob pressed hard upon the sons of Esau in the mountains of Seir, and bowed their necks so that they became servants of the sons of Jacob. 11. And they sent to their father (to inquire) whether they should make peace with them or slay them. 12. And Jacob sent word to his sons that they should make peace, and they made peace with them, and placed the yoke of servitude upon them, so that they paid tribute to Jacob and to his sons always. 13. And they continued to pay tribute to Jacob until the day that he went down into Egypt.[2] 14. And the sons of Edom have not got quit of the yoke of servitude which the twelve sons of Jacob had imposed on them until this day.[3]

[1] A city in Idumaea (Edom) identical with the "Adora" mentioned in 1 Macc. xiii. 20. It was captured by John Hyrcanus and forced to accept circumcision. In *Test. Judah* ix. 3 the name appears as *Anoniram*.

[2] For 11–13 cf. *Test. Judah* ix. 7–8.

[3] *i. e.* the author's day. Edom was finally made tributary to Israel by John Hyrcanus.

The Kings of Edom (xxxviii. 15–24; cf. Gen. xxxvi. 31–39).

15. And these are the kings that reigned in Edom before there reigned any king over the children of Israel [until this day] in the land of Edom. 16. And Bâlâq,[1] the son of Beor, reigned in Edom, and the name of his city was Danâbâ.[2] 17. And Bâlâq died, and Jobab, the son of Zârâ of Bôsêr,[3] reigned in his stead. 18. And Jobab died, and 'Asâm,[4] of the land of Têmân, reigned in his stead. 19. And 'Asâm died, and 'Adâth,[5] the son of Barad,[6] who slew Midian in the field of Moab, reigned in his stead, and the name of his city was Avith. 20. And 'Adâth died, and Salman,[7] from 'Amâsêqâ,[8] reigned in his stead. 21. And Salman died, and Saul of Râ'abôth [9] (by the) river, reigned in his stead. 22. And Saul died, and Ba'êlûnân,[10] the son of Achbor, reigned in his stead. 23. And Ba'êlûnân, the son of Achbor, died, and 'Adâth [11] reigned in his stead, and the name of his wife was Maiṭabîth,[12] the daughter of Mâṭarat,[13] the daughter of Mêtabêdzâ'ab.[14] 24. These are the kings who reigned in the land of Edom.

Joseph's Service with Potiphar ; his Purity and Imprisonment (xxxix. 1–13; cf. Gen. xxxix.).

XXXIX. And Jacob dwelt in the land of his father's sojournings in the land of Canaan. 2. These are the generations of Jacob. And Joseph was seventeen years old [15] when they took him down into the land of Egypt, and Potiphar, an eunuch of Pharaoh,

---

[1] LXX (Gen. xxxvi. 22) Βάλακ = Heb. *Belă.*
[2] MT *Dinhabah.*   [3] MT *Bozrah.*
[4] LXX 'Ασόμ, MT *Husham.*   [5] MT *Hadad.*
[6] LXX Βαράδ, MT *Bedad.*   [7] LXX Σαλαμά, MT *Samlah.*
[8] MT *Masrekah.*   [9] LXX 'Ροωβώθ, MT *Rehoboth.*
[10] LXX Βαλαεννάν, MT *Baal-hanan.*   [11] MT *Hadar.*
[12] MT *Mehetabel.*   [13] MT *Matred* (LXX Ματραείθ).
[14] MT *Me-zahab.*   [15] Cf. Gen. xxxvii. 2.

the chief cook [1] bought him. 3. And he set Joseph over all his house, and the blessing of the Lord came upon the house of the Egyptian on account of Joseph, and the Lord prospered him in all that he did. 4. And the Egyptian committed everything into the hands of Joseph; for he saw that the Lord was with him, and that the Lord prospered him in all that he did. 5. And Joseph's appearance was comely and very beautiful was his appearance, and his master's wife lifted up her eyes and saw Joseph, and she loved him, and besought him to lie with her. 6. But he did not surrender his soul, and he remembered the Lord and the words which Jacob, his father, used to read from amongst the words of Abraham,[2] that no man should commit fornication with a woman who hath a husband; that for him the punishment of death hath been ordained in the heavens before the Most High God, and the sin will be recorded against him in the eternal books continually before the Lord. 7. And Joseph remembered these words and refused to lie with her. 8. And she besought him for a year, but he refused and would not listen. 9. But she embraced him and held him fast in the house in order to force him to lie with her, and closed the doors of the house and held him fast; but he left his garment in her hands and broke through the door and fled without from her presence. 10. And the woman saw that he would not lie with her, and she calumniated him in the presence of his lord, saying : " Thy Hebrew servant, whom thou lovest, sought to force me so that he might lie with me; and it came to pass when I lifted up my voice that he fled and left his garment in my hands when I held him, and he brake through the door." 11. And the Egyptian saw the garment of Joseph and the broken door, and heard the words of his wife, and cast Joseph into prison into the place where the prisoners were kept whom the king imprisoned. 12. And he was there in the prison; and the Lord gave Joseph favour in the sight of the chief

---

[1] Cf. xxxiv. 11 (note).   [2] Cf. xx. 4, xxv. 7.

of the prison guards and compassion before him, for
he saw that the Lord was with him, and that the Lord
made all that he did to prosper.   13. And he committed all things into his hands, and the chief of the
prison guards knew of nothing that was with him,[1]
for Joseph did everything, and the Lord perfected it.

Joseph interprets the Dreams of the Chief Butler and the Chief Baker (xxxix. 14-18; cf. Gen. xl.).

14. And he remained there two years.[2]   And in
those days Pharaoh, king of Egypt, was wroth against
his two eunuchs, against the chief butler and against
the chief baker, and he put them in ward in the house
of the chief cook,[3] in the prison where Joseph was
kept.   15. And the chief of the prison guards appointed Joseph to serve them; and he served before
them.   16. And they both dreamed a dream, the chief
butler and the chief baker, and they told it to Joseph.
17. And as he interpreted to them so it befell them,
and Pharaoh restored the chief butler to his office,
and the (chief) baker he slew, as Joseph had interpreted to them.   18. But the chief butler forgot
Joseph in the prison, although he had informed him
what would befall him, and did not remember to
inform Pharaoh how Joseph had told him for he
forgot.

Pharaoh's Dreams and their Interpretation. Joseph's Elevation and Marriage (xl. 1-13; cf. Gen. xli.).

XL. And in those days Pharaoh dreamed two
dreams in one night concerning a famine which was
to be in all the land, and he awoke from his sleep and
called all the interpreters of dreams that were in
Egypt, and magicians, and told them his two dreams,

---

[1] Cf. Gen. xxxix. 8.   [2] Cf. Gen. xli. 1.
[3] Cf. xxxiv. 11 (note).

and they were not able to declare (them). 2. And then the chief butler remembered Joseph and spake of him to the king, and he brought him forth from the prison, and he told his two dreams before him. 3. And he said before Pharaoh that his two dreams were one, and he said unto him : " Seven years will come (in which there will be) plenty over all the land of Egypt, and after that seven years of famine, such a famine as hath not been in all the land. 4. And now let Pharaoh appoint overseers [1] in all the land of Egypt, and let them store up food in every city throughout the days of the years of plenty, and there will be food for the seven years of famine, and the land will not perish through the famine, for it will be very severe." 5. And the Lord gave Joseph favour and mercy in the eyes of Pharaoh, and Pharaoh said unto his servants : " We shall not find such a wise and discreet man as this man, for the spirit of the Lord is with him." 6. And he appointed him the second in all his kingdom and gave him authority over all Egypt, and caused him to ride in the second chariot of Pharaoh. 7. And he clothed him with byssus garments, and he put a gold chain upon his neck, and (a herald) proclaimed before him " 'El 'El wa' Abîrĕr,"[2] and he placed a ring on his hand and made him ruler over all his house, and magnified him, and said unto him : " Only on the throne shall I be greater than thou." 8. And Joseph ruled over all the land of Egypt, and all the princes of Pharaoh, and all his servants, and all who did the king's business loved him, for he walked in uprightness, for he was without pride and arrogance, and he had no respect of persons, and did not accept gifts, but he judged in uprightness all the people of the land. 9. And the

---

[1] Cf. Gen. xli. 34.

[2] *'El 'El wa 'Abîrĕr* = Heb. *'el 'el wa'ăbîr 'el*, " God, God, the mighty one of God." This is a peculiar amplification of the Hebrew *'abrēk* (R.V. " bow the knee ") of Gen. xli. 43. " Mighty one of God " may be a technical term for a great magician; cf. Acts viii. 10.

land of Egypt was at peace before Pharaoh because of Joseph, for the Lord was with him, and gave him favour and mercy for all his generations before all those who knew him and those who heard concerning him, and Pharaoh's kingdom was well ordered, and there was no Satan [1] and no evil person (therein). 10. And the king called Joseph's name Sĕphânṭî-phâns,[2] and gave Joseph to wife the daughter of Potiphar, the daughter of the priest of Heliopolis, the chief cook.[3] 11. And on the day that Joseph stood before Pharaoh he was thirty years old [when he stood before Pharaoh]. 12. And in that year Isaac died. And it came to pass as Joseph had said in the interpretation of his two dreams, according as he had said it, there were seven years of plenty over all the land of Egypt, and the land of Egypt produced abundantly, one measure (producing) eighteen hundred measures. 13. And Joseph gathered food into every city until they were full of corn until they could no longer count and measure it for its multitude.

Judah's Incest with Tamar ; his Repentance and Forgiveness (xli. 1–28 ; Cf. Gen. xxxviii.).

2165 A.M. XLI. And in the forty-fifth jubilee, in the second week, (and) in the second year, Judah took for his first-born Er, a wife from the daughters of Aram,[4] named Tamar. 2. But he hated, and did not lie with her, because his mother was of the daughters of Canaan, and he wished to take him a wife of the kinsfolk of his mother, but Judah, his father, would not permit him. 3. And this Er, the first-born of

---

[1] A sign of great felicity ; cf. xxiii. 29.

[2] i. e. Zaphenath-paneah (Gen. xli. 45).

[3] The author identifies Potiphar of Gen. xxxvii. 36 with Potiphera of Gen. xli. 45. In later Jewish legend Asenath (Joseph's wife) is represented as a Jewess, a daughter of Dinah, who was brought up in the family of Potiphera (cf. Pirḳe de R. Eliezer xxxviii.). The difficulty of Joseph's heathen marriage is thus removed.

[4] Cf. Test. Judah x. (" from Mesopotamia ").

Judah, was wicked, and the Lord slew him. 4. And Judah said unto Onan, his brother : " Go in unto thy brother's wife and perform the duty of a husband's brother unto her,[1] and raise up seed unto thy brother." 5. And Onan knew that the seed would not be his, (but) his brother's only, and he went into the house of his brother's wife, and spilt the seed on the ground, and he was wicked in the eyes of the Lord, and He slew him. 6. And Judah said unto Tamar, his daughter-in-law : " Remain in thy father's house as a widow till Shelah my son be grown up, and I shall give thee to him to wife." 7. And he grew up ; but Bêdsû'êl,[2] the wife of Judah, did not permit her son Shelah to marry. And Bêdsû'êl, the wife of Judah, died in the fifth year of this week. 8. And in the sixth year Judah went up to shear his sheep at Timnah. And they told Tamar : " Behold thy father-in-law goeth up to Timnah to shear his sheep." 9. And she put off her widow's clothes, and put on a veil, and adorned herself, and sat in the gate adjoining the way to Timnah. 10. And as Judah was going along he found her, and thought her to be an harlot, and he said unto her : " Let me come in unto thee " ; and she said unto him : " Come in," and he went in. 11. And she said unto him : " Give me my hire " ; and he said unto her : " I have nothing in my hand save my ring that is on my finger, and my necklace, and my staff which is in my hand." 12. And she said unto him : " Give them to me until thou dost send me my hire " ; and he said unto her : " I will send unto thee a kid of the goats " ; and he gave them to her, (and he went in unto her,) and she conceived by him. 13. And Judah went unto his sheep, and she went to her father's house. 14. And Judah sent a kid of the goats by the hand of his shepherd, an Adullamite, and he found her not ; and he asked the people of the place, saying : " Where is the harlot who was here ? " And they said unto him : " There

2168 A.M.
2169 A.M.

---

[1] Cf. Gen. xxxviii. 8 ; Deut. xxv. 5.
[2] i. e. Bathshua ; cf. xxxiv. 20.

is no harlot here with us." 15. And he returned and informed him, and said unto him that he had not found her; " I asked the people of the place, and they said unto me : ' There is no harlot here.' " And he said : " Let her keep (them) lest we become a cause of derision." 16. And when she had completed three months, it was manifest that she was with child, and they told Judah, saying : " Behold Tamar, thy daughter-in-law, is with child by whoredom." 17. And Judah went to the house of her father, and said unto her father and her brothers : " Bring her forth, and let them burn her,[1] for she hath wrought unclean-ness in Israel." 18. And it came to pass when they brought her forth to burn her that she sent to her father-in-law the ring and the necklace, and the staff, saying : " Discern whose are these, for by him am I with child." 19. And Judah acknowledged, and said : " Tamar is more righteous than I am. And therefore let them burn her not." 20. And for that reason she was not given to Shelah, and he did not again approach her. 21. And after that she bare 2170 A.M. two sons, Perez and Zerah, in the seventh year of this second week. 22. And thereupon the seven years of fruitfulness were accomplished, of which Joseph spake to Pharaoh.[2] 23. And Judah acknow-ledged that the deed which he had done was evil, for he had lain with his daughter-in-law, and he esteemed it hateful in his eyes, and he acknowledged that he had transgressed and gone astray; for he had un-covered the skirt of his son, and he began to lament and to supplicate before the Lord because of his transgression. 24. And we told him in a dream that it was forgiven him because he supplicated earnestly, and lamented, and did not again commit it. 25. And he received forgiveness because he turned from his

---

[1] The punishment appointed for such an offence on the part of a priest's daughter (Lev. xxi. 9); cf. xxx. 7 above. According to the Targum (Ps.-Jon.), on Gen. xxxviii. 6, 24, Tamar was the daughter of a priest.

[2] Cf. Gen. xli. 53.

sin and from his ignorance, for he transgressed
greatly before our God; and every one that acteth
thus, every one who lieth with his mother-in-law, let
them burn him with fire that he may burn therein,[1]
for there is uncleanness and pollution upon them;
with fire let them burn them. 26. And do thou
command the children of Israel that there be no
uncleanness amongst them, for every one who lieth
with his daughter-in-law [2] or with his mother-in-law
hath wrought uncleanness; with fire let them burn
the man who hath lain with her, and likewise the
woman, and He will turn away wrath and punishment
from Israel. 27. And unto Judah we said that his
two sons had not lain with her, and for this reason
his seed was established for a second generation,
and would not be rooted out. 28. For in singleness
of eye he had gone and sought for punishment, namely,
according to the judgment of Abraham,[3] which he had
commanded his sons, Judah had sought to burn her
with fire.

The Two Journeys of the Sons of Jacob to Egypt (xlii. 1–25; cf. Gen. xlii., xliii.).

XLII.   And in the first year of the third week of 2171 A.M.
the forty-fifth jubilee the famine began to come into
the land, and the rain refused to be given to the earth,
for none whatever fell. 2. And the earth grew
barren, but in the land of Egypt there was food, for
Joseph had gathered the seed of the land in the seven
years of plenty and had preserved it.[4] 3. And the
Egyptians came to Joseph that he might give them
food, and he opened the storehouses where was the
grain of the first year, and he sold it to the people of
the land for gold.[5] 4. (Now the famine was very sore
in the land of Canaan), and Jacob heard that there

[1] Cf. Lev. xx. 14.
[2] Cf. Lev. xviii. 15, xx. 12 (mode of death not specified;
but Gen. xxxviii. 24 presupposes burning by fire).
[3] Cf. xx. 4 (note).   [4] Cf. Gen. xli. 54.   [5] Cf. Gen. xli. 56.

was food in Egypt, and he sent his ten sons that they should procure food for him in Egypt; but Benjamin he did not send, and (the ten sons of Jacob) arrived (in Egypt) among those that went (there.) 5. And Joseph recognized them, but they did not recognize him, and he spake unto them and questioned them, and he said unto them: "Are ye not spies, and have ye not come to explore the approaches of the land?" And he put them in ward. 6. And after that he set them free again, and detained Simeon alone and sent off his nine brothers. 7. And he filled their sacks with corn, and he put their gold in their sacks, and they did not know. 8. And he commanded them to bring their younger brother, for they had told him their father was living and their younger brother. 9. And they went up from the land of Egypt and they came to the land of Canaan; and they told their father all that had befallen them, and how the lord of the country had spoken roughly to them, and had seized Simeon till they should bring Benjamin. 10. And Jacob said: "Me have ye bereaved of my children! Joseph is not and Simeon also is not, and ye will take Benjamin away. On me hath your wickedness come."[1] 11. And he said: "My son will not go down with you lest perchance he fall sick; for their mother gave birth to two sons, and one hath perished, and this one also ye will take from me. If perchance he took a fever on the road,[2] ye would bring down my old age with sorrow unto death." 12. For he saw that their money had been returned to every man in his sack, and for this reason he feared to send him. 13. And the famine increased and became sore in the land of Canaan, and in all lands save in the land of Egypt, for many of the children of the Egyptians had stored up their seed for food from the time when they saw Joseph gathering seed together

---

[1] ? An interpretation of Gen. xlii. 36 ("All these things are against me").

[2] "If mischief befall him by the way in the which ye go" (Gen. xlii. 38).

and putting it in storehouses and preserving it for the
years of famine. 14. And the people of Egypt fed
themselves thereon during the first year of their
famine. 15. But when Israel saw that the famine was
very sore in the land, and there was no deliverance,
he said unto his sons : " Go again, and procure food
for us that we die not." 16. And they said : " We
shall not go ; unless our youngest brother go with us,
we shall not go." 17. And Israel saw that if he did
not send him with them, they should all perish by
reason of the famine. 18. And Reuben said :
" Give him into my hand, and if I do not bring him
back to thee, slay my two sons instead of his soul."
And he said unto him : " He will not go with thee."
19. And Judah came near and said : " Send him with
me, and if I do not bring him back to thee, let me
bear the blame before thee all the days of my life." 20.
And he sent him with them in the second year of this 2172 A.M.
week on the first day of the month, and they came to
the land of Egypt with all those who went, and (they
had) presents in their hands, stacte and almonds and
terebinth nuts and pure honey. 21. And they went
and stood before Joseph, and he saw Benjamin his
brother, and he knew him, and said unto them : " Is
this your youngest brother ? " And they said unto
him : " It is he." And he said : " The Lord be
gracious to thee, my son ! " 22. And he sent him
into his house and he brought forth Simeon unto
them and he made a feast for them, and they presented
to him the gift which they had brought in their hands.
23. And they ate before him and he gave them all a
portion, but the portion of Benjamin was seven times
larger than that of any of theirs. 24. And they ate
and drank and arose and remained with their asses.
25. And Joseph devised a plan whereby he might
learn their thoughts as to whether thoughts of peace
prevailed amongst them, and he said to the steward
who was over his house : " Fill all their sacks with
food, and return their money unto them into their
vessels, and my cup, the silver cup out of which I

drink, put it in the sack of the youngest, and send them away." [1]

Joseph finally tests his Brethren, and then makes himself known to them (xliii. 1–24; cf. Gen. xliv., xlv.).

XLIII. And he did as Joseph had told him, and filled all their sacks for them with food and put their money in their sacks, and put the cup in Benjamin's sack. 2. And early in the morning they departed, and it came to pass that, when they had gone from thence, Joseph said unto the steward of his house : " Pursue them, run and seize them, saying, ' For good ye have requited me with evil; you have stolen from me the silver cup out of which my lord drinks.' And bring back to me their youngest brother, and fetch (him) quickly before I go forth to my seat of judgment." 3. And he ran after them and said unto them according to these words. 4. And they said unto him : " God forbid that thy servants should do this thing, and steal from the house of thy lord any utensil, and the money also which we found in our sacks the first time, we thy servants brought back from the land of Canaan. 5. How then should we steal any utensil? Behold here are we and our sacks; search, and wherever thou findest the cup in the sack of any man amongst us, let him be slain, and we and our asses will serve thy lord." 6. And he said unto them : " Not so, the man with whom I find, him only shall I take as a servant, and ye will return in peace unto your house." 7. And as he was searching in their vessels, beginning with the eldest and ending with the youngest, it was found in Benjamin's sack. 8. And they rent their garments, and laded their asses, and returned to the city and came to the house of Joseph, and they all bowed themselves on their faces to the ground before him. 9. And Joseph said unto them : " Ye have done evil." And they

[1] Cf. Gen. xliv. 1, 2.

said : " What shall we say and how shall we defend ourselves ? Our lord hath discovered the transgression of his servants; behold we are the servants of our lord, and our asses also." 10. And Joseph said unto them : " I too fear the Lord; as for you, go ye to your homes and let your brother be my servant, for ye have done evil. Know ye not that a man delighteth in his cup as I with this cup ?[1] And yet ye have stolen it from me." 11. And Judah said : " O my lord, let thy servant, I pray thee, speak a word in my lord's ear; two brothers did thy servant's mother bear to our father; one went away and was lost, and hath not been found, and he alone is left of his mother, and thy servant our father loveth him, and his life also is bound up with the life of this (lad). 12. And it will come to pass, when we go to thy servant our father, and the lad is not with us, that he will die, and we shall bring down our father with sorrow unto death. 13. Now rather let me, thy servant, abide instead of the boy as a bondsman unto my lord, and let the lad go with his brethren, for I became surety for him at the hand of thy servant our father, and if I do not bring him back, thy servant will bear the blame to our father for ever." 14. And Joseph saw that they were all accordant in goodness one with another, and he could not refrain himself, and he told them that he was Joseph. 15. And he conversed with them in the Hebrew tongue [2] and fell on their neck and wept. But they knew him not and they began to weep. 16. And he said unto them : " Weep not over me, but hasten and bring my father to me; and ye see that it is my mouth that speaketh and the eyes of my brother Benjamin see. 17. For behold this is the second year of the famine, and there are still five years without harvest or fruit of trees or ploughing. 18. Come down quickly ye and your households, so that ye perish not through the famine,

---

[1] Gen. xliv. 15 (" Know ye not that such a man as I can indeed divine ? "). The change in our text may be deliberate.
[2] A Midrashic touch; so *Bereshith rabba* xciii.

and do not be grieved for your possessions, for the Lord
sent me before you to set things in order that many
people might live.   19. And tell my father that I am
still alive, and ye, behold, ye see that the Lord hath
made me as a father to Pharaoh, and ruler over his
house and over all the land of Egypt.   20. And tell
my father of all my glory, and all the riches and glory
that the Lord hath given me."   21. And by the
command of the mouth of Pharaoh he gave them
chariots and provisions for the way, and he gave them
all many-coloured raiment and silver.   22. And to
their father he sent raiment and silver and ten asses
which carried corn, and he sent them away.   23. And
they went up and told their father that Joseph was
alive, and was measuring out corn to all the nations
of the earth, and that he was ruler over all the land of
Egypt.   24. And their father did not believe it,
for he was beside himself in his mind ; but when he
saw the wagons which Joseph had sent, the life of his
spirit revived, and he said : " It is enough for me if
Joseph liveth ; I will go down and see him before I
die."

Jacob celebrates the Feast of First-fruits and journeys to Egypt. List of his Descendants.
(xliv. 1–34 ; cf. Gen. xlvi. 1–28).

XLIV. And Israel took his journey from † Haran † [1]
from his house on the new moon of the third month,
and he went on the way of the Well of the Oath,[2]
and he offered a sacrifice to the God of his father Isaac
on the seventh of this month.   2. And Jacob remembered the dream that he had seen at Bethel,[3]
and he feared to go down into Egypt.   3. And while
he was thinking of sending word to Joseph to come
to him, and that he would not go down, he remained
there seven days, if perchance he should see a vision
as to whether he should remain or go down.   4. And

[1] Probably corrupt for " Hebron " ; cf. Gen. xxxvii. 14.
[2] Beersheba.   [3] Cf. xxvii. 22.

he celebrated the harvest festival of the first-fruits [1]
with old grain, for in all the land of Canaan there was
not a handful of seed (in the land), for the famine
was over all the beasts and cattle and birds, and also
over man. 5. And on the sixteenth the Lord appeared unto him, and said unto him, " Jacob, Jacob " ;
and he said, " Here am I." And He said unto him :
" I am the God of thy fathers, the God of Abraham
and Isaac ; fear not to go down into Egypt, for I will
there make of thee a great nation. 6. I shall go
down with thee, and I shall bring thee up [2] (again),
and in this land wilt thou be buried, and Joseph
will put his hands upon thy eyes. Fear not ; go
down into Egypt." 7. And his sons rose up, and
his sons' sons, and they placed their father and their
possessions upon wagons. 8. And Israel rose up from
the Well of the Oath on the sixteenth of this third
month, and he went to the land of Egypt. 9. And
Israel sent Judah before him to his son Joseph to
examine [3] the Land of Goshen, for Joseph had told
his brothers that they should come and dwell there
that they might be near him. 10. And this was the
goodliest (land) in the land of Egypt, and near to
him, for all (of them) and also for the cattle. 11. And
these are the names of the sons of Jacob who went
into Egypt with Jacob their father. 12.[4] Reuben,
the first-born of Israel ; and these are the names of
his sons : Enoch, and Pallu, and Hezron and Carmi
—five.[5] 13. Simeon and his sons ; and these are
the names of his sons : Jemuel, and Jamin, and Ohad,

[1] Cf. Gen. xlvi. 1 (the feast was celebrated on the 15th of
the third month).

[2] Cf. xxvii. 24, xxxii. 23.

[3] " To show the way " (Gen. xlvi. 28).

[4] The number 70, according to our text, includes Jacob
with his descendants. Another reckoning makes up the
number by excluding Jacob himself : cf. Exod. i. 5 and
Gen. xlvi. 15, 18, 21, 25, 27. The number 75, in Acts vii. 14.
is due to the LXX of Exod. i. 5 and Deut. x. 22. There
are certain differences in detail between the list in our text
and the details given in Genesis ; see Charles *ad loc*.

[5] The father is included in each case.

and Jachin, and Zohar, and Shaul, the son of the Zephathite [1] woman—seven. 14. Levi and his sons; and these are the names of his sons : Gershon, and Kohath, and Merari—four. 15. Judah and his sons; and these are the names of his sons : Shela, and Perez, and Zerah—four. 16. Issachar and his sons; and these are the names of his sons : Tola, and Phûa,[2] and Jâsûb,[3] and Shimron—five. 17. Zebulon and his sons; and these are the names of his sons : Sered, and Elon, and Jahleel—four. 18. And these are the sons of Jacob, and their sons, whom Leah bore to Jacob in Mesopotamia, six, and their one sister, Dinah : and all the souls of the sons of Leah, and their sons, who went with Jacob their father into Egypt, were twenty-nine, and Jacob their father being with them, they were thirty. 19. And the sons of Zilpah, Leah's handmaid, the wife of Jacob, whom she bore unto Jacob, Gad and Asher. 20. And these are the names of their sons who went with him into Egypt : the sons of Gad : Ziphion, and Haggi, and Shuni, and Ezbon, (and Eri) and Areli, and Arodi —eight. 21. And the sons of Asher : Imnah, and Ishvah, (and Ishvi), and Beriah, and Serah, their one sister—six. 22. All the souls were fourteen, and all those of Leah were forty-four. 23. And the sons of Rachel, the wife of Jacob : Joseph and Benjamin. 24. And there were born to Joseph in Egypt before his father came into Egypt, those whom Asenath, daughter of Potiphar priest of Heliopolis bare unto him, Manasseh, and Ephraim—three. 25. And the sons of Benjamin : Bela and Becher, and Ashbel, Gera, and Naaman, and Ehi, and Rosh, and Muppim, and Huppim, and Ard—eleven. 26. And all the souls of Rachel were fourteen. 27. And the sons of Bilhah, the handmaid of Rachel, the wife of Jacob, whom she

---

[1] *i. e.* a native of the Canaanite city Zephath; cf. Judg. i. 17.
[2] So LXX, Sam. and other versions. MT *Puvah* (Gen. xlvi. 13).
[3] So Sam. (Gen. xlvi. 13) and LXX = MT *Iob*.

bare to Jacob, were Dan and Naphtali. 28. And
these are the names of their sons who went with them
into Egypt. And the sons of Dan were Hushim, and
Sâmôn, and Asûdî, and 'Îjâka, and Salômôn—six.
29. And they died the year in which they entered
into Egypt, and there was left to Dan Hushim alone.[1]
30. And these are the names of the sons of Naphtali :
Jahziel, and Guni, and Jezer, and Shallum, and
'Îv.[2] 31. And 'Îv, who was born after the years
of famine, died in Egypt. 32. And all the souls of
Rachel were twenty-six. 33. And all the souls of
Jacob which went into Egypt were seventy souls.
These are his children and his children's children, in all seventy; but five died in Egypt before
Joseph, and had no children. 34. And in the land of
Canaan two sons of Judah died, Er and Onan, and
they had no children, and the children of Israel
buried those who perished, and they were reckoned
among the seventy Gentile nations.

Joseph receives Jacob. The Land of Egypt is acquired for Pharaoh. Jacob's Death and Burial (xlv. 1–16; cf. Gen. xlvi. 28 ff., xlvii. 11 ff.).

XLV. And Israel went into the country of Egypt, 2172 A M.
into the land of Goshen, on the new moon of the
fourth month, in the second year of the third week
of the forty-fifth jubilee. 2. And Joseph went to
meet his father Jacob, to the land of Goshen, and he
fell on his father's neck and wept. 3. And Israel
said unto Joseph : " Now let me die since I have seen
thee, and now may the Lord God of Israel be blessed,
the God of Abraham and the God of Isaac who hath
not withheld His mercy and His grace from His
servant Jacob. 4. It is enough for me that I have
seen thy face whilst †I am† [3] yet alive ; yea, true is
the vision which I saw at Bethel. Blessed be the

---

[1] In Gen. xlvi. 23 " Hushim " (MT) is mentioned alone.

[2] Cf. Gen. xlvi. 24 and 1 Chron. vii. 13 : 'Iv is omitted in
both texts.

[3] MT (Gen. xlvi. 30) " that thou art."

Lord my God for ever and ever, and blessed be His name." 5. And Joseph and his brothers ate bread before their father and drank wine, and Jacob rejoiced with exceeding great joy because he saw Joseph eating with his brothers and drinking before him, and he blessed the Creator of all things who had preserved him, and had preserved for him his twelve sons. 6. [1] And Joseph had given to his father and to his brothers as a gift the right of dwelling in the land of Goshen and in Rameses and all the region round about, which he ruled over before Pharaoh. And Israel and his sons dwelt in the land of Goshen, the best part of the land of Egypt; and Israel was one hundred and thirty years old when he came into Egypt. 7. And Joseph nourished his father and his brethren and also their possessions with bread as much as sufficed them [2] for the seven years of the famine. 8. And the land of Egypt suffered by reason of the famine, and Joseph acquired all the land of Egypt for Pharaoh in return for food, and he got possession of the people and their cattle and everything for Pharaoh. 9. And the years of the famine were accomplished, and Joseph gave to the people in the land seed and food that they might sow (the land) in the eighth year, for the river had overflowed all the land of Egypt. 10. For in the seven years of the famine it had not overflowed and had irrigated only a few places on the banks of the river, but now it overflowed and the Egyptians sowed the land, and it bore much corn that year. 11. And this was the 2178 A.M. first year of the fourth week of the forty-fifth jubilee. 12. And Joseph took of the corn of the harvest the fifth part for the king and left four parts for them for food and for seed, and Joseph made it an ordinance for the land of Egypt until this day. 13. And Israel lived in the land of Egypt seventeen years, and all the days which he lived were three jubilees, one hundred and forty-seven years, and he died in the

---

[1] Cf. Gen. xlvii. 11.

[2] MT (Gen. xlvii. 12) " according to their families."

fourth year of the fifth week of the forty-fifth jubilee. 2188 A.M.
14. And Israel blessed his sons before he died and
told them everything[1] that would befall them in the
land of Egypt; and he made known to them what
would come upon them in the last days, and blessed
them and gave to Joseph two portions[2] in the land.
15. And he slept with his fathers, and he was buried
in the double cave in the land of Canaan, near Abraham his father in the grave which he dug for himself
in the double cave in the land of Hebron.[3] 16. And
he gave all his books and the books of his fathers to
Levi his son that he might preserve them and renew
them for his children until this day.[4]

The Death of Joseph. The Bones of Jacob's Sons (except Joseph) interred at Hebron. The Oppression of Israel by Egypt (xlvi. 1–16; cf. Gen. l.; Exod. i.).

XLVI. And it came to pass that after Jacob died
the children of Israel multiplied in the land of Egypt,
and they became a great nation, and they were of
one accord in heart, so that brother loved brother
and every man helped his brother, and they increased
abundantly and multiplied exceedingly, ten weeks 2242 A.M.
of years, all the days of the life of Joseph.[5] 2. And
there was no Satan[6] nor any evil all the days of the
life of Joseph which he lived after his father Jacob,
for all the Egyptians honoured the children of Israel
all the days of the life of Joseph. 3. And Joseph
died being a hundred and ten years old;[7] seventeen
years he lived in the land of Canaan, and ten years
he was a servant, and three years in prison, and
eighty years he was under the king, ruling all the land

---

[1] Cf. Gen. xlix. 1 ff.　　　[2] Cf. Gen. xlviii. 22.
[3] Cf. Gen. l. 13.
[4] Note that the tribal traditions are represented by our
author as in the keeping of the priests (Levi and his
descendants).
[5] Cf. Exod. i. 7.　　　　　[6] Cf. xxiii. 29.
[7] Cf. Gen. l. 22, 26; Exod. i. 6.

of Egypt. 4. And he died and all his brethren and all that generation. 5. And he commanded the children of Israel before he died that they should carry his bones with them when they went forth from the land of Egypt.[1] 6. And he made them swear regarding his bones, for he knew that the Egyptians would not again bring forth and bury him in the land of Canaan,[2] for Mâkamârôn,[3] king of Canaan, while dwelling in the land of Assyria, fought in the valley with the king of Egypt and slew him there, and pursued after the Egyptians to the gates of 'Êrmôn.[4] 7. But he was not able to enter, for another, a new king, had become king of Egypt,[5] and he was stronger than he, and he returned to the land of Canaan, and the gates of Egypt were closed, and none went out and none came into Egypt. 8. And Joseph died 2242 A.M. in the forty-sixth jubilee, in the sixth week, in the second year, and they buried him in the land of Egypt, and all his brethren died after him. 9. And the king of Egypt went forth to war with the king of 2263 A.M. Canaan in the forty-seventh jubilee, in the second week in the second year, and the children of Israel brought forth all the bones of the children of Jacob save the bones of Joseph, and they buried them in the field in the double cave in the mountain. 10. And the most (of them) returned to Egypt, but a few of them remained in the mountains of Hebron, and

[1] Cf. Gen. l. 25.

[2] Cf. *Test. Simeon* viii. 3 f. (" For the bones of Joseph the Egyptians guarded in the tombs of the kings. For the sorcerers told them that on the departure of the bones of Joseph there should be throughout all the land darkness and gloom," etc.).

[3] Identification unknown.

[4] *i. e.* Heroônpolis (close to the desert).

[5] ? Rameses III (1202–1171), founder of the 20th dynasty, who repulsed an invasion of peoples from the north and twice marched through Canaan, and in North Canaan defeated the invaders. The war between Egypt and Canaan, mentioned in our text, is referred to in *Test. Simeon* viii. 2. A war between Cush and Egypt, in which Moses led the Egyptians, is referred to by Josephus (*Ant.* ii. 10). In *Chron. Jerahmeel* xlv. it is between Cush and Syria.

Amram thy father remained with them[1]. 11. And
the king of Canaan was victorious over the king of
Egypt, and he closed the gates of Egypt. 12. And
he devised an evil device against the children of
Israel of afflicting them; and he said unto the people
of Egypt: 13. " Behold the people of the children
of Israel have increased and multiplied more than we.
Come and let us deal wisely with them before they
become too many, and let us afflict them with slavery
before war come upon us and before they too fight
against us; else they will join themselves unto our
enemies and get them up out of our land, for their
hearts and faces are towards the land of Canaan."
14. And he set over them taskmasters to afflict them
with slavery; and they built strong [2] cities for
Pharaoh, Pithom and Raamses, and they built all
the walls and all the fortifications which had fallen
in the cities of Egypt. 15. And they made them
serve with rigour, and the more they dealt evilly
with them, the more they increased and multiplied.
16. And the people of Egypt abominated the children
of Israel.

The Birth and Early Years of Moses
(xlvii. 1-12; cf. Exod. ii.).

XLVII. And in the seventh week, in the seventh 2303 A.M
year, in the forty-seventh jubilee, thy father [3] went
forth from the land of Canaan, and thou wast born
in the fourth week, in the sixth year thereof, in the 2330 A.M.
forty-eighth jubilee; this was the time of tribulation
on the children of Israel. 2. And Pharaoh, king of
Egypt, issued a command regarding them that they

---

[1] This interesting statement apparently implies that some
of the Hebrew tribes were already in Canaan before the
Exodus. Or is it a reminiscence of the fact that the tribe
of Judah absorbed some South Canaanitish tribes which were
never in Egypt? Cf. Burney in *Journal of Theological Studies*,
1908, pp. 321–352.
[2] So LXX (Exod. i. 11); MT = ? " store cities."
[3] *i. e*, Moses' father, Amram.

should cast all their male children which were born
into the river.   3. And they cast them in for seven
months until the day that thou wast born.   And thy
mother hid thee for three months, and they told
regarding her.   4. And she made an ark for thee, and
covered it with pitch and asphalt, and placed it in
the flags on the bank of the river, and she placed thee
in it seven days, and thy mother came by night and
suckled thee, and by day Miriam, thy sister, guarded
thee from the birds.   5. And in those days Tharmuth,[1]
the daughter of Pharaoh, came to bathe in the river,
and she heard thy voice crying, and she told her
maidens to bring thee forth, and they brought thee
unto her.   6. And she took thee out of the ark, and
she had compassion on thee.   7. And thy sister said
unto her : " Shall I go and call unto thee one of the
Hebrew women to nurse and suckle this babe for
thee ? "   And she said (unto her) : " Go." 8. And
she went and called thy mother Jochebed,[2] and she
gave her wages, and she nursed thee.   9. And afterwards, when thou wast grown up, they brought thee
unto the daughter of Pharaoh, and thou didst become
her son, and Amram thy father taught thee writing,[3]
and after thou hadst completed three weeks they
brought thee into the royal court.   10. And thou
2351-2372 wast three weeks of years at court until the time
A.M. when thou didst go forth from the royal court and
didst see an Egyptian smiting thy friend who was of
the children of Israel, and thou didst slay him and
hide him in the sand.   11. And on the second day
thou didst find two of the children of Israel striving
together, and thou didst say to him who was doing
the wrong : " Why dost thou smite thy brother ? "
12. And he was angry and indignant, and said :
" Who made thee a prince and a judge over us ?
Thinkest thou to kill me as thou killedst the Egyptian
yesterday ? "   And thou didst fear and flee on account
of these words.

---

[1] Thermuthis (Josephus, *Ant.* ii. 9, 5, 7).
[2] Cf. Exod. vi. 20; Num. xxvi. 59.   [3] Contrast Acts vii. 22.

From the Flight of Moses to the Exodus
(xlviii. 1–19; cf. Exod. ii. 15 ff., iv. 19–24, vii.–xiv.).

XLVIII. And in the sixth year of the third week 2372 A.M. of the forty-ninth jubilee thou didst depart and dwell in the land of Midian [1] five weeks and one year. And thou didst return into Egypt [2] in the second week in the second year in the fiftieth jubilee. 2. 2410 A.M. And thou thyself knowest what He spake unto thee on Mount Sinai, and what prince Mastêmâ [3] desired to do with thee when thou wast returning into Egypt on the way when thou didst meet him at the lodging-place. 3. Did he not with all his power seek to slay thee and deliver the Egyptians out of thy hand when he saw that thou wast sent to execute judgment and vengeance on the Egyptians? [4] 4. And I delivered thee out of his hand, and thou didst perform the signs and wonders which thou wast sent to perform in Egypt against Pharaoh, and against all his house, and against his servants and his people. 5. And the Lord executed a great vengeance on them for Israel's sake, and smote them through (the plagues of) blood and frogs, lice and dog-flies, and malignant boils breaking forth in blains; and their cattle by death; and by hail-stones, thereby He destroyed everything that grew for them; and by locusts which devoured the residue which had been left by the hail, and by darkness; and (by the death) of the first-born of men and animals, and on all their idols the Lord took vengeance and burned them with fire. [5] 6. And everything was sent through thy hand,

---

[1] Cf. Exod. ii. 15.   [2] Cf. Exod. iv. 19.

[3] Notice here the substitution of Satanic agency where the original text of Scripture ascribes the action directly to Jahveh (cf. Exod. iv. 24); another instance in our Book is xvii. 16. The same tendency can be illustrated from 1 Chron. xxi. 1 compared with 2 Sam. xxiv. 1.

[4] This explanation of the incident described in Exod. iv. 24 ff. seems to be peculiar to our author, the real explanation being that Moses had failed to circumcise his son (so Targ. Ps.-Jon. in loc.).

[5] An enumeration of the ten plagues.

that thou shouldst declare (these things) before they were done, and thou didst speak with the king of Egypt before all his servants and before his people. 7. And everything took place according to thy words; ten great and terrible judgments came on the land of Egypt that thou mightest execute vengeance on it for Israel. 8. And the Lord did everything for Israel's sake, and according to His covenant, which He had ordained with Abraham that He would take vengeance on them as they had brought them by force into bondage.[1] 9. And the prince of the Mastêmâ stood up against thee, and sought to cast thee into the hands of Pharaoh, and he helped the Egyptian sorcerers, and they stood up and wrought before thee. 10. The evils indeed we permitted them to work, but the remedies we did not allow to be wrought by their hands. 11. And the Lord smote them with malignant ulcers, and they were not able to stand,[2] for we destroyed them so that they could not perform a single sign. 12. And notwithstanding all (these) signs and wonders the prince of the Mastêmâ was not put to shame because he took courage and cried to the Egyptians to pursue after thee with all the powers of the Egyptians, with their chariots, and with their horses, and with all the hosts of the peoples of Egypt.[3] 13. And I stood between the Egyptians and Israel, and we delivered Israel out of his hand, and out of the hand of his people, and the Lord brought them through the midst of the sea as if it were dry land. 14. And all the peoples whom he brought to pursue after Israel, the Lord our God cast them into the midst of the sea, into the depths of the abyss beneath the children of Israel, even as the people of Egypt had cast their children into the river.[4] He took vengeance on 1,000,000 of them, and one thousand strong and energetic men were

---

[1] Cf. Gen. xv. 13, 14.   [2] Cf. Exod. ix. 11.   [3] Cf. Ex. xiv. 8 ,9.

[4] Another example of the *lex talionis* (cf. iv 31), though a distinction may be drawn between ' eye for eye ' (a principle of human justice) and ' measure for measure' (a theory of divine retribution) ; cf. Abrahams, *Studies in Pharisaism and the Gospels*, p. 154 (series i).

destroyed on account of one suckling of the children of thy people which they had thrown into the river.[1] 15. And on the fourteenth day and on the fifteenth and on the sixteenth and on the seventeenth and on the eighteenth the prince of the Mastêmâ was bound and imprisoned behind the children of Israel that he might not accuse them. 16. And on the nineteenth we let them loose that they might help the Egyptians and pursue the children of Israel. 17. And he [2] hardened their hearts and made them stubborn, and the device was devised by the Lord our God that He might smite the Egyptians and cast them into the sea. 18. And on the fourteenth we bound him that he might not accuse the children of Israel on the day when they asked the Egyptians for vessels and garments, vessels of silver, and vessels of gold, and vessels of bronze, in order to despoil the Egyptians [3] in return for the bondage in which they had forced them to serve. 19. And we did not lead forth the children of Israel from Egypt empty handed.

Regulations regarding the Passover (xlix. 1–23; cf. Exod. xii.).

XLIX. Remember the commandment which the Lord commanded thee concerning the passover, that thou shouldst celebrate it in its season on the fourteenth of the first month, that thou shouldst kill it before it is evening, and that they should eat it by night on the evening [4] of the fifteenth from the time of the setting of the sun. 2. For on this night—the beginning of the festival and the beginning of the joy —ye were eating the passover in Egypt, when all the powers of Mastêmâ [5] had been let loose to slay all the first-born in the land of Egypt, from the first-born of Pharaoh to the first-born of the captive

---

[1] Cf. Wisdom xviii. 5.
[2] *i. e.* the prince of the Mastêmâ (substituted for Jahveh in Exod. xiv. 8).
[3] Cf. Exod. xii. 35 f.   [4] Cf. Exod. xii. 6.
[5] In Exod. xii. 29 it is Jahveh Himself who smites all the first-born.

maidservant in the mill, and to the cattle. 3. And this is the sign which the Lord gave them : Into every house on the lintels of which they saw the blood of a lamb of the first year, into (that) house they should not enter to slay, but should pass by (it), that all those should be saved that were in the house because the sign of the blood was on its lintels. 4. And the powers of the Lord did everything according as the Lord commanded them, and they passed by all the children of Israel, and the plague came not upon them to destroy from amongst them any soul either of cattle, or man, or dog. 5. And the plague was very grievous in Egypt, and there was no house in Egypt where there was not one dead, and weeping and lamentation. 6. And all Israel was eating the flesh of the paschal lamb, and drinking the wine,[1] and was lauding and blessing, and giving thanks to the Lord God of their fathers, and was ready to go forth from under the yoke of Egypt, and from the evil bondage. 7. And remember thou this day all the days of thy life, and observe it from year to year all the days of thy life, once a year, on its day, according to all the law thereof, and do not adjourn (it) from day to day, or from month to month. 8. For it is an eternal ordinance, and engraven on the heavenly tables regarding all the children of Israel that they should observe it every year on its day once a year, throughout all their generations;[2] and there is no limit of days, for this is ordained for ever. 9. And the man who is free from uncleanness, and doth not come to observe it on occasion of its day, so as to bring an acceptable offering before the Lord, and to eat and to drink before the Lord on the day of its festival, that man who is clean and close at hand will be cut off; because he offered not the oblation of the Lord in its appointed season, he will

---

[1] The use of wine at the Passover feast is attested here for the first time. For the later prescriptions about the four cups of wine drunk at the feast see Mishna, *Pesaḥim* x.

[2] For 7–8 cf. vi. 20, 22.

take the guilt upon himself.[1] 10. Let the children of Israel come and observe the passover on the day of its fixed time, on the fourteenth day of the first month, between the evenings, from the third part of the day to the third part of the night, for two portions of the day are given to the light, and a third part to the evening.[2] 11. That is that which the Lord commanded thee that thou shouldst observe it between the evenings. 12. And it is not permissible to slay it during any period of the light, but during the period bordering on the evening,[3] and let them eat it at the time of the evening until the third part of the night,[4] and whatever is left over of all its flesh from the third part of the night and onwards, let them burn it with fire. 13. And they shall not cook it with water, nor shall they eat it raw, but roast on the fire :[5] they shall eat it with diligence,[6] its head with the inwards thereof[7] and its feet they shall roast with fire, and not break any bone thereof ;[8] for †of the children of Israel no bone shall be crushed†.[9] 14. For this reason the Lord commanded the children of Israel to observe the passover on the day of its fixed time, and they shall not break a bone thereof ; for it is a festival day, and a day commanded, and

[1] Cf. Num. ix. 13.

[2] The Jews divided the night into three parts, or watches (6–10 p.m., 10 p.m.–2 a.m., 2–6 a.m.). The corresponding parts of the day would be 6–10 a.m., 10 a.m.–2 p.m., and 2 p.m.–6 p.m. Our text says the last of these was " given " to the evening.

[3] This is an interpretation of the Biblical phrase "between the two evenings " (Exod. xii. 6; cf. R.V. marg.). This was interpreted by the Sadducees and Samaritans to mean between sunset and complete darkness (and may possibly have had that meaning here), but by the Pharisees it was understood to refer to the earlier afternoon (3–6).

[4] *i. e.* any time between 6 p.m. and 6 a.m. The Rabbis limited the eating to midnight.

[5] Cf. Exod. xii. 9.

[6] Cf. LXX ($\sigma\pi o\upsilon\delta\alpha\acute{\iota}\omega\varsigma$) : Heb. (Exod. xii. 11), " in haste."

[7] Cf. Exod. xii. 9.   [8] Cf. Exod. xii. 46.

[9] The Latin, which is to be preferred, reads : " There shall be no tribulation among the sons of Israel on this day."

there may be no passing over from day to day, and month to month, but on the day of its festival let it be observed. 15. And do thou command the children of Israel to observe the passover throughout their days, every year, once a year on the day of its fixed time, and it will come for a memorial well pleasing before the Lord, and no plague will come upon them to slay or to smite [1] in that year in which they celebrate the passover in its season in every respect according to His command. 16. And they shall not eat it outside the sanctuary [2] of the Lord, but before the sanctuary of the Lord, and all the people of the congregation of Israel shall celebrate it in its appointed season. 17. And every man who hath come upon its day shall eat it in the sanctuary of your God before the Lord from twenty years old [3] and upward; for thus is it written and ordained that they should eat it in the sanctuary of the Lord. 18. And when the children of Israel come into the land which they are to possess, into the land of Canaan, and set up the tabernacle of the Lord in the midst of the land in one of their tribes until the sanctuary of the Lord hath been built in the land, let them come and celebrate the passover in the midst of the tabernacle of the Lord, and let them slay it before the Lord from year to year. 19. And in the days when the house hath been built in the name of the Lord in the land of their inheritance, they shall go there and slay the passover in the evening, at sunset, at the third part of the day. 20. And they will offer its blood on the threshold of the altar, and shall place its fat on the fire which is upon the altar, and they shall eat its flesh roasted with fire in the court of the house [4] which hath been sanctified in

---

[1] Cf. Exod. xii. 13.   [2] Cf. 20 below.

[3] *i. e.* the age when maturity is first attained; cf. Exod. xxx. 14; Num. i. 32.

[4] Cf. Deut. xvi. 7. In later times the Passover lamb was slaughtered in the Temple, but eaten at home, *i. e.* in a house in Jerusalem. The vast numbers of pilgrims present necessitated this extension (cf. Josephus, *War*, vi. 9, 3. ii. 14, 3).

the name of the Lord. 21. And they may not celebrate the passover in their cities,[1] nor in any place save before the tabernacle of the Lord, or before His house where His name hath dwelt; and they will not go astray from the Lord. 22. And do thou, Moses, command the children of Israel to observe the ordinances of the passover, as it was commanded unto thee; declare thou unto them every year †and the day of its days, and†[2] the festival of unleavened bread, that they should eat unleavened bread seven days, (and) that they should observe its festival, and that they bring an oblation every day during those seven days of joy before the Lord on the altar of your God. 23. For ye celebrated this festival with haste[3] when ye went forth from Egypt till ye entered into the wilderness of Shur;[4] for on the shore of the sea ye completed it.

Laws regarding the Jubilees and the Sabbath
(l. 1–13).

L. And after this law I made known to thee the days of the Sabbaths in the desert of Sin[ai], which is between Elim and Sinai.[5] 2. And I told thee of the Sabbaths of the land on Mount Sinai, and I told thee of the jubilee years[6] in the sabbaths of years : but the year thereof have I not told thee till ye enter the land which ye are to possess. 3. And the land also will keep its sabbaths while they dwell upon it,[7] and they will know the jubilee year. 4. Wherefore I have ordained for thee the year-weeks[8] and the years and the jubilees : there are forty-nine jubilees from the days of Adam until this day, and one week 2410 A.M. and two years : and there are yet forty years to come (lit. " distant ") for learning the commandments of 2450 A.M.

[1] Cf. Deut. xvi. 5.
[2] Read with the Latin " during its days and during."
[3] Cf. Exod. xii. 11.   [4] Cf. Exod. xv. 22.
[5] Cf. Exod. xvi. 1 (" the wilderness of Sin . . . between Elim and Sinai ").   [6] Cf. Lev. xxv. 8.
[7] Cf. Lev. xxvi. 34.   [8] A " year-week " = seven years.

the Lord, until they pass over into the land of Canaan, crossing the Jordan to the west. 5. And the jubilees will pass by, until Israel is cleansed from all guilt of fornication, and uncleanness, and pollution, and sin, and error, and dwelleth with confidence in all the land, and there will be no more a Satan or any evil one, and the land will be clean from that time for evermore.[1]

6. And behold the commandment regarding the Sabbaths—I have written (them) down for thee—and all the judgments of its laws. 7. Six days wilt thou labour, but on the seventh day is the Sabbath of the Lord your God.[2] In it ye shall do no manner of work, ye and your sons, and your men-servants and your maid-servants, and all your cattle and the sojourner also who is with you. 8. And the man that doeth any work on it shall die : [3] whoever desecrateth that day, whoever lieth with (his) wife,[4] or whoever saith he will do something on it, that he will set out on a journey thereon [5] in regard to any buying or selling : [6] and whoever draweth water thereon [7] which he had not prepared for himself on the sixth day, and whoever taketh up any burden to carry it out of his tent [8] or out of his house shall die. 9. Ye shall do no work whatever on the Sabbath day save that ye have prepared for yourselves on the sixth day, so as to eat, and drink, and rest, and keep Sabbath from all work on that day, and to bless the Lord your God, who has given you a day of festival, and a holy day : and a day of the holy kingdom for all Israel is this day among their days for ever. 10. For great is the

---

[1] The Messianic Age is referred to; cf. i. 29, xxiii. 26 ff.

[2] Cf. Exod. xx. 9–10.   [3] Cf. Exod. xxxv. 2.

[4] This ascetic practice is still followed by the Samaritans, but not by the Jews. The exact opposite is enjoined in the Mishna; see Charles *ad loc*.

[5] Cf. Exod. xvi. 29. It was allowed to go a distance of 2000 cubits by Rabbinical law; cf. the "Sabbath day's journey" of Acts i. 12.

[6] Prohibited by Nehemiah (cf. Neh. x. 31, xiii. 16, 17).

[7] This is prohibited by the Ḳaraite Jews.   [8] Cf. ii. 29.

honour which the Lord hath given to Israel that they should eat and drink and be satisfied on this festival day, and rest thereon from all labour [1] which belongeth to the labour of the children of men, save burning frankincense and bringing oblations and sacrifices before the Lord for days and for Sabbaths. 11. This work alone shall be done on the Sabbath-days [2] in the sanctuary of the Lord your God; that they may atone for Israel with sacrifice continually from day to day for a memorial well-pleasing before the Lord, and that He may receive them always from day to day according as thou hast been commanded. 12. And every man who doeth any work thereon, or goeth a journey, or tilleth (his) farm,[3] whether in his house or any other place,[4] and whoever lighteth a fire,[5] or rideth on any beast,[6] or travelleth by ship on the sea, and whoever striketh or killeth anything, or slaughtereth [7] a beast or a bird, or whoever catcheth an animal or a bird or a fish, or whoever fasteth or maketh war on the Sabbaths:[8] 13. The man who doeth any of these things on the Sabbath shall die, so that the children of Israel shall observe the Sabbaths according to the commandments regarding the Sabbaths of the land, as it is written in the tables, which He gave into my hands that I should write out for thee the laws of the seasons, and the seasons according to the division of their days.

Herewith is completed the account of the division of the days.

[1] Cf. ii. 21.

[2] Cf. Matt. xii. 5 (Num. xxviii. 9, 10).

[3] Forbidden; cf. Exod. xxxiv. 21 (Mishna, *Shabb.* vii. 2).

[4] Perhaps this clause should follow " any work thereon " (Charles).

[5] Forbidden; Exod. xxxv. 3; cf. Num. xv. 32 f.

[6] Forbidden by the Jewish oral law.

[7] " Slaughtering " on the Sabbath is forbidden in the Mishna (*Shabb.* vii. 2).

[8] This rule was at first rigidly observed in the Maccabean wars (cf. 1 Macc. ii. 31–38), but afterwards relaxed (cf. 1 Macc. ii. 41).

INDEX